As Per NEP Syllabus (NEP) BCU/BC/BU

DESIGN AND ANALYSIS OF ALGORITHMS

[For BCA & B.Sc. 5th and 6th Semester Students of Universities of Karnataka state]

HELARIA MARIA
MCA, M.Phil. (Ph.D.)
Senior Assistant Professor,
Department of Computer Science,
New Horizon College, KASTURINAGAR

DR. R PREMA
Senior Assistant Professor,
New Horizon College, KASTURINAGAR

KALYANI PUBLISHERS

LUDHIANA – NEW DELHI – NOIDA (U.P.) – HYDERABAD – CHENNAI
KOLKATA – CUTTACK – GUWAHATI – KOCHI – BENGALURU

KALYANI PUBLISHERS

Head Office

3251/B, Street No. 5, Near Sandhu Tower, Gurdev Nagar, **Ludhiana-**141 001 • Ph : 0161-2760031
E-mail : kalyanibooks@yahoo.co.in **Website :** www.kalyanipublishers.co.in

Administrative Office

4779/23, Ansari Road, Daryaganj, **New Delhi-**110 002 • Ph : 011-23271469, 23274393
E-mail : kalyani_delhi@kalyanipublishers.in

Works

B-16, Sector-8, **NOIDA** (U.P.)

Branches

1, Mahalakshmi Street, T. Nagar, **Chennai-**600 017 • Ph : 044-24344684
Gopabandhu Lane, Behind Govt. Bus Stand, Badambadi,
Cuttack-753 012 (Odisha) • Ph : 0671-2311391
4-3-65/2/A, Behind HVS Public School, Raghunath Bagh
Sultan Bazar, **Hyderabad-**500 095 • Ph : 040-24750368
10/2B, Ramanath Mazumdar Street, **Kolkata-**700 009 • Ph : 033-35571565
Arunalaya, 1st Floor, Saraswati Road, Pan Bazar, **Guwahati-**781 001 • Ph : 0361-2731274
Koratti Parambil House, Convent Road, **Kochi-**682 035 • Ph : 0484-2367189
No. 24 & 25, 1st Floor, Hameed Shah Complex, Cubbonpet Main Road, **Bengaluru-**560 002

T 40417 03 12 + 272 = 284 Pages 20" x 30" 35.5 Forms

Gautam Graphic Printers
(MISC-2024-DAA-BNU)

PRINTED IN INDIA
At Kalyani Printings, B-15, Sector 8, NOIDA

Preface

This book is designed as a textbook to sufficiently full fill the needs of the students, who study computer sciences as one of their major subjects, it conforms to the latest syllabus proposed by the National Education Policy (NEP) for Bangalore North University, Bangalore Central University and Bangalore University.

This book is complete reference for V Semester, VI Semester BCA Students. Explanation of fundamental algorithms and complexity of an algorithm are clear and simple. There is a Systematic approach in presenting the topics from simple to complex.

Constructive Suggestions from teachers and students to improve this book is always welcome.

2024

Helaria Maria
Dr. R Prema

Syllabus

CA-C17f: THE DESIGN AND ANALYSIS OF ALGORITHMS

Total Teaching Hours: 48 *No. of Hours / Week: 03*

UNIT – I *[12 Hours]*

Introduction: Algorithms, Fundamentals of Algorithmic Problem Solving, Important Problem Types, Fundamental Data Structures. Fundamentals of the Analysis of Algorithm Efficiency: The Analysis Framework, Asymptotic Notations and Basic Efficiency Classes, Mathematical Analysis of Non-recursive and Recursive Algorithms, Empirical Analysis of Algorithms

UNIT – II *[12 Hours]*

Brute Force Method: Selection Sort and Bubble Sort, Sequential Search, Brute-Force String Matching, Exhaustive Search, Depth-First Search and Breadth-First Search. Decrease and Conquer: Insertion Sort, Topological Sorting, Algorithms for Generating Combinatorial Objects, Decrease–by-a-Constant-Factor Algorithms. Divide and Conquer: Merge Sort, Quick Sort, Binary Tree Traversals and Related Properties, Strassen's Matrix Multiplication.

UNIT – III *[12 Hours]*

Space and Time Tradeoffs: Sorting by Counting, Input Enhancement in String Matching, Hashing. Dynamic programming: Binomial Coefficient, Principle of Optimality, Optimal Binary Search Trees, Knapsack Problem and Memory Functions, Warshall 's and Floyd's Algorithms. Greedy Technique: Prim's Algorithm, Kruskal's Algorithm, Dijkstra's Algorithm, Huffman Trees.

UNIT – IV *[12 Hours]*

Limitations of Algorithm Power: Lower-Bound Arguments, Decision Trees, P, NP and NP Complete Problems. Coping with the Limitations of Algorithm Power: Back Tracking: n Queens problem, Hamiltonian Circuit Problem, Subset-Sum Problem. Branch-and-Bound: Assignment Problem, Knapsack Problem, Travelling Salesman Problem.

Program Name	BCA	Semester	V
Course Title	Design and Analysis of Algorithm (Theory)		
Course Code:	DSC13	No. of Credits	04
Contact hours	52 Hours	Duration of SEA/Exam	2:30 hours
Formative Assessment Marks	40	Summative Assessment Marks	60

Course Outcomes (COs): After the successful completion of the course, the student will be able to:

1. Understand the fundamental concepts of algorithms and their complexity, including time and space complexity, worst-case and average-case analysis, and Big-O notation. BL (L_1, L_2)

2. Design algorithms for solving various types of problems, such as Sorting, Searching, Graph traversal, Decrease-and-Conquer, Divide-and-Conquer and Greedy Techniques. BL (L_1, L_2, L_3)

3. Analyze and compare the time and space complexity of algorithms with other algorithmic techniques. BL (L_1, L_2, L_3, IA)

4. Evaluate the performance of Sorting, Searching, Graph traversal, Decrease-and-Conquer, Divide-and-Conquer and Greedy Techniques using empirical testing and benchmarking, and identify their limitations and potential improvements. BL (L_1, L_2, L_3, *IA)*

5. Apply various algorithm design to real-world problems and evaluate their effectiveness and efficiency in solving them. BL (L_1, L_2, L_3)

Note: Blooms Level (BL): L_1 = Remember, L_2 = Understand, L_3 = Apply, IA=Analyze, L_5 = Evaluate, L_6=Create

Contents	*52 Hrs*
Introduction: What is an Algorithm? Fundamentals of Algorithmic problem solving, Fundamentals of the Analysis of Algorithm Efficiency, Analysis Framework, Measuring the input size, Units for measuring Running time, Orders of Growth, Worst-case, Best : case and Average-case efficiencies.	10
Asymptotic Notations and Basic Efficiency : Classes, Informal Introduction, O-notation, Ω-notation, θ-notation, mathematical analysis of non-recursive algorithms, mathematical analysis of recursive algorithms.	10
Brute Force & Exhaustive Search: Introduction to Brute Force approach, Selection Sort and Bubble Sort, Sequential search, Exhaustive Search- Travelling Salesman Problem and Knapsack Problem, Depth First Search, Breadth First Search	11

Decrease-and-Conquer: Introduction, Insertion Sort, Topological Sorting **Divide-and-Conquer:** Introduction, Merge Sort, Quick Sort, Binary Search, Binary Tree traversals and related properties.	**11**
Greedy Technique: Introduction, Prim's Algorithm, Kruskal's Algorithm, Dijkstra's Algorithm, Lower-Bound Arguments, Decision Trees, P Problems, NP Problems, NP– Complete Problems, Challenges of Numerical Algorithms.	**10**

Course Articulation Matrix: Mapping of Course Outcomes (COs) with Program Outcomes (POs 1-15)

Course Outcomes (COs) I Program Outcomes (POs)	**Program Outcomes (POs)**														
	1	**2**	**3**	**4**	**5**	**6**	**7**	**8**	**9**	**10**	**11**	**12**	**13**	**14**	**15**
Course Outcomes (COs) I Program Outcomes (POs)															
Discuss the fundamentals algorithms.															
Describe the analysis of algorithm efficiency using different notations.															
Discuss various problems using Brute force technique.															
Describe various problems using Divide and-Conquer Technique.															
Describe various problems using Decrease-and-Conquer.															
Discuss Greedy Techniques.															
Devise an algorithm using appropriate design strategies for problem solving.															
Estimate the computational complexity of different algorithms.															
Demonstrate the hardness of simple NP-complete problems.															

Pedagogy: Lecture/ PPT/ Videos/ Animations/ Role Plays/ Think-Pair-Share/ Predict-Observe- Explain/ Demonstration/ Concept mapping/ Case Studies examples/ Tutorial/ Activity/ Flipped Classroom/ Jigsaw/ Field based Learning/ Project Based Learning/ Mini Projects/ Hobby Projects/ Forum Theatre/ Dance/ Problem Based Learning/ Game Based Learning/ Group Discussion/ Collaborative Learning/ Experiential Learning/ Self Directed Learning etc.

Formative Assessment for Theory	
Assessment Occasion/ type	**Marks**
Internal Assessment Test I	10%
Internal Assessment Test 2	10%
Quiz/ Assignment/ Small Project	10%
Seminar	10%
Total	**40 Marks**
Formative Assessment as per guidelines.	

Course Title	**Design and Analysis of Algorithms Laboratory (Practical)**	**Practical Credits**	**02**
Course Code	**DSC13-Lab**	**Contact Hours**	**4 Hours/wk**
Formative Assessment	**25 Marks**	**Summative Assessment**	**25 Marks**

PRACTICAL CONTENT

1. Write a program to sort a list of N elements using Selection Sort Technique.
2. Write a program to perform Travelling Salesman Problem
3. Write program to implement Dynamic Programming algorithm for the 0/1 Knapsack problem.
4. Write a program to perform Knapsack Problem using Greedy Solution
5. Write program to implement the DFS and BFS algorithm for a graph.
6. Write a program to find minimum and maximum value in an array using divide and conquer.
7. Write a test program to implement Divide and Conquer Strategy. Eg: Quick sort algorithm for sorting list of integers in ascending order.

8. Write a program to implement Merge sort algorithm for sorting a list of integers in ascending order.
9. Sort a given set of n integer elements using Merge Sort method and compute its time complexity. Run the program for varied values of n> 5000, and record the time taken to sort.
10. Sort a given set of n integer elements using Quick Sort method and compute its time complexity. Run the program for varied values of n> 5000 and record the time taken to sort.
11. Write C program that accepts the vertices and edges for a graph and stores it as an adjacency matrix.
12. Implement function to print In-Degree, Out-Degree and to display that adjacency matrix.
13. Write program to implement backtracking algorithm for solving problems like N queens.
14. Write a program to implement the backtracking algorithm for the sum of subsets problem
15. Write program to implement greedy algorithm for job sequencing with deadlines.
16. Write program to implement Dynamic Programming algorithm for the Optimal Binary Search Tree Problem.
17. Write a program that implements Prim's algorithm to generate minimum cost spanning Tree.
18. Write a program that implements K.ruskal's algorithm to generate minimum cost spanning tree.

Pedagogy: Demonstration, Hands-on, Simulation

Formative Assessment for Practical	
Assessment Occasion/ type	**Marks**
Total	**25 Marks**
Formative Assessment as per guidelines.	

CA-C19L: Algorithms Lab

1. Write a program to implement linear search algorithm. Repeat the experiment for different values of *n*, the number of elements in the list to be searched and plot a graph of the time taken versus *n*.

2. Write a program to implement binary search algorithm. Repeat the experiment for different values of *n*, the number of elements in the list to be searched and plot a graph of the time taken versus *n*.

3. Write a program to solve towers of honai problem and execute it for different number of disks

4. Write a Program to Sort a given set of numbers using selection sort algorithm. Repeat the experiment for different values of *n*, the number of elements in the list to be sorted and plot a graph of the time taken versus *n*. The elements can be read from a file or can be generated using the random number generator.

5. Write a program to find the value of *a*• (where a and n are integers) using both brute-force based algorithm and divide and conquer based algorithm

6. Write a Program to Sort a given set of elements using quick sort algorithm. Repeat the experiment for different values of n, the number of elements in the list to be sorted and plot a graph of the time taken versus n.

7. Write a Program to find the binomial co-efficient C(*n*, *k*}, [where *n* and *k* are integers and $n > k$] using brute force based algorithm and also dynamic programming based algorithm

8. Write a Program to implement Floyd's algorithm and find the lengths of the shortest paths from every pairs of vertices in a given weighted graph

9. Write a program to evaluate a polynomial using brute-force based algorithm and using Horner's rule and compare their performances

10. Write a Program to solve the string matching problem using Boyer-Moore approach.

11. Write a Program to solve the string matching problem using KMP algorithm

12. Write a program to implement BFS traversal algorithm

13. Write a program to find the minimum spanning tree of a given graph using Prim's algorithm

14. Write a Program to obtain the topological ordering of vertices in a given digraph. Compute the transitive closure of a given directed graph using Warshall's algorithm.

15. Write a Program to Find a subset of a given sets = $\{s_1, s_2, , s_n\}$ of *n* positive integers whose ..... sum is equal to a given positive integer d. For example, if S= {1, 2, 5, 6, 8} and $d = 9$ there are two solutions {1, 2, 6} and {1, 8}. A suitable message is to be displayed if the given problem instance doesn't have a solution.

Contents

UNIT

1

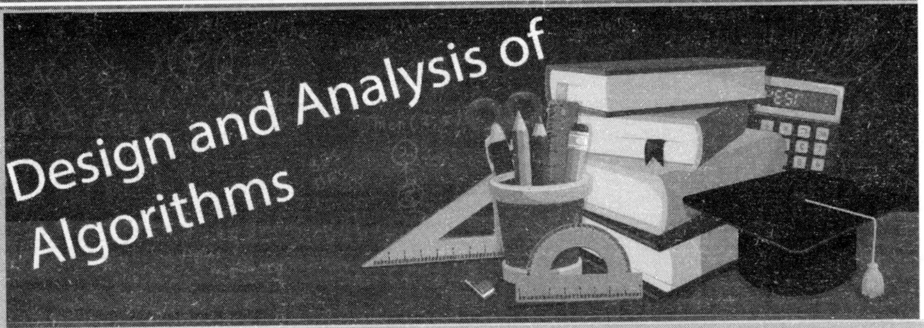

INTRODUCTION

WHAT IS AN ALGORITHM?

1.1 ALGORITHM

Informally, an algorithm is any well-defined computational procedure that takes some values as "input" and produces some value, or set of values, as "output". An algorithm is thus "a sequence of computational steps that transform the input into the output."

We can also view an algorithm as a tool for solving a well-specified "computational problem". The statement of the problem specifies in general terms the desired input/output relationship.

In simple terms we can say that "An algorithm is a step–by–step procedure for performing some task in a finite amount of time".

Definition:

An algorithm is a finite set of steps each of which may require one or more operations. Every operation may be characterized as either a simple or complex.

Notions of an Algorithms: Pictorial representation of an algorithm.

1.1.1 NEED OF THE ALGORITHMS:

Algorithms are used to solve problems or automate tasks in a systematic and efficient manner. They are a set of instructions or rules that guide the computer or software in performing a particular task or solving a problem.

1. **Efficiency:** Algorithms can perform tasks quickly and accurately, making them an essential tool for tasks that require a lot of calculations or data processing.
2. **Consistency:** Algorithms are repeatable and produce consistent results every time they are executed. This is important when dealing with large amounts of data or complex processes.
3. **Scalability:** Algorithms can be scaled up to handle large datasets or complex problems, which makes them useful for applications that require processing large volumes of data.
4. **Automation:** Algorithms can automate repetitive tasks, reducing the need for human intervention and freeing up time for other tasks.
5. **Standardization:** Algorithms can be standardized and shared among different teams or organizations, making it easier for people to collaborate and share knowledge.

1.1.2. The Essential Characteristics of an Algorithm

1. Every step of an algorithm should perform a single task.
2. Ambiguity (Confusion) should not be included at any stage in an algorithm.
3. An algorithm should involve a finite number of steps to arrive at a solution.
4. Simple statement and structures should be used in the development of the algorithm.
5. Every algorithm should lead to a unique solution of the problem.
6. An algorithm should have the capability to handle some unexpected situations, which may arise during the solution of a problem (For example, division by zero).

1.1.3 Properties of an Algorithm

All algorithms must satisfy the following criteria:

1. **Input:** Zero or more quantities are externally supplied.
2. **Output:** At least one Output is produced.
3. **Definiteness:** Each instruction should be simple and clear.
4. **Finiteness:** If we trace out the instruction of an algorithm, then for all cases, the algorithm terminates after a finite number of steps.
5. **Effectiveness:** Every instruction must be very basic so that it can be carried out, in principal, by a person using only pencil and paper

1.1.4 Advantages of Algorithm

1. It is a step–by–step representation of a solution to a given problem, which is very easy to understand.
2. It has got a definite procedure, which can be executed within a set period of time.
3. It is easy to first develop an algorithm, and then convert it into a flowchart and then into a computer program.
4. It is independent of programming language.
5. It is easy to debug as every step has got its own logical sequence.

Disadvantages of Algorithm

It is time consuming and cumbersome as an algorithm is developed first which is converted into a flowchart and then into a computer program.

1.2 FUNDAMENTALS OF ALGORITHMIC PROBLEM SOLVING

A sequence of steps involved in designing and analyzing an algorithm is shown in the figure below.

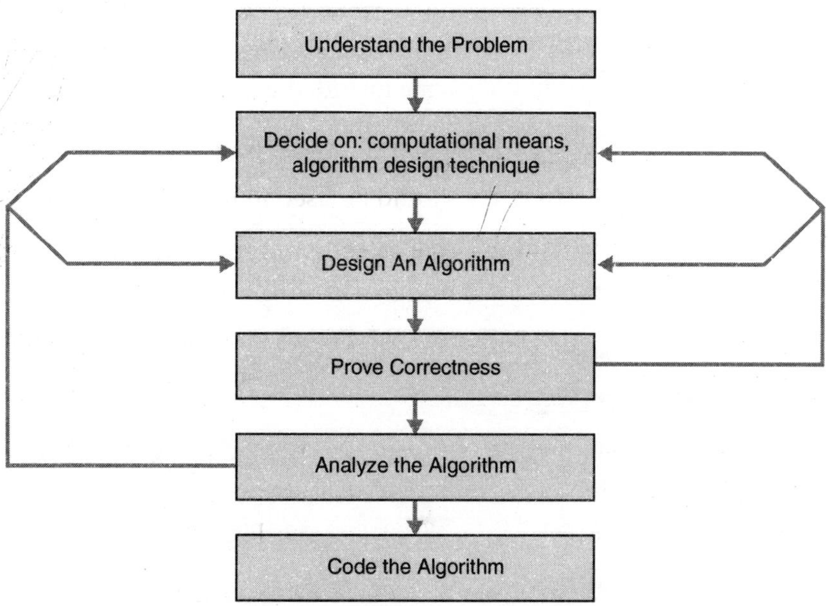

Fig. Flow diagram of designing and analyzing an algorithm

(i) Understanding the Problem

- This is the first step in designing of algorithm.
- Read the problem's description carefully to understand the problem statement completely.

- Ask questions for clarifying the doubts about the problem.
- Identify the problem types and use existing algorithm to find solution.
- Input (instance) to the problem and range of the input get fixed.

(ii) Decision making

The Decision making is done on the following:

(a) Ascertaining the Capabilities of the Computational Device

- In random–access machine (RAM), instructions are executed one after another (The central assumption is that one operation at a time). Accordingly, algorithms designed to be executed on such machines are called sequential algorithms.
- In some newer computers, operations are executed concurrently, i.e., in parallel. Algorithms that take advantage of this capability are called parallel algorithms.
- Choice of computational devices like Processor and memory is mainly based on space and time efficiency.

(b) Choosing between Exact and Approximate Problem Solving

- The next principal decision is to choose between solving the problem exactly and solving it approximately.
- An algorithm used to solve the problem exactly and produce correct result is called an exact algorithm.
- If the problem is so complex and not able to get exact solution, then we must choose an algorithm called an approximation algorithm. i.e., produces an approximate answer. E.g., extracting square roots, solving nonlinear equations, and evaluating definite integrals.

(c) Algorithm Design Techniques

- An algorithm design technique (or "strategy" or "paradigm") is a general approach to solving problems algorithmically that is applicable to a variety of problems from different areas of computing.

Algorithms+ Data Structures = Programs

- Though Algorithms and Data Structures are independent, but they are combined to develop program. Hence the choice of proper data structure is required before designing the algorithm.
- Implementation of algorithm is possible only with the help of Algorithms and Data Structures

- Algorithmic strategy / technique / paradigm are a general approach by which many problems can be solved algorithmically. E.g., Brute Force, Divide and Conquer, Dynamic Programming, Greedy Technique and so on.

(iii) Methods of Specifying an Algorithm There are three ways to specify an algorithm.

(a) Natural language

(b) Pseudo code

(c) Flowchart

(iv) Proving an Algorithm's Correctness

(a) Once an algorithm has been specified then its correctness must be proved.

(b) An algorithm must yields a required result for every legitimate input in a finite amount of time. For example, the correctness of Euclid's algorithm for computing the greatest common divisor stems from the correctness of the equality $gcd(m, n) = gcd(n, m \bmod n)$.

(c) A common technique for proving correctness is to use mathematical induction because an algorithm's iterations provide a natural sequence of steps needed for such proofs.

(d) The notion of correctness for approximation algorithms is less straightforward than it is for exact algorithms. The error produced by the algorithm should not exceed a predefined limit

(v) Analyzing an Algorithm

(a) For an algorithm the most important is efficiency. In fact, there are two kinds of algorithm efficiency. They are:

(b) Time efficiency, indicating how fast the algorithm runs, and

(c) Space efficiency, indicating how much extra memory it uses.

(d) The efficiency of an algorithm is determined by measuring both time efficiency and space efficiency.

(e) So factors to analyze an algorithm are:

- Time efficiency of an algorithm
- Space efficiency of an algorithm
- Simplicity of an algorithm
- Generality of an algorithm

(vi) Coding an Algorithm

(a) The coding / implementation of an algorithm is done by a suitable programming language like C, C++, JAVA.

(b) The transition from an algorithm to a program can be done either incorrectly or very inefficiently. Implementing an algorithm correctly is necessary. The Algorithm power should not reduce by inefficient implementation.

(c) Standard tricks like computing a loop's invariant (an expression that does not change its value) outside the loop, collecting common sub–expressions, replacing expensive operations by cheap ones, selection of programming language and so on should be known to the programmer.

(d) Typically, such improvements can speed up a program only by a constant factor, whereas a better algorithm can make a difference in running time by orders of magnitude.

(e) It is very essential to write an optimized code (efficient code) to reduce the burden of compiler.

Role of algorithms in computing

The most important problem types related to computing are:

1. *Sorting*: The sorting problem is to rearrange the items of a given list in non–decreasing (ascending) order.
2. *Searching:* The searching problem deals with finding a given value, called a search key, in a given set.
3. *String processing:* A string is a sequence of characters from an alphabet. Strings comprise letters, numbers, and special characters; bit strings, which comprise zeros and ones; and gene sequences, which can be modeled by strings of characters from the four character alphabet {A, C,G, T}. It is very useful in bioinformatics. Searching for a given word in a text is called string matching.
4. *Graph problems*: A graph is a collection of points called vertices, some of which are connected by line segments called edges. Some of the graph problems are graph traversal, shortest path algorithm, topological sort, traveling sales man problem and the graph–coloring problem and so on.
5. *Combinatorial problems*: These are problems that ask, explicitly or implicitly, to find a combinatorial object such as a permutation, a combination, or a subset that satisfies certain constraints.

6. *Geometric problems:* Geometric algorithms deal with geometric objects such as points, lines, and polygons. Geometric algorithms are used in computer graphics, robotics, and topography.

7. *Numerical problems*: There are problems that involve mathematical equations, systems of equations, computing definite integrals, evaluating functions, and so on. The majority of such mathematical problems can be solved only approximately.

Algorithms as a Technology.

There are a huge number of real life applications where, algorithms play the major and vital role. Few of such applications are discussed below.

- The ***Internet*** without which it is difficult to imagine a day is the result of *clever and efficient algorithms*. With the aid of these algorithms, various sites on the Internet are able to manage and manipulate this large volume of data. Finding good routes on which the data will travel and using search engine to find pages on which particular information is present.
- Another great milestone is the Human Genome Project which has great progress towards the goal of identification of the 100000 genes in human DNA, determining the sequences of the 3 billion chemical base pairs that make up the human DNA, storing this *huge amount of information* in databases, and developing tools for data analysis. Each of these steps required *sophisticated and efficient algorithms.*
- The day–to–day ***electronic commerce*** activities is hugely dependent on our personal information such as credit/debit card numbers, passwords, bank statements, OTPs and so on. The core technologies used include public–key crypto currency and digital signatures which are based on numerical algorithms and number theory.
- The approach of **linear programming** is also one such technique which is widely used like
    - In *manufacturing* and other commercial enterprises where resources need to be allocated scarcely in the most beneficial way.
    - Or a institution may want to determine where to spend money buying advertising in order to *maximize* the chances of their institution to grow.
- **Shortest path algorithm** also has an extensive use as
    - In a *transportation* firm such as a trucking or railroad company, may have financial interest in finding shortest path through a road or rail network because taking shortest path result in lower labour or fuel costs.

- Or a *routing node* on the Internet may need to find the shortest path through the network in order to route mess age quickly.

- Even an application that does not require algorithm content at the application level relies heavily on algorithms as the application depends on *hardware, GUI, networking or object orientation* and all of these make an extensive use of algorithms.

1.3 IMPORTANT PROBLEM TYPES IN DESIGN AND ANALYSIS OF ALGORITHM

In the design and analysis of algorithms, several important problem types are frequently encountered. These encompass various categories and approaches to problem–solving. Some of the key problem types include:

Sorting and Searching:

Sorting algorithms: Organizing elements in a specific order (e.g., numerical or lexicographical).

Searching algorithms: Finding an element within a collection or data structure efficiently (e.g., binary search).

Graph Algorithms:

Shortest path algorithms: Finding the most efficient path between two points in a graph (e.g., Dijkstra's algorithm).

Minimum spanning tree: Determining the smallest possible tree that connects all nodes in a graph (e.g., Prim's algorithm, Kruskal's algorithm).

Graph traversal: Visiting all nodes or vertices in a graph (e.g., Depth–First Search (DFS), Breadth–First Search (BFS)).

Dynamic Programming:

Optimization problems: Finding the best solution among a set of possible solutions, often using memoization or bottom–up approaches.

Longest common subsequence, Knapsack problem, Matrix chain multiplication are classic examples.

Greedy Algorithms:

Optimization problems: Making a series of choices that seem the best at the moment, hoping they will lead to a globally optimal solution (e.g., Dijkstra's algorithm, Huffman coding).

Divide and Conquer:

Recursive problem–solving technique: Dividing a problem into smaller sub–problems until they can be solved directly.

Examples include merge sort, quicksort, and Strassen's matrix multiplication algorithm.

String Algorithms:

String matching: Finding occurrences or patterns within strings (e.g., KMP algorithm, Rabin–Karp algorithm).

Computational Geometry:

Geometric algorithms: Solving problems related to geometric shapes and structures (e.g., convex hull, line intersection).

Network Flow and Linear Programming:

Solving optimization problems involving flows in networks or linear programming models.

Randomized Algorithms:

Algorithms that use randomness in their computation to solve problems or improve efficiency (e.g., randomized quicksort, randomized algorithms in graph theory).

Fundamental of the Data Structure

A data structure is a specialized format of data for arranging and storing data so that any user can easily access and worked within an appropriate data to run a program efficiently. Computer memory data can be organized logically or mathematically, and this process is known as a **data structure**.

Fundamentals of data structures encompass the basic building blocks and principles used to organize and manage data efficiently within computer programs. Here are some fundamental concepts in data structures:

- **Arrays:** Ordered collections of items stored at contiguous memory locations. Elements can be accessed by index.
- **Linked Lists:** A linear collection of elements where each element points to the next one in the sequence, forming a chain. Types include singly linked lists, doubly linked lists, and circular linked lists.
- **Stacks:** A Last–In, First–Out (LIFO) structure where elements are inserted and removed from the same end. Operations include push (insert) and pop (remove).
- **Queues:** A First–In, First–Out (FIFO) structure where elements are inserted at the rear

end and removed from the front end. Operations include enqueue (insert) and dequeue (remove).

- **Trees:** Hierarchical data structures consisting of nodes, typically with one designated as the root, and each node having zero or more child nodes. Examples include binary trees, AVL trees, red–black trees, and B–trees.
- **Graphs:** Non–linear data structures comprising nodes (vertices) and edges that connect these nodes. Graphs can be directed or undirected and may have various properties like cycles, paths, etc.
- **Hash Tables:** Data structures that store data in an associative manner, using a hash function to map keys to values. They offer efficient insertion, deletion, and retrieval operations.
- **Heaps:** Specialized trees used to implement priority queues. Heaps often follow the heap property (either max–heap or min–heap) where the parent node is larger/smaller than its children.
- **Trie:** A tree–like structure often used to store strings in a way that allows for efficient prefix–based searches.
- **Graph Algorithms:** Various algorithms applied to graphs such as Depth–First Search (DFS), Breadth–First Search (BFS), Dijkstra's algorithm, Kruskal's algorithm, etc., to solve problems related to graphs.

1.4 DATA STRUCTURES VS DESIGN AND ANALYSIS OF ALGORITHM

Data structures and the design and analysis of algorithms are two interconnected but distinct concepts within computer science.

Data Structures refer to the way data is organized, stored, and managed in a computer's memory or storage. They focus on representing and managing data efficiently to perform various operations (such as insertion, deletion, searching, sorting) on that data. Examples of data structures include arrays, linked lists, stacks, queues, trees, graphs, hash tables, and more. Understanding data structures involves knowing how to select the appropriate structure for storing data based on the requirements of specific applications and performing operations efficiently.

Design and Analysis of Algorithms deals with creating step–by–step procedures or methods to solve problems using computational processes. It involves the study of designing algorithms to efficiently solve computational problems, analyzing their efficiency in terms of time complexity (how long an algorithm takes to run) and space complexity (how much memory an algorithm uses), and proving their correctness. This field focuses on devising algorithms that perform tasks optimally or near–optimally, given specific constraints and requirements. It covers various algorithmic techniques such as divide and conquer, dynamic programming, greedy algorithms, graph algorithms, and more.

While data structures deal with organizing and managing data, algorithms deal with creating procedures to manipulate that data efficiently. However, they are interconnected because the choice of data structure often greatly influences the efficiency of algorithms and their performance. For instance, the selection of an appropriate data structure (e.g., array, hash table, tree) can significantly impact the efficiency of algorithms that operate on that data.

In summary, data structures are about organizing and storing data, while the design and analysis of algorithms are about devising efficient methods to solve computational problems. Both are essential components of computer science and are closely related, as the choice of data structure often affects the design and efficiency of algorithms used to manipulate that data.

Fundamentals of the Analysis of Algorithm Efficiency

The efficiency of an algorithm can be in terms of time and space. The algorithm efficiency can be analyzed by the following ways.

(a) Analysis Framework.

(b) Asymptotic Notations and its properties.

(c) Mathematical analysis for Recursive algorithms.

(d) Mathematical analysis for Non–recursive algorithms.

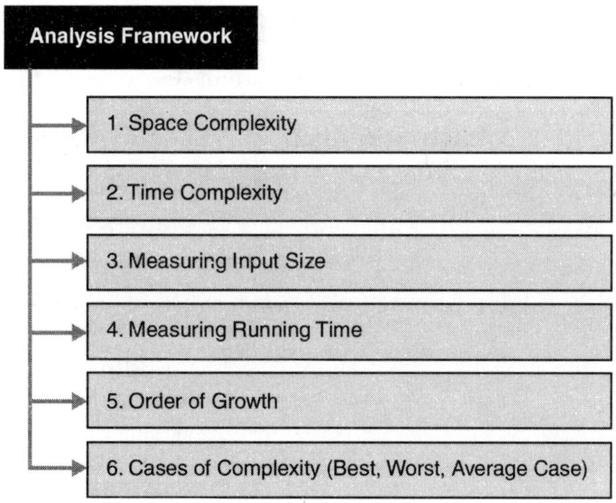

Algorithm analysis is an important part of computational complexity theory, which provides theoretical estimation for the required resources of an algorithm to solve a specific computational problem. Most algorithms are designed to work with inputs of arbitrary length.

Analysis of algorithms is the determination of the amount of time and space resources required to execute it.

The complexity of an algorithm describes the efficiency of the algorithm in terms of the amount of the memory required to process the data and the processing time.

Complexity of an algorithm is analyzed in two perspectives: **Time** and **Space**.

(a) Time Complexity

It's a function describing the amount of time required to run an algorithm in terms of the size of the input. "Time" can mean the number of memory accesses performed, the number of comparisons between integers, the number of times some inner loop is executed, or some other natural unit related to the amount of real time the algorithm will take.

Algorithm 1: Consider the algorithm to sum *n* element contained in an array *x*.

Statement	Statement count	Frequency/repetition	Total Steps
1. Int sum(x,n)	0	0	0
2. {	0	0	0
3. Total =0	1	1	1
4. For i=1 to n do	1	N +1	N+1
5. Total=total+x[i];	1	N	N
6. Return Total;	1	1	1
7. }	0	0	0
Total Steps			**(2n+3)**

Algorithm 2: Consider the algorithm to add two matrices.

Statement	Statement count	Frequency/repetition	Total Steps
1. Algorithm ADD(a,b,c,m,n)	0	0	0
2. {	0	0	0
3. for i=1 to m do	1	1	M+1
4. for j=1 to n do	1	M+1	Mn+m
5. c[i,j]=a[i,j] + b[i,j]	1	M(n+1)	Mn
6. }	0	Mn	0
		0	
Total Steps			**(2mn+2m+1)**

Step count: step counts method we attempt to find the time spent in all parts of the program. A step is any computation unit that is independent of the selected characters any program step must be systematically and semantically meaningful.

For an example:

```
(i)  X = a+b;                          // step count = 1
(ii) For(i=1; i<=n; i++)
          X = a+b;                     // step count = n
(iii) For(i=1; i<=n; i++)
          For(j=1;j<=n;j++)
               X=a+b;                  // step count = n^2
```

Let us study some more complicated examples:

EXAMPLE 1: We find out the sum of all array elements by using iterative teachnique.

```
Int Isum (int a [] , int n)
{
  Int sum:
  Int I;
  Sum_count ++;
  For (I=0;I<n;I++)
   {
 For_count++;
      Sum += a[];
 Assign_count++;
   }
 for_count++;
 return_count++;
    return sum;
 }
```

Note: the step count for sum = 1

The step count for statement = n + 1

The step count for assignment = n

The step count for return = 1

The total step = 2n + 3

EXAMPLE 2: Matrix addition

Let A and B are two matrices of order m x n. The resultant matrix 'C' is $C(m \times n)=A(m \times n) + B(m \times n)$

```
For(i=0; i<m; i++)                    // step count = m+1

For (j=0; j<n; j++)                   // step count = m (n+1)
    C[i] [j] = A[i][j] +B[i][j]       // step count = m*n

Total steps = (m+1) + m(n+1) + (m*n)
            = m+1 + mn + m + mn
            = 2 mn + 2m + 1
```

In the above example, first for loop executed m + 1 times. The second for loop executes m(n+1) times.

(b) Space Complexity

It's a function describing the amount of memory an algorithm takes in terms of the size of input to the algorithm. We often speak of "extra" memory needed, not counting the memory needed to store the input itself. Again, we use natural (but fixed–length) units to measure this.

Space complexity is sometimes ignored because the space used is minimal and/or obvious, how ever some times it becomes as important an issue as time.

So the space complexity of an algorithm is defined as the amount of memory is needs to run 2 completion.

The space needed by an algorithm consist of the following components:

(a) The fixed static part that is independent of the characteristics example number size of the input and outputs. This part typically includes the instruction space *i.e.* space for code, space for simple variables and fixed size component variable space for constants etc.

(b) A variable dynamic part, that consist of the space needed by component variable whose size is dependent on the problem instead at runtime being solved, the space needed by referred variables and the recursion stack space depends on instant characteristics.

The Space complexity can be calculated in 2 ways:

Constant Space Complexity: Its for a simple program or fixed steps.

Eg1: int square(int a, int b)

```
{
  Return a*b;
}
```

Here in this above algorithm fixed amount of space for all the input values so, this type of complexity called as constant.

S (square) = 2

Eg2: int XYZ(X, Y, Z)

```
{
  Return (X + Y + Y*Z + (X+Y–Z)) / ((X+Y) +40);
}
```

In the above algorithm, here are no instance characteristics and the space needed by X, Y, Z is independent of instance characteristics therefore we can write

S (XYZ) = 3 + 0 = 3

Linear Space Complexity: the space needed for algorithm like size of the variable, array of values, loop variable and sum variable.

Ex1: int add(X, n)

```
{
Total = 0;
For i=1 to n do
        Total = Total + X[i];
Return Total;
}
```

For the above program we make some assumption that one word of space needed for N and the space needed by X is the space needed by the variable of type array of floating point numbers this is at least N words since X must be larger enough to hold the NL comment to be summed here the problem instance is characterized by N the number of elements to be summed so we can write.

S(add) = $(n + 3)$

Where n → is for array X [ ]

3 → one each for n, I and total.

EXAMPLE 2:

```
Algorithm Rsum(X, n)
{
 If(n<=0) then return 0;
 Else return (Rsum (X, n–1) + a[n]);
}
```

Since the above problem uses recursion, stack space includes space for the formal parameters, Local variables and the return address.

Here the problem instances are characterized by 'n' assumption we make here is the return address requires one word of memory. Each call are 'Rsum' requires at least three words this includes space for the value of n, the return address and a pointera[]. Depth of recursion is $n + 1$. Hence the space needed is

S (Rsum) = 3(n+1) = 3n +3

The Need for Analysis

The need for analysis of algorithms and how to choose a better algorithm for a particular problem as one computational problem can be solved by different algorithms.

Algorithms are often quite different from one another, though the objective of these algorithms are the same. For example, we know that asset of numbers can be sorted using different algorithms. Number of comparisons performed by one algorithm may vary with others for the same input. Hence, time complexity of those algorithms may differ. At the same time, we need to calculate the memory space required by each algorithm.

The algorithm analysis framework consists of the following:

- Measuring an Input's Size
- Units for Measuring Running Time
- Orders of Growth
- Worst–Case, Best–Case, and Average–Case Efficiencies

Measuring an Input's Size:

An algorithm's efficiency is defined as a function of some parameter n indicating the algorithm's input size. In most cases, selecting such a parameter is quite straight forward. For example, it will be the size of the list for problems of sorting, searching.

Almost all algorithms run longer on larger inputs. For example, it takes to sort larger arrays, multiply larger matrices and so on. It is important to investigate an algorithm's efficiency as a function of some parameter n indicating the algorithm's input size. For example, it will be the size of the list for problems of sorting, searching etc. For the problem of evaluating a polynomial $p(x)$ = an x^n+ ——— + $a0$ of degree n, it will be the polynomial's degree or the number of its coefficients, which is larger by one than its degree.

The size is also influenced by the operations of the algorithm. For example in a spell–check algorithm, it examines individual characters of its input, then we measure the size by the number of characters or words.

Note: Measuring size of inputs for algorithms involving properties of numbers. For such algorithms, computer scientists prefer measuring size by the number b of bits in the n's binary representation.

$$b = \log 2^{n+1}.$$

Units for Measuring Running Time:

We can use some standard unit of time to measure the running time of a program implementing the algorithm. The drawbacks to such an approach are : the dependence on the speed of a particular computer, the quality of a program implementing the algorithm.

The drawback to such an approach are : the dependence on the speed of a particular computer, the quality of a program implementing the algorithm, the compiler used to generate its machine code and the difficulty in clocking the actual running time of the program. Here, we do not consider these extraneous factors for simplicity.

One possible approach is to count the number of times each of the algorithm's operations is executed. The simple way, is to identify the most important operation of the algorithm, called the basic operation, the operation contributing the most to the total running time and compute the number of times the basic operation is executed.

The basic operation is usually the most time consuming operation in the algorithm's innermost loop. For example, most sorting algorithm works by comparing elements (keys), of a list being sorted with each other; for such algorithms, the basic operation is the key comparison.

Let Cop be the time of execution of an algorithm's basic operation on a particular computer and let $c(n)$ be the number of times this operations needs to be executed for this algorithm. Then we can estimate the running time, T (n) as: T $(n) \sim$ Cop $c(n)$

Here, the count $c(n)$ does not contain any information about operations that are not basic and intact, the count it self is often computed only approximately. The constant Cop is also an approximation whose reliability is not easy to assess. If this algorithm is executed in a machine which is ten times faster than one we have, the running time is also ten times or assuming that $C(n) = \frac{1}{2} n(n-1)$, how much longer will the algorithm run if we doubt its in put size? The answer is four times longer. Indeed, for all but very small values of n,

$$C(n) = \frac{1}{2} n(n-1) = \frac{1}{2} n^2 - \frac{1}{2} n \approx \frac{1}{2} n^2$$

and therefore,

	T(2n)	Cop C(2n)	$\frac{1}{2}(2n)^2 = 4$
		Cop	
	$T(n) \approx$	C(n)	$\approx \frac{1}{2}(2n)^2$

Here Cop is unknown, but still we got the result, the value is cancelled out in the ratio. Also, ½ the multiplicative constant is also cancelled out. Therefore, the efficiency analysis framework ignores multiplicative constants and concentrates on the counts' order of growth to within a constant multiple for large size inputs.

Running time of algorithms is typically measured using units that represent the amount of time or computational work performed by the algorithm. Common units include:

- **Seconds:** Measuring running time in seconds is a straightforward way to express how long an algorithm takes to execute. like the speed of the computer's processor, available resources, and system load.
- **Operations:** This unit counts the number of basic operations (such as arithmetic operations, comparisons, or memory accesses) performed by the algorithm.
- **Instructions:** In low–level programming and assembly language, running time can be measured in terms of the number of machine instructions executed by the algorithm. This unit is closely related to the hardware and architecture.
- **Clock Cycles:** In the context of microprocessor or hardware–level analysis, running time can be measured in clock cycles. Each machine instruction may take a certain number of clock cycles to execute.
- **Comparisons:** For sorting algorithms and search algorithms, the number of comparisons between elements or keys is a common unit of measurement.
- **Memory Accesses:** In cases where memory access patterns significantly affect performance, the number of memory accesses can be a critical metric.
- **I/O Operations:** In input/output–bound tasks, measuring running time in terms of read and write operations can be relevant.

Orders of Growth

- Orders of growth, also known as algorithmic complexity or computational complexity, are a way to analyze and describe the efficiency of algorithms.
- Orders of growth provide a high–level to categorize algorithms based on their efficiency and predict how they will perform when the input size grows.

O(1) – Constant Time:

- Algorithms with constant time complexity
- It takes same amount of time to complete, regardless of the input size.
- Running time is not dependent on the size of the input data
- E.g. Performing basic arithmetic operations are examples of O(1) operations.

O(n) – Linear Time:

- Algorithms with linear time complexity have a running time that scales linearly with the size of the input data.
- If the input size doubles, the running time also doubles.

E.g. Linear search through an unsorted list or iterating through an array are common examples of $O(n)$ operations.

$O(n^2)$, $O(n^3)$, etc. – Polynomial Time

- Algorithms with polynomial time complexity have running times that depend on the input size to some power.
- For example, an algorithm with $O(n^2)$ time complexity means that its running time is proportional to the square of the input size.

E.g: sorting algorithms like bubble sort and selection sort have $O(n^2)$ complexity.

O(log n) logarithmic time

e.g., binary search

- In binary search, you repeatedly divide the search space in half, making it a very efficient way to find an item in a sorted list or array.
- This process of halving the search space leads to a logarithmic growth in running time.
- the running time of an algorithm grows in proportion to the logarithm of the input size (n).
- This is a highly desirable characteristic for algorithms when dealing with large datasets because they tend to be much more efficient than algorithms with linear or polynomial time complexity.

$O(n^2)$ – Quadratic Time

- Its a category of algorithmic efficiency where the running time of an algorithm grows quadratic ally with the input size (n).
- As the input size increases, the running time of the algorithm increases by the square of the input size.
- Quadratic time complexity is still efficient for small input sizes, but it can become slow for larger datasets. It's often used when more efficient solutions are not available.

E.g. Sorting algorithms like the Bubble Sort and certain types of nested loop-based searching algorithms often have quadratic time complexity.

O(2^n) for exponential time complexity

- This notation indicates that the running time of the algorithm grows exponentially with the input size.
- The "2" in O(2^n) implies that the running time doubles as the input size increases by one, which is a characteristic of exponential growth.
- E.g: Traveling Salesman Problem (TSP).
- Certain types of recursive algorithms.

O(n log n) – Linearithmic Time:

- Algorithms with linearithmic time complexity are often efficient for sorting and other divide–and–conquer problems. They are faster than pure linear time in many cases.

Values of several functions important for analysis of algorithms:

n	log 2 n	n	n log 2n	n^2	n^3	2n	$n!$
10	3.3	10^1	$3.3x10^1$	10^2	10^3	10^3	$3.6 x10^6$
10^2	6.6	10^2	$6.6x10^2$	10^4	10^6	$1.3 x10^{30}$	$9.3 x10^{157}$
10^3	10	10^3	$1.0x10^4$	10^6	10^9		
10^4	13	10^4	$1.3x10^5$	10^8	10^{12}		
10^5	17	10^5	$1.7x10^6$	10^{10}	10^{15}		
10^6	20	10^6	$2.0x10^7$	10^{12}	10^{18}		

The function growing slowly is the logarithmic function, logarithmic basic–operation count to run practically instantaneously on inputs of all realistic sizes. Although specific values of such a count depend, of course, in the logarithm's base, the formula.

Makes it possible to switch from one base to another, leaving the count logarithmic but with a new multiplicative constant.

On the other end, the exponential function 2^n and the factorial function n! grows of as even for small values of n. These two functions are required to as exponential–growth functions. "Algorithms that require an exponential number of operations are practical for solving only problems of very small sizes."

Another way to appreciate the qualitative difference among the orders of growth of the functions is to consider how they react to, say, a twofold increase in the value of their argument n. The function log 2n increases in value by just 1 (since log22n = log22 + log2n = 1 + log2n); the linear function increases twofold; then log n increases slightly more than twofold; the quadratic n^2 as fourfold (since $(2n)^2= 4n^2$) and the cubic function n^3 as eight fold (since $(2n)^3 = 8n^3$); the value of 2^n is squared (since $2^{2n}=(2^n)^2$ and n! increases much more than that.

Worst–case, Best–case and Average–case efficiencies:

Best Case:

- The best–case represents the most favorable conditions under which an algorithm can operate.
- It is the situation where the algorithm performs with the least amount of work or in the shortest amount of time.
- Best–case analysis provides the lower bound of an algorithm's performance. It helps understand the ideal efficiency under specific circumstances.
- However, best–case scenarios are often theoretical and may not reflect real–world performance accurately. Algorithms are generally designed to perform well on average or in the worst–case scenarios

Worst Case:

- The worst–case represents the most unfavorable conditions or the input data that would make the algorithm perform with the maximum amount of work or take the longest time.
- It serves as an upper bound on an algorithm's performance. It helps understand how bad the algorithm's performance can be in the most challenging situations.

Average Case:

- The average–case represents the expected or typical performance of an algorithm when provided with random or statistically likely input data.
- It is often the most relevant analysis for real–world applications since it considers the common or typical usage of the algorithm.
- Average–case analysis considers various input distributions and their probabilities to calculate the expected running time or resource usage.

EXAMPLE: The running time not only depends on the input size but also on the specifics of a particular input. Consider the example, sequential search. It's a straightforward algorithm that searches for a given item (search key K) in a list of n elements by checking successive elements of the list until either a match with these arch key is found or the list is exhausted.

The psuedocode is as follows.

```
Algorithm sequential search {A[0. .n–1] , k}
//Searches for a given value in a given array by Sequential search
//Input: An array A[0..n–1]and a search key K
//Output: Returns the index of the first element of A that matches K or–1 if there is
// no match
i← o
while i<n and A[ i]≠K do i←i+1
if i<n
return i
else
return–1
```

Clearly, the running time of this algorithm can be quite different for the same list size n. In the worst case, when there are no matching elements or the first matching element happens to be the last one on the list, the algorithm makes the largest number of key comparisons among all possible inputs of size n; C worst $(n) = n$.

The worst–case efficiency of an algorithm is its efficiency for the worst–case input of size n, which is an input of size n for which the algorithm runs the longest among all possible inputs of that size. The way to determine is, to analyze the algorithm to see what kind of inputs yield the largest value of the basic operation's count $c(n)$ among all possible inputs of size n and then compute this worst–case value C worst(n).

The best– case efficiency of an algorithm is its efficiency for the best–case input of size n, which is an input of size n for which the algorithm runs the fastest among all inputs of that size. First, determine the kind of inputs for which the count C(n) will be the smallest among all possible inputs of size n. Then ascertain the value of C(n) on the most convenient inputs. For example, for the searching with input size n, if the first element equals to a search key, C best(n) = 1.

Neither the best–case nor the worst–case gives the necessary information about an algorithm's behaviour on a typical or random input. This is the information that the average–case efficiency seeks to provide. To analyze the algorithm's average–case efficiency, we must make some assumptions about possible inputs of size n.

EXAMPLE: Let us consider a gain sequential search. The standard assumptions are that:

1. the probability of a successful search is equal to p$(0 \le p \le 1)$,and,
2. the probability of the first match occurring in the ith position is same for every i.

Accordingly, the probability of the first match occurring in the ith position of the list is p/n for every i, and the no. of comparisons is i for a successful search. In case of unsuccessful search, the number of comparisons is n with probability of such a search being $(1 - p)$.Therefore,

$$\text{Cavg}(n) = [1 .p/n + 2 . p/n + \ldots\ldots\ldots i . p/n + \ldots\ldots\ldots\ldots\ldots n. p/n] + n . (1 - p)$$

$$= p/n\ [1 + 2 + \ldots\ldots. i + \ldots\ldots\ldots\ldots + n] + n . (1 - p)$$

$$= p/n . [n (n + 1)]/2 + n .(1 - p) \text{ [sum of } 1^{st}\ n \text{ natural number formula]}$$

$$= [p(n + 1)]/2 + n .(1 - p)$$

This general formula yields the answers. For example, if $p = 1$ (i.e., successful), the average number of key comparisons made by sequential search is $(n + 1)/2$; i.e., the algorithm will inspect, on an average, about half of the list's elements. If $p = 0$ (i.e., unsuccessful), the average number of key comparisons will be 'n' because the algorithm will inspect all n elements on all such inputs.

The average–case is better than the worst–case, and it is not the average of both best and worst–cases.

Another type of efficiency is called amortized efficiency. It applies not to a single run of an algorithm but rather to a sequence of operations performed on the same data structure. In some situations a single operation can be expensive, but the total time for an entire sequence of such n operations is always better than the worst–case efficiency of that single operation multiplied by n. It is considered in algorithms for finding unions of disjoint sets

RECAPS OF ANALYSIS FRAMEWORK :

1. Both time and space efficiencies are measured as functions of the algorithm's i/p size.
2. Time efficiency is measured by counting the number of times the algorithm's basic operation is executed. Space efficiency is measured by counting the number of extra memory units consumed by the algorithm.
3. The efficiencies of some algorithms may differ significantly for input of the same size. For such algorithms, we need to distinguish between the worst–case, average–case and best–case efficiencies.
4. The frame work's primary interest lies in the order of growth of the algorithm's running time as its input size goes to infinity.

❍❍❍

UNIT

2

ASYMPTOTIC NOTATION AND BASIC EFFICIENCY CLASSES

ASYMPTOTIC NOTATION:

Asymptotic notations are the mathematical notations used to describe the running time of an algorithm when the input tends towards a particular value or a limiting value. Execution time of an algorithm depends on the instruction set, processor speed, disk I/O speed, etc. Hence, we estimate the efficiency of an algorithm asymptotically.

Let $t(n)$ and $g(n)$ can be any non-negative functions defined on the set of natural numbers. The algorithm's running time $t(n)$ usually indicated by its basic operation count $C(n)$, and $g(n)$, some simple function to compare with the count.

Different types of asymptotic notations are used to represent the complexity of an algorithm.

Following asymptotic notations are used to calculate the running time complexity of an algorithm.

O – Big Oh

Ω – Big omega

θ – Big theta

Why is Asymptotic Notation Important?

Asymptotic Notation is a very important part involved in algorithm design and analysis. Some of the main reasons of importance include:

- **Comparing Efficiency** – We can easily compare the efficiency of the algorithms by analysing their average, best, and worst–case complexities.
- **Problem–Solving** – Time and Space complexities are a very important part of problem–solving in computer science. These notations help the programmer predict the program's expected time and space requirements.
- **Standardization** – Asymptotic notation provides the users with a standardized **way to differentiate between multiple algorithms for the same task.**
- **Optimization** – We can also use the asymptotic notations to analyze our program and further optimize it for better performance.
- **Scaling** – Asymptotic Notation also helps us check whether our algorithm can work efficiently on larger datasets.

Properties of Asymptotic Notations

Some of the properties of asymptotic notations are:

Symmetric

If $f(n)$ equals theta($g(n)$, then $g(n)$ equals theta($f(n)$).

Transpose symmetric

If $f(n)$ equals Big–Oh($g(n)$), then $g(n)$ equals Omega($f(n)$).

Transitive

If $f(n)$ equals Big–Oh($g(n)$) and $g(n)$ equals Big–Oh($h(n)$), then $f(n)$ = Big – Oh($h(n)$).

Reflexive

If $f(n)$ is given, it means $f(n)$ is Big–Oh($f(n)$).

Big Oh (O): Asymptotic Upper Bound

'O' (Big Oh) is the most commonly used notation. A function $f(n)$ can be represented is the order of $g(n)$ that is O($g(n)$), if there exists a value of positive integer n as $n0$ and a positive constant c such that –

$$f(n) \leq c.g(n) \text{ for } n > n0 \text{ in all case}$$

Hence, function $g(n)$ is an upper bound for function $f(n)$, as $g(n)$ grows faster than $f(n)$.

EXAMPLE : Let us consider a given function, $f(n) = 4 .n^3 +10. 4 . n^2 + 5 . n + 1$

Considering $g(n) = n^3$,

$$f(n) \leq 5. g(n) \text{ for all the values of } n > 2$$

Hence, the complexity of $f(n)$ can be represented as $O(g(n))$, i.e. $O(4 . n^3)$

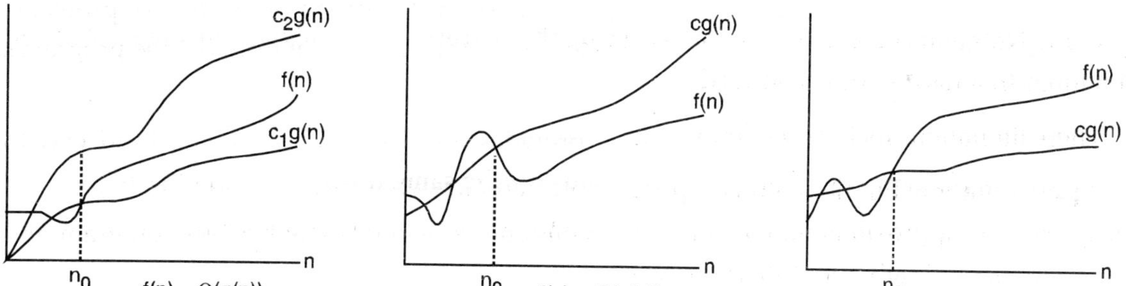

f(n) = Θ(g(n)) (a) f(n) = O(g(n)) (b) f(n) = Ω(g(n)) (c)

The Use of Big O Notation in Real–World Applications

Big O Notation is widely used in computer science and software engineering to analyze and compare the performance of algorithms. This notation is used in various real–world applications to determine algorithms' efficiency, scalability, and stability and to make informed decisions about which algorithm to use for a specific problem.

Some of the common real–world applications where Big O Notation is used include:

Database Optimization: Big O Notation is used to analyze and optimize the performance of database operations, such as query execution and indexing. Understanding the time complexity of different database operations makes it possible to make informed decisions about which algorithms to use and how to design the database to achieve the desired performance.

Sorting and Searching: Big O Notation is used to analyze the performance of sorting and searching algorithms and to compare the efficiency of different algorithms. Understanding the time complexity of sorting and searching algorithms makes it possible to make informed decisions about which algorithm to use for a specific problem.

Graph Algorithms: Big O Notation is used to analyze the performance of graph algorithms, such as breadth–first search and depth–first search. Understanding the time complexity of different graph algorithms makes it possible to make informed decisions about which algorithm to use for a specific problem.

Computer Graphics: Big O Notation is used to analyze the performance of algorithms used in computer graphics, such as rendering and image processing algorithms. Understanding the time complexity of different computer graphics algorithms makes it possible to make informed decisions about which algorithm to use for a specific problem.

The Limitations of Big O Notation

Big O Notation is a useful tool for analysing the performance of algorithms, but it has some limitations that need to be considered.

These limitations include the following:

Approximation: Big O Notation approximates an algorithm's running time rather than the exact time. The approximation may only sometimes accurately reflect the actual running time of an algorithm, especially for small input sizes.

Overestimation: Big O Notation tends to overestimate the running time of an algorithm, as it only considers the worst–case scenario. This can lead to an overestimation of the actual running time of an algorithm, especially for algorithms with better average–case time complexity.

Constant Factors: Big O Notation ignores constant factors, such as the efficiency of the hardware and the compiler used to run the algorithm. These constant factors can significantly impact the actual running time of an algorithm, but they are not taken into account by Big O Notation.

Unrepresentative Inputs: Big O Notation assumes that the input size is the only factor affecting an algorithm's running time. However, this is only sometimes the case, as the input data distribution can also significantly impact the running time of an algorithm.

Omega (Ω): Asymptotic Lower Bound

We say that $f(n) = \Omega(g(n))$ when there exists constant c that $f(n) \geq c \cdot g(n)$ for all sufficiently large value of n. Here n is a positive integer. It means function g is a lower bound for function f; after a certain value of n, f will never go below g.

EXAMPLE : Let us consider a given function, $f(n) = 4 \cdot n^3 + 10.\ 4 \cdot n^2 + 5 \cdot n + 1$

Considering $g(n) = 3$, $f(n) \geq 4 .g(n)$ for all the values of $n > 0$

Hence, the complexity of $f(n)$ can be represented as $\Omega(g(n))$, i.e. $\Omega(3)$

Theta (θ): Asymptotic Tight Bound

We say that $f(n) = \theta(g(n))$ when there exist constants c_1 and c_2 that $1.g(n) \leq f(n) \leq 2 \cdot g(n)$ for all sufficiently large value of n. Here n is a positive integer. This means function g is a tight bound for function f.

EXAMPLE : Let us consider a given function, $f(n) = 4 . n^3 + 10 . 4 . n^2 + 5 . n + 1$

Considering $g(n) = 3$, $4 . g(n) \leq f(n) \leq 5 . g(n)$ for all the large values of n.

Hence, the complexity of $f(n)$ **can be represented** as $\theta(g(n))$, i.e. $\theta(n^3)$.

What is the difference between Big O, Big Omega, and Big Theta Asymptotic Notations:

The property is used in analyzing algorithms that consists of two consecutively executed parts:

THEOREM : If $t_1(n)) \in O(g_1(n))$ and $t_2(n) \in O(g_2(n))$ then $t_1(n) + t_2(n) \in O(\max\{g_1(n), g_2(n)\})$.

PROOF (As we shall see, the proof will extend to orders of growth the following simple fact about four arbitrary real numbers a_1 , b_1 , a_2, and b_2: if $a_1 < b_1$ and $a_2 < b_2$ then $a_1 + a_2 < 2 \max\{ b_1, b_2\}$.) Since $t_1(n) \in O(g_1(n))$, there exist some constant c and some non-negative integer n_1 such that $t_1(n) < c_1 g_1(n)$ for all $n > n_1$ since $t_2(n) \in O(g_2(n))$, $t_2(n) < c_2 g_2(n)$ for all $n > n_2$.

Let us denote $c_3 = \max fc_1, c_2\}$ and consider $n > \max \{n_1, n_2\}$ so that we can use both inequalities. Adding the two inequalities above yields the following:

$t_1(n) + t_2(n) < c_1 g_1(n) + c_2 g_2(n)$

$< c_3 g_1(n) + c_3 g_2(n) = c_3[g_1(n) + g_2(n)]$

$< c_{32} \max\{g_1(n), g_2(n)\}$.

Hence, $t_1(n) + t_2(n)) \in O(\max \{g_1(n) , g_2(n)\})$, with the constants c and n_0 required by the O definition being $2c_3 = 2 \max\{c_1, c_2\}$ and $\max\{ n_1, n_2\}$, respectively. This implies that the algorithm's overall efficiency will be determined by the part with a larger order of growth, i.e., its least efficient part:

$t_1(n) \in O(g_1(n))$

$t_2(n) \in O(g_2(n))$ then $t_1(n) + t_2(n) \in O(\max\{g_1(n), g_2(n)\})$.

For example, we can check whether an array has identical elements by means of the following two–part algorithm: first, sort the array by applying some known sorting algorithm; second, scan the sorted array to check its consecutive elements for equality. If, for example, a sorting algorithm used in the first part makes no more than $1/2n(n - 1)$ comparisons (and hence is in $O(n_2)$) while the second part makes no more than $n - 1$ comparisons (and hence is in $O(n\})$, the efficiency of the entire algorithm will be in $(O(\max\{n_2, n\}) = O(n_2)$.

Using Limits for Comparing Orders of Growth:

The convenient method for doing the comparison is based on computing the limit of the ratio of two functions in question. Three principal cases may arise:

$t(n)$ 0 implies that $t(n)$ has a smaller order of growth than $g(n)$ lim= c implies that $t(n)$ has the same order of growth as $g(n)$ $n \to \infty$ $g(n)$ ∞ implies that $t(n)$ has a larger order of growth than $g(n)$.

Note that the first two cases mean that $t(n) \in O(g(n))$, the last two mean that $t(n) \in \Omega(g(n))$, and the second case means that $t(n) \in \Theta(g(n))$.

EXAMPLE 1. Compare orders of growth of 1/2 $n(n - 1)$ and $n2$. (This is one of the examples we did above to illustrate the definitions.)

lim 1/2 $n(n - 1)$ = ½ lim $n^2 - n$ = 1/2 lim $(1 - 1/n)$ = ½ $n \to \infty$ $n2$ $n \to \infty$ n^2 $n \to \infty$

Since the limit is equal to a positive constant, the functions have the same order of growth or, symbolically, 1/2 $n(n - 1) \in \Theta(n^2)$

Basic Efficiency Classes:

Even though the efficiency analysis framework puts together all the functions whose orders of growth differ by a constant multiple, there are still infinitely many such classes. (For example, the exponential functions an have different orders of growth for different values of base a.) Therefore, it may come as a surprise that the time efficiencies of a large number of algorithms fall into only a few classes. These classes are listed in Table in increasing order of their orders of growth, along with their names and a few comments.

You could raise a concern that classifying algorithms according to their asymptotic efficiency classes has little practical value because the values of multiplicative constants are usually left unspecified. This leaves open a possibility of an algorithm in a worse efficiency class running faster than an algorithm in a better efficiency class for inputs of realistic sizes. For example, if the running time of one algorithm is $n3$ while the running time of the other is $106n2$, the cubic algorithm will outperform the quadratic algorithm unless n exceeds 106. A few such anomalies are indeed known. For example, there exist algorithms for matrix multiplication with a better asymptotic efficiency than the cubic efficiency of the definition–based algorithm Because of their much larger multiplicative constants, however, the value of these more sophisticated algorithms is mostly theoretical.

Fortunately, multiplicative constants usually do not differ that drastically. As a rule, you should expect an algorithm from a better asymptotic efficiency class to outperform an algorithm from a worse class even for moderately sized inputs. This observation is especially true for an algorithm with a better than exponential running time versus an exponential (or worse) algorithm.

Class	Name	Comments
1	Constant	Short of best case efficiency when its input grows the time also grows to infinity.
Logn	Logarithmic	It cannot take into account all its input, any algorithm that does so will have atleast linear running time.
N	Linear	Algorithms that scan a list of size *n*, e.g., sequential Search
nlogn	Nlogn	Many divide & conquer algorithms including Merger sort quick sort fall into this class
n^2	Quadratic	Characterizes with two embedded loops, mostly sorting and matrix operations.
N^3	Cubic	Efficiency of algorithms with three embedded loops,
2^n	Exponential	Algorithms that generate all subsets of an *n*–element set
n!	factorial	Algorithms that generate all permutations of an *n*–element set

Types of Time Complexity

Some Common Algorithmic Runtimes. (from fastest to slowest)

O(1)	Constant Time Complexity	**Example:** Sum of two numbers.
O(log*n*)	Logarithmic Time Complexity	**Example:** Finding an element in a sorted array by using binary search.
O(*n*)	Linear Time Complexity	**Example:** Finding the sum of an array of size *n*.
O(*n* log*n*)	Log–Linear Time Complexity	**Example:** Sorting the array using merge sort.
O(n^2)	Quadratic Time Complexity	**Example:** Finding the sum of every pair of elements in an array.

O(2*n*)	Exponential Time Complexity	**Example:** Finding all the subsets.
O(*n*!)	Factorial Time Complexity	**Example:** Finding all the permutations of a given array.

Big O	Big Omega	Big Theta
It gives the worst–case complexity.	It gives the best–case complexity.	It gives the average–case complexity.
The actual complexity must be less than the Big O complexity.	The actual complexity must be more than the Big Ω complexity.	The actual complexity is often the Big Θ complexity.
It provides an upper bound.	It provides a lower bound.	It provides both an upper and a lower bound.
It is mathematically represented as: $O(g(n)) = f(n)$, such that there $0 \le f(n) \le c \cdot g(n)$ for all $n \ge n0$, where c and $n0$ are positive constants.	It is mathematically represented as: $\Omega(g(n)) = f(n)$, such that there $0 \le c.g(n) \le f(n)$ for all $n \ge n0$, where c and $n0$ are positive constants.	It is mathematically represented as : $\Theta(g(n)) = f(n)$, such that there $0 \le c_1.g(n) \le f(n) \le c_2.g(n)$ for all $n \ge n0$, where c_1, c_2 and $n0$ are positive constants.

Time Complexity Cheat Sheet

Algorithm	Best Case Time Complexity	Average Case Time Complexity	Worst Case Time Complexity
Linear Search	O(1)	O(*n*)	O(*n*)
Binary Search	O(1)	O(log *n*)	O(log *n*)
Bubble Sort	O(*n*)	O(*n*^2)	O(*n*^2)
Selection Sort	O(*n*^2)	O(*n*^2)	O(*n*^2)
Insertion Sort	O(*n*)	O(*n*^2)	O(*n*^2)
Merge Sort	O(*n*log*n*)	O(*n*log*n*)	O(*n*log*n*)
Quick Sort	O(*n*log*n*)	O(*n*log*n*)	O(*n*^2)
Heap Sort	O(*n*log*n*)	O(*n*log*n*)	O(*n*log*n*)
Bucket Sort	O(*n*+ *k*)	O(*n* + *k*)	O(*n*^2)
Radix Sort	O(*nk*)	O(*nk*)	O(*nk*)
Tim Sort	O(*n*)	O(*n*log*n*)	O(*n*log*n*)
Shell Sort	O(*n*)	O((*n*log*n*)^2)	O(1)

MATHEMATICAL ANALYSIS OF NON–RECURSIVE ALGORITHMS:

The general framework outlined is applied to analyze the efficiency of non recursive algorithms. Let us start with a very simple example that demonstrates the entire principal steps typically taken in analyzing such algorithms.

EXAMPLE 1. Consider the problem of finding the value of the largest element in a list of n numbers. For simplicity, we assume that the list is implemented as an array. The following is a pseudocode of a standard algorithm for solving the problem.

ALGORITHM Max Element(A[0,..n – 1])

//Determines the value of the largest element in a given array //Input:

An array A[0..n – 1] of real numbers

//Output: The value of the largest element in A maxval <– A[0]

for i <– 1 to n – 1 do

if A[i] > maxval maxval <– A[i] return maxval

The obvious measure of an input's size here is the number of elements in the array, i.e., n. The operations that are going to be executed most often are in the algorithm's for loop. There are two operations in the loop's body: the comparison A[i] > maxval and the assignment maxval ← A[i]. Since the comparison is executed on each repetition of the loop and the assignment is not, we should consider the comparison to be the algorithm's basic operation. (Note that the number of comparisons will be the same for all arrays of size n; therefore, in terms of this metric, there is no need to distinguish among the worst, average, and best cases here.)

Let us denote C(n) the number of times this comparison is executed and try to find a formula expressing it as a function of size n. The algorithm makes one comparison on each execution of the loop, which is repeated for each value of the loop's variable i within the bounds between 1 and n – 1 (inclusively). Therefore, we get the following sum for C(n): $C(n) = \sum_{i=1}^{n-1} 1$

This is an easy sum to compute because it is nothing else but 1 repeated n–1 times. Thus,

$$C(n) = \sum^{n-1} 1 = n - 1 \in \theta(n)$$

Here is a general plan to follow in analyzing non recursive algorithms.

General Plan for Analyzing Efficiency of Non–recursive Algorithms

1. Decide on a parameter (or parameters) indicating an input's size.

2. Identify the algorithm's basic operation. (As a rule, it is located in its inner most loop.)
3. Check whether the number of times the basic operation is executed depends only on the size of an input. If it also depends on some additional property, the worst–case, average–case, and, if necessary, best–case efficiencies must be investigated separately.
4. Setup a sum expressing the number of times the algorithm's basic operation is executed.
5. Using standard formulas and rules of sum manipulation either find a closed–form formula for the count or, at the very least, establish its order of growth.

In particular, we use especially frequently two basic rules of sum manipulation

$$\sum_{i=1}^{u} c\, ai = c \sum_{i=1}^{u} ai \quad \text{........ } (R_1)$$

$$\sum_{i=1}^{u} (ai \pm bi) = \sum_{i=1}^{u} ai \pm \sum_{i=1}^{u} bi \quad \text{........ } (R_2)$$

and two summation formulas

$$\sum_{i=1}^{u} 1 = u - 1 + 1 \text{ where } 1 \le u \text{ are some lower and upper integer limits} \quad \text{— } (S_1)$$

$$\sum_{i=0}^{n} i = 1 + 2 + ... + n = [n(n+1)]/2 \approx \tfrac{1}{2} n_2 \in \theta(n_2) \quad (S_2)$$

(Note that the formula which we used in Example 1, is a special case of formula (S_1) for l= = 0 and $n = n - 1$)

EXAMPLE 2. Consider the element uniqueness problem: Check whether all the elements in a given array are distinct. This problem can be solved by the following straightforward algorithm.

```
ALGORITHM Unique Elements (A[0..n– 1])
//Checks whether all the elements in a given array are distinct//Input:
An array A[0..n–1]
//"false" otherwise.
for i «– 0 to n – 2 do for
j' <– i: + 1 to n – 1 do
if A[i] = A[j]
return false
return true
```

The natural input's size measure here is again the number of elements in the array, i.e., n. Since the innermost loop contains a single operation (the comparison of two elements), we should consider it as the algorithm's basic operation. Note, however, that the number of element comparisons will depend not only on n but also on whether there are equal elements in the array and, if there are, which array positions they occupy. We will limit our investigation to the worst case only.

By definition, the worst case input is an array for which the number of element comparisons Cworst(n) is the largest among all arrays of size n. An inspection of the innermost loop reveals that there ate two kinds of worst–case inputs (inputs for which the algorithm does not exit the loop prematurely): arrays with no equal elements and arrays in which the last two elements are the only pair of equal elements. For such inputs, one comparison is made for each repetition of the innermost loop, i.e., for each value of the loop's variable j between its limits $i + 1$ and $n - 1$; and this is repeated for each value of the outer loop, i.e., for each value of the loop's variable i between its limits 0 and $n - 2$. Accordingly, we get

$$C\text{ worst }(n) = \sum_{i=0}^{n-2} \sum_{j=i+1}^{n-1} = \sum_{i=0}^{n-2} [(n-1) - (i+1) + 1] = \sum_{i=0}^{n-2} (n-1-i)$$

$$= \sum_{i=0}^{n-2} (n-1) - \sum_{i=0}^{n-2} i = (n-1) \sum_{i=0}^{n-2} 1 - [(n-2)(n-1)]/2$$

$$= (n-1)\, 2 - [(n-2)(n-1)]/2 = [(n-1)n]/2 \approx \tfrac{1}{2} n^2 \in \theta(n^2)$$

Also it can be solved as (by using S_2) $\sum^{n-2} (n-1-i) = (n-1) + (n-2) + \ldots\ldots + 1$

$$= [(n-1)n]/2 \approx \tfrac{1}{2} n^2 \in \theta(n^2) \; i=0$$

Note that this result was perfectly predictable: in the worst case, the algorithm needs to compare all n(n – 1)/2 distinct pairs of its n elements.

MATHEMATICAL ANALYSIS OF RECURSIVE ALGORITHMS

In this section, we systematically apply the general framework to analyze the efficiency of recursive algorithms. Let us start with a very simple example that demonstrates all the principal steps typically taken in analyzing recursive algorithms.

EXAMPLE 1: Compute the factorial function F(n) = n! for an arbitrary non negative integer n. Since, $n! = 1 * 2 * \ldots\ldots * (n-1) * n = n(n-1)!$ For $n \geq 1$ and $0! = 1$ by definition, we can compute $F(n) = F(n-1).\, n$ with the following recursive algorithm.

```
ALGORITHM F(n)
// Computes n! recursively
// Input: A nonnegative integer n
// Output: The value of n! if n =0 return 1
else return F(n – 1) * n
```

For simplicity, we consider n itself as an indicator of this algorithm's input size (rather than the number of bits in its binary expansion). The basic operation of the algorithm is multiplication, whose number of executions we denote $M(n)$. Since the function $F(n)$ is computed according to the formula

$$F(n) = F(n-1) - n \qquad \text{for } n > 0,$$

the number of multiplications $M(n)$ needed to compute it must satisfy the equality

$$M(n) = M(n-1) + 1 \qquad \text{for } n > 0.$$

to compute to multiply

$F(n-1)$ $F(n-1)$ by n

Indeed, $M(n - 1)$ multiplications are spent to compute $F(n - 1)$, and one more multiplication is needed to multiply the result by n.

The last equation defines the sequence $M(n)$ that we need to find. Note that the equation defines $M(n)$ not explicitly, i.e., as a function of n, but implicitly as a function of its value at another point, namely $n - 1$. Such equations are called recurrence relations or, for brevity, recurrences. Recurrence relations play an important role not only in analysis of algorithms but also in some areas of applied mathematics. Our goal now is to solve the recurrence relation $M(n) = M(n-1) + 1$, i.e., to find an explicit formula for the sequence $M(n)$ in terms of n only.

Note, however, that there is not one but infinitely many sequences that satisfy this recurrence. To determine a solution uniquely, we need an initial condition that tells us the value with which the sequence starts. We can obtain this value by inspecting the condition that makes the algorithm stop its recursive calls:

if $n = 0$ return 1.

This tells us two things. First, since the calls stop when $n = 0$, the smallest value of n for which this algorithm is executed and hence $M(n)$ defined is 0. Second, by inspecting the code's exiting line, we can see that when $n = 0$, the algorithm performs no multiplications.

Thus, the initial condition we are after is:

$$M(0) = 0.$$

the calls stop when $n = 0$, no multiplications when $n = 0$ Thus, we succeed in setting up the recurrence relation and initial condition for the algorithm's number of multiplications $M(n)$:

$$M(n) = M(n-1) + 1 \text{ for } n > 0, \quad (2.1)$$

$$M(0) = 0.$$

Before we embark on a discussion of how to solve this recurrence, let us pause to reiterate an important point. We are dealing here with two recursively defined functions. The first is the factorial function $F(n)$ itself; it is defined by the recurrence

$$F(n) = F(n-1) \bullet n \text{ for every } n > 0, F(0) = 1.$$

The second is the number of multiplications $M(n)$ needed to compute $F(n)$ by the recursive algorithm whose pseudo code was given at the beginning of the section. As we just showed, $M(n)$ is defined by recurrence (2.1). And it is recurrence (2.1) that we need to solve now.

Though it is not difficult to "guess" the solution, it will be more useful to arrive at it in a systematic fashion. Among several techniques available for solving recurrence relations, we use what can be called the method of backward substitutions. The method's idea (and the reason for the name) is immediately clear from the way it applies to solving there currency:

$M(n) = M(n-1) + 1$ + substitute $M(n-1)$ $= M(n-2) + 1$

$= [M(n-2)$ $+1]$ 1 $= M(n-2) + 2$ substitute $M(n-2)$ $= M(n-3) + 1$

+

$= [M(n-3)$ $+1]$ 2 $= M(n-3) + 3.$

After inspecting the first three lines, we see an emerging pattern, which makes it possible to predict not only the next line (what would it be?) but also a general formula for the pattern: $M(n) = M(n-i) + i$. Strictly speaking, the correctness of this formula should be proved by mathematical induction, but it is easier to get the solution as follows and then verify its correctness.

What remains to be done is to take advantage of the initial condition given. Since it is specified for $n = 0$, we have to substitute $i = n$ in the pattern's formula to get the ultimate result of our backward substitutions:

$$M(n) = M(n-1) + 1 = \bullet \bullet \bullet = M(n-i) + i = = M(n-n) + n = n.$$

The benefits of the method illustrated in this simple example will become clear very soon, when we have to solve more difficult recurrences. Also note that the simple iterative algorithm that accumulates the product of n consecutive integers requires the same number of multiplications, and it does so without the overhead of time and space used for maintaining the recursion's stack.

The issue of time efficiency is actually not that important for the problem of computing n!, however. The function's values get so large so fast that we can realistically compute its values only for very small *n*'s. Again, we use this example just as a simple and convenient vehicle to introduce the standard approach to analyzing recursive algorithms.

Generalizing our experience with investigating the recursive algorithm for computing n!, we can now outline a general plan for investigating recursive algorithms.

A General Plan for Analyzing Efficiency of Recursive Algorithms

1. Decide on a parameter (or parameters) indicating an input's size.
2. Identify the algorithm's basic operation.
3. Check whether the number of times the basic operation is executed can vary on different inputs of the same size; if it can, the worst–case, average–case, and best–case efficiencies must be investigated separately.
4. Set up a recurrence relation, with an appropriate initial condition, for the number of times the basic operation is executed.
5. Solve the recurrence or at least ascertain the order of growth of its solution.

EXAMPLE 2: The algorithm to find the number of binary digits in the binary representation of a positive decimal integer.

```
ALGORITHM BinRec(n) : – //Input: A positive decimal integer n
//Output: The number of binary digits in n's binary representation if n
= 1 return 1
else return BinRec(n/2) + 1
```

Let us set up a recurrence and an initial condition for the number of additions A(n) made by the algorithm. The number of additions made in computing BinRec(n/2) is A(n/2), plus one more addition is made by the algorithm to increase the returned value by 1. This leads to the recurrence

$$A(n) = A(n/2) + 1 \text{ for } n > 1. \quad (2.2)$$

Since the recursive calls end when n is equal to 1 and there are no additions made then, the initial condition is A(1) = 0.

The presence of [n/2] in the function's argument makes the method of backward substitutions stumble on values of n that are not powers of 2. Therefore, the standard approach to solving such a recurrence is to solve it only for $n - 2k$ and then take advantage of the theorem called the smoothness rule which claims that under very broad assumptions the order of growth observed for $n = 2k$ gives a correct answer about the order of growth for all values of n. (Alternatively, after getting a solution for powers of 2, we can sometimes fine tune this solution to get a formula valid for an arbitrary n.) So let us apply this recipe to our recurrence, which for $n = 2k$ takes the form.

$$A(2\,k) = A(2\,k-1\,) + 1 \text{ for } k > 0,\ A(2\,0\,) = 0$$

Now backward substitutions encounter no problems:

$$A(2\,k) = A(2\,k-1\,) + 1 \text{ substitute } A(2k-1) = A(2k-2) + 1$$

$$= [A(2k-2\,) + 1] + 1 = A(2k-2) + 2 \text{ substitute } A(2k-2)$$

$$= A(2k-3) + 1 = [A(2\,k-3) + 1] + 2 = A(2\,k-3) + 3$$

....

$$= A(2\,k-i) + i$$

....

$$= A(2\,k-k) + k$$

Thus, we end up with $A(2k) = A\,(\,1\,) + k = k$ or, after returning to the original variable $n = 2k$ and, hence, $k = \log 2\ n$, $A\,(n) = \log 2\ n \in \theta\ (\log n)$.

Example: Fibonacci numbers

In this section, we consider the Fibonacci numbers, a sequence of numbers as 0, 1, 1, 2, 3, 5, 8, ... That can be defined by the simple recurrence

$$F(n) = F(n-1) + F(n-2) \text{ for n} > 1 \qquad (2.3)$$

and two initial conditions

$$F(0) = 0,\ F(1) = 1 \qquad (2.4)$$

The Fibonacci numbers were introduced by Leonardo Fibonacci in 1202 as a solution to a problem about the size of a rabbit population. Many more examples of Fibonacci–like numbers have since been discovered in the natural world, and they have even been used in predicting prices of stocks and commodities. There are some interesting applications of the Fibonacci numbers in computer science as well. For example, worst–case inputs for Euclid's algorithm happen to be consecutive elements of the Fibonacci sequence. Our discussion goals are quite limited here, however. First, we find an explicit formula for the nth Fibonacci number $F(n)$, and then we briefly discuss algorithms for computing it.

Explicit Formula for the nth Fibonacci Number

If we try to apply the method of backward substitutions to solve recurrence (2.6), we will fail to get an easily discernible pattern. Instead, let us take advantage of a theorem that describes solutions to a homogeneous second–order linear recurrence with constant coefficients

$$ax(n) + bx(n-1) + cx(n-2) = 0, \tag{2.5}$$

where a, b, and c are some fixed real numbers ($a \neq 0$) called the coefficients of the recurrence and $x(n)$ is an unknown sequence to be found. According to this theorem–see Theorem 1 in Appendix B–recurrence (2.5) has an infinite number of solutions that can be obtained by one of the three formulas. Which of the three formulas applies for a particular case depends on the number of real roots of the quadratic equation with the same coefficients as recurrence (2.5):

$$ar^2 + br + c = 0. \tag{2.6}$$

Quite logically, equation (2.6) is called the characteristic equation for recurrence (2.5). Let us apply this theorem to the case of the Fibonacci numbers.

$$F(n) - F(n-1) - F(n-2) = 0. \tag{2.7}$$

Its characteristic equation is $r^2 - r - 1 = 0$, with the roots $r1,2 = (1 \pm \sqrt{1-4(-1)})/2 = (1 \pm \sqrt{5})/2$

Algorithms for Computing Fibonacci Numbers

Though the Fibonacci numbers have many fascinating properties, we limit our discussion to a few remarks about algorithms for computing them. Actually, the sequence grows so fast that it is the size of the numbers rather than a time–efficient method for computing them that should be of primary concern here. Also, for the sake of simplicity, we consider such operations as additions and multiplications at unit cost in the algorithms that follow. Since the Fibonacci numbers grow infinitely large (and grow rapidly), a more detailed analysis than the one offered here is warranted. These caveats notwithstanding, the algorithms we outline and their analysis are useful examples for a student of design and analysis of algorithms.

To begin with, we can use recurrence (2.3) and initial condition (2.4) for the obvious recursive algorithm for computing $F(n)$.

```
ALGORITHM F(n)
//Computes the nth Fibonacci number recursively by using its definition //Input: A nonnegative integer n
//Output: The nth Fibonacci number
if n < 1 return n
else return F(n – 1) + F(n – 2)
```

Analysis:

The algorithm's basic operation is clearly addition, so let $A(n)$ be the number of additions performed by the algorithm in computing $F(n)$. Then the numbers of additions needed for computing $F(n-1)$ and $F(n-2)$ are $A(n-1)$ and $A(n-2)$, respectively, and the algorithm needs one more addition to compute their sum. Thus, we get the following recurrence for $A(n)$:

$$A(n) = A(n-1) + A(n-2) + 1 \text{ for } n > 1, \quad (2.8)$$

$$A(0) = 0, A(1) = 0.$$

The recurrence $A(n) - A(n-1) - A(n-2) = 1$ is quite similar to recurrence (2.7) but its right–hand side is not equal to zero. Such recurrences are called inhomogeneous recurrences. There are general techniques for solving inhomogeneous recurrences (see Appendix B or any textbook on discrete mathematics), but for this particular recurrence, a special trick leads to a faster solution. We can reduce our inhomogeneous recurrence to a homogeneous one by rewriting it as

$$[A(n) + 1] - [A(n-1) + 1] - [A(n-2) + 1] = 0 \text{ and}$$

substituting $B(n) = A(n) + 1$: $B(n) - B(n-1) - B(n-2) = 0$

$$B(0) = 1, B(1) = 1.$$

This homogeneous recurrence can be solved exactly in the same manner as recurrence (2.7) was solved to find an explicit formula for $F(n)$.

We can obtain a much faster algorithm by simply computing the successive elements of the Fibonacci sequence iteratively, as is done in the following algorithm.

```
ALGORITHM Fib(n)
//Computes the nth Fibonacci number iteratively by using its definition
//Input: A nonnegative integer n
//Output: The nth Fibonacci number F[0]<–0; F[1]<–1
```

```
for i <– 2 to n do
F[i]«–F[i–1]+F[i–2]
return F[n]
```

This algorithm clearly makes $n - 1$ additions. Hence, it is linear as a function of n and "only" exponential as a function of the number of bits b in n 's binary representation. Note that using an extra array for storing all the preceding elements of the Fibonacci sequence can be avoided: storing just two values is necessary to accomplish the task.

The third alternative for computing the nth Fibonacci number lies in using a formula. The efficiency of the algorithm will obviously be determined by the efficiency of an exponentiation algorithm used for computing $\theta\ n$. If it is done by simply multiplying ø by itself $n - 1$ times, the algorithm will be in $\theta\ (n) = \theta\ (2b)$. There are faster algorithms for the exponentiation problem. Note also that special care should be exercised in implementing this approach to computing the nth Fibonacci number. Since all its intermediate results are irrational numbers, we would have to make sure that their approximations in the computer are accurate enough so that the final round–off yields a correct result.

Finally, there exists a θ (log n) algorithm for computing the nth Fibonacci number that manipulates only integers. It is based on the equality

$F(n-1)$	$F(n)$	0	1^n	
$F(n)$	$F(n+1)$	1	1	for $n \geq 1$

And an efficient way of computing matrix powers

Empirical Analysis of Algorithms

Empirical analysis of algorithms involves the practical study and evaluation of algorithms through experimentation, often using computational resources to observe and measure their performance in real–world scenarios. This approach is crucial for understanding how algorithms behave under different conditions and for assessing their efficiency in practice.

Here's an overview of how empirical analysis of algorithms is conducted:

Implementation: The first step involves implementing the algorithm(s) of interest in a programming language. This implementation should be accurate, efficient, and reflect the algorithm's intended functionality.

Experimental Setup: Define specific test cases or datasets that cover a range of scenarios relevant to the algorithm's use. Vary the input sizes, data distributions, or other relevant parameters to test the algorithm under different conditions. The choice of test cases should reflect the algorithm's expected usage patterns.

Performance Metrics: Identify and define appropriate metrics for measuring the algorithm's performance. Common metrics include time complexity (measuring how execution time grows with input size), space complexity (memory usage), accuracy, scalability, and any other relevant measures specific to the problem or application domain.

Data Collection: Run the algorithm on the defined test cases while recording relevant data, such as execution times, memory usage, or any other specified metrics.

Analysis and Interpretation: Analyze the collected data to draw conclusions about the algorithm's behavior. This involves interpreting trends, identifying patterns, and drawing comparisons between different algorithms or variations of the same algorithm. Visualization tools and statistical methods can aid in presenting and analyzing the data effectively.

Validation and Conclusion: Validate the observations made during the analysis phase. Draw conclusions about the algorithm's strengths, weaknesses, efficiency, and suitability for different scenarios based on empirical evidence.

Reiteration and Optimization: Based on the findings, refine the algorithm or its implementation to improve performance in specific areas if necessary. Then, conduct further experiments to validate any improvements achieved.

Empirical analysis complements theoretical analysis (analyzing algorithms mathematically) by providing practical insights into an algorithm's behavior in real–world situations. It helps in understanding how algorithms perform on different datasets and input sizes, guiding the selection of algorithms based on their empirical efficiency for specific applications.

This empirical approach is particularly useful when theoretical analysis may be challenging due to complex scenarios, real–world data, or when practical performance matters more than asymptotic theoretical bounds.

QUESTIONS

Short Answers

1. Define Asymptotic Notations.
2. What are Basic efficiency classes.

3. What is Big O – Notation ? Given an example.
4. What is Ω–Notation? Given an example.
5. What is θ–notation? Given an example.
6. Define non– recursive algorithms.
7. Define recursive algorithms.

Long Answers

1. Explain Algorithm Analysis and Algorithm design.
2. Explain the General Plan for Analyzing the Time Efficiency of Non–recursive Algorithms.
3. Explain Recurrence relations.
4. Write the Factorial algorithm and Analyzing the Time Efficiency of Recursive Algorithms.
5. Explain the concept of Asymptotic Notation with an example.

UNIT

3

BRUTE FORCE APPROACHES

INTRODUCTION

A brute force approach is an approach that finds all the possible solutions to find a satisfactory solution to a given problem. The brute force algorithm tries out all the possibilities till a satisfactory solution is not found.

Let's understand the brute force search through an example.

Suppose we have converted the problem in the form of the tree shown as below:

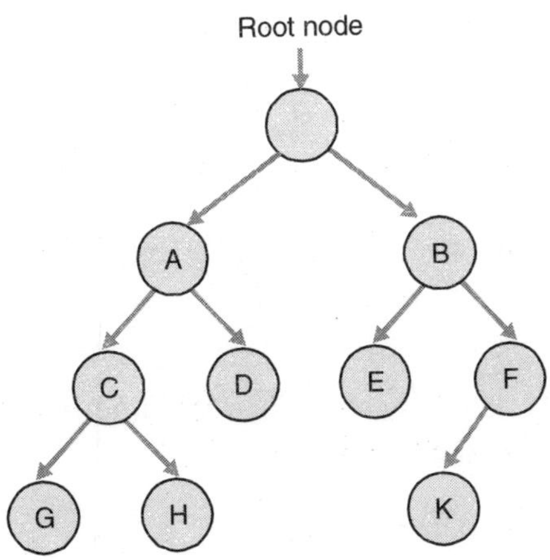

Brute force search considers each and every state of a tree, and the state is represented in the form of a node. As far as the starting position is concerned, we have two choices, i.e., A state and B state. We can either generate state A or state B. In the case of B state, we have two states, i.e., state E and F.

In the case of brute force search, each state is considered one by one. As we can observe in the above tree that the brute force search takes 12 steps to find the solution.

On the other hand, backtracking, which uses Depth–First search, considers the below states only when the state provides a feasible solution. Consider the above tree, start from the root node, then move to node A and then node C. If node C does not provide the feasible solution, then there is no point in considering the states G and H. We backtrack from node C to node A. Then, we move from node A to node D. Since node D does not provide the feasible solution, we discard this state and backtrack from node D to node A.

We move to node B, then we move from node B to node E. We move from node E to node K; Since k is a solution, so it takes 10 steps to find the solution. In this way, we eliminate a greater number of states in a single iteration. Therefore, we can say that backtracking is faster and more efficient than the brute force approach.

NOTE: Brute Force Method

The straightforward method of solving a given problem based on the problems statement and definition is called Brute Force method.

Ex : Selection Sort, Bubble Sort, Linear Search etc.

PROS AND CONS OF BRUTE FORCE METHOD :

Pros:

- The brute force approach is a guaranteed way to find the correct solution by listing all the possible candidate solutions for the problem.
- It is a generic method and not limited to any specific domain of problems.
- The brute force method is ideal for solving small and simpler problems.
- It is known for its simplicity and can serve as a comparison benchmark.

Cons:

- The brute force approach is inefficient. For real–time problems, algorithm analysis often goes above the O(N!) order of growth.
- This method relies more on compromising the power of a computer system for solving a problem than on a good algorithm design.
- Brute force algorithms are slow.
- Brute force algorithms are not constructive or creative compared to algorithms that are constructed using some other design paradigms.

BRUTE FORCE STRING MATCHING

Brute force string matching, also known as naive string matching, is a simple algorithm used to find occurrences of a pattern within a larger text or string. This algorithm methodically checks for a pattern's occurrence in the text by examining all possible alignments.

The basic idea behind brute force string matching involves comparing the pattern to the text character by character, starting from each possible position in the text. At each position, it checks if the pattern matches the substring of the text starting from that position.

Here's a basic outline of the brute force string matching algorithm:

Input: Text string (T) and a pattern string (P).

Procedure:

For each position *i* in the text T, from 0 to len(T) – len(P) (where len(P) is the length of the pattern):

Compare the characters of the pattern P with the characters of the text T starting from position *i*.

If a mismatch occurs at any character, move to the next position in the text.

If all characters in the pattern match the corresponding characters in the text, a match is found at position *i*.

Output: Positions or indices in the text where the pattern occurs.

While the brute force string matching algorithm is straightforward and easy to implement, its efficiency can be poor for larger texts or patterns due to its time complexity. The worst–case time complexity of this algorithm is $O((n - m + 1) * m)$, where:

n is the length of the text.

m is the length of the pattern.

This means that in the worst case, the algorithm might need to check every character of the text multiple times, resulting in higher time complexity, especially when the pattern occurs frequently or when both the text and pattern are long.

More sophisticated algorithms like the Knuth–Morris–Pratt (KMP) algorithm, Boyer–Moore algorithm, or Rabin–Karp algorithm are often used for more efficient string matching, especially when dealing with large texts, as they can significantly reduce the number of character comparisons required to find occurrences of a pattern within a text.

Here's an example of a brute force string matching algorithm implemented in C:

```
#include <stdio.h>
#include <string.h>

void brute_force_string_matching(const char* text, const char* pattern) {
  int n = strlen(text);
  int m = strlen(pattern);
  int i, j;

  for (i = 0; i<= n – m; i++) {
    for (j = 0; j < m; j++) {
      if (text[i + j] != pattern[j])
break; // If mismatch, break out of the loop
    }
    if (j == m) {
printf("Pattern found at index: %d\n", i);
    }
  }
}

int main() {
const char text[] = "ABCDEFABCDE";
const char pattern[] = "CDE";

printf("Text: %s\n", text);
printf("Pattern: %s\n", pattern);

printf("Occurrences:\n");
brute_force_string_matching(text, pattern);

  return 0; }
```

This C program defines a function brute_force_string_matching that searches for occurrences of a pattern within a text using a brute force approach. The main function demonstrates how to use this function by providing a sample text and pattern. When executed, it searches for occurrences of the pattern within the text and prints the indices where the pattern is found in the text.

Let's say we have the following input:

Text: "ABCDEFABCDE"

Pattern: "CDE"

Output:

Text: ABCDEFABCDE

Pattern: CDE

Pattern found at index: 5

SELECTION SORT AND BUBBLE SORT

Selection Sort

Selection sort is a simple sorting algorithm. This sorting algorithm, like insertion sort, is an in–place comparison–based algorithm in which the list is divided into two parts, the sorted part at the left end and the unsorted part at the right end. Initially, the sorted part is empty and the unsorted part is the entire list.

The smallest element is selected from the unsorted array and swapped with the leftmost element, and that element becomes a part of the sorted array. This process continues moving unsorted array boundaries by one element to the right.

This algorithm is not suitable for large data sets as its average and worst case complexities are of **$O(n^2)$**, where n is the number of items.

Selection Sort Algorithm

This type of sorting is called Selection Sort as it works by repeatedly sorting elements. That is: we first find the smallest value in the array and exchange it with the element in the first position, then find the second smallest element and exchange it with the element in the second position, and we continue the process in this way until the entire array is sorted.

Step 1 – Set MIN to location 0

Step 2 – Search the minimum element in the list

Step 3 – Swap with value at location MIN

Step 4 – Increment MIN to point to next element

Step 5 – Repeat until the list is sorted

Algorithm: Selection–Sort (A)

```
fori← 1 to n–1 do
  min j ←i;
  min x ← A[i]
  for j ←i + 1 to n do
    if A[j] < min x then
      min j ← j
      min x ← A[j]
A[min j] ← A [i]
  A[i] ← min x
```

Analysis

Selection sort is among the simplest of sorting techniques and it works very well for small files. It has a quite important application as each item is actually moved at the most once.

Section sort is a method of choice for sorting files with very large objects (records) and small keys. The worst case occurs if the array is already sorted in a descending order and we want to sort them in an ascending order.

Nonetheless, the time required by selection sort algorithm is not very sensitive to the original order of the array to be sorted: the test if **A[*j*] < A[*j*] < min *x*** is executed exactly the same number of times in every case.

Selection sort spends most of its time trying to find the minimum element in the unsorted part of the array. It clearly shows the similarity between Selection sort and Bubble sort.

- Bubble sort selects the maximum remaining elements at each stage, but wastes some effort imparting some order to an unsorted part of the array.
- Selection sort is quadratic in both the worst and the average case, and requires no extra memory.

For each i from 1 to $n - 1$, there is one exchange and $n - i$ comparisons, so there is a total of $n - 1$ exchanges and $(n - 1) + (n - 2) + ... + 2 + 1 = n(n - 1)/2$ comparisons.

These observations hold, no matter what the input data is.

In the worst case, this could be quadratic, but in the average case, this quantity is **O(n log n)**. It implies that the **running time of Selection sort is quite insensitive to the input**.

EXAMPLE : Consider the following depicted array as an example.

0	1	2	3	4	5	6	7
14	33	27	10	35	19	44	42

For the first position in the sorted list, the whole list is scanned sequentially. The first position where 14 is stored presently, we search the whole list and find that 10 is the lowest value.

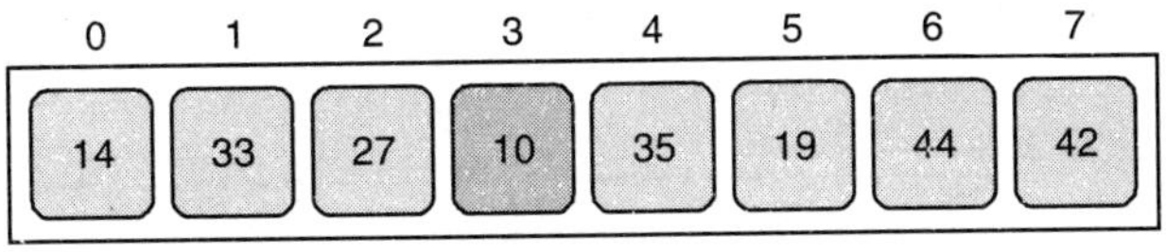

So we replace 14 with 10. After one iteration 10, which happens to be the minimum value in the list, appears in the first position of the sorted list.

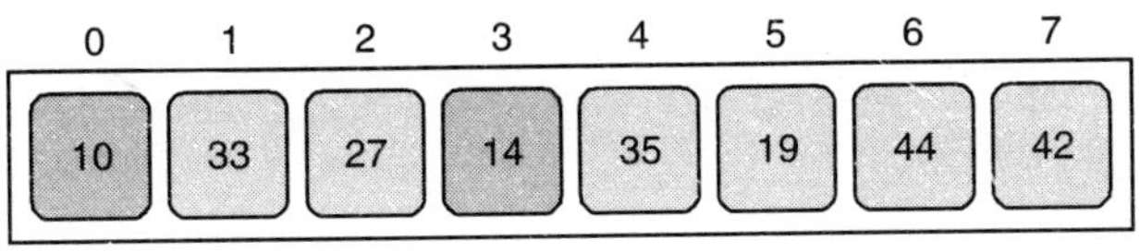

For the second position, where 33 is residing, we start scanning the rest of the list in a linear manner.

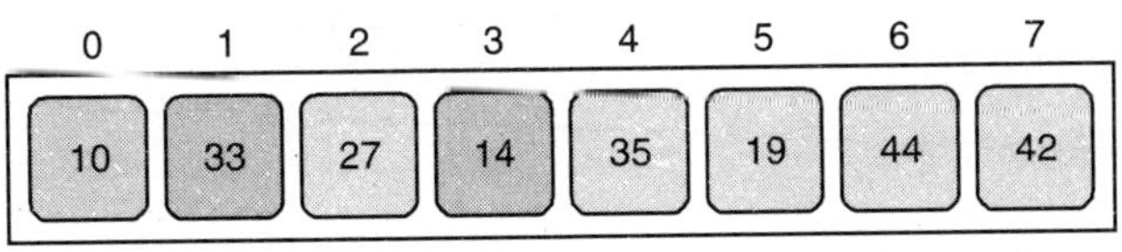

We find that 14 is the second lowest value in the list and it should appear at the second place. We swap these values.

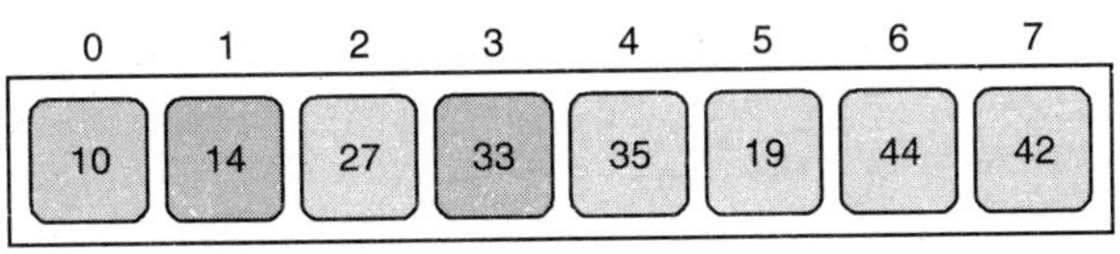

After two iterations, two least values are positioned at the beginning in a sorted manner.

The same process is applied to the rest of the items in the array –

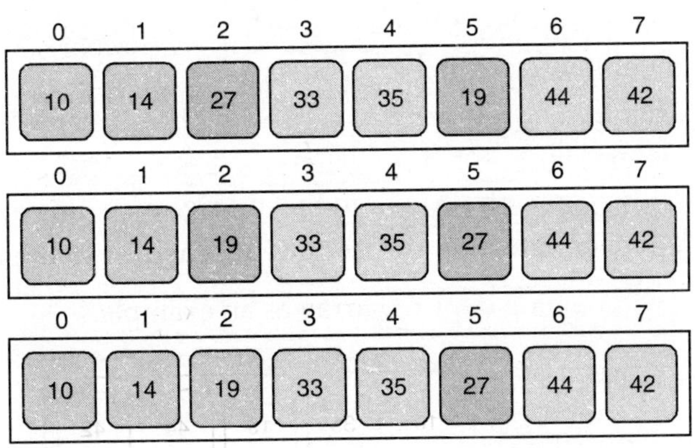

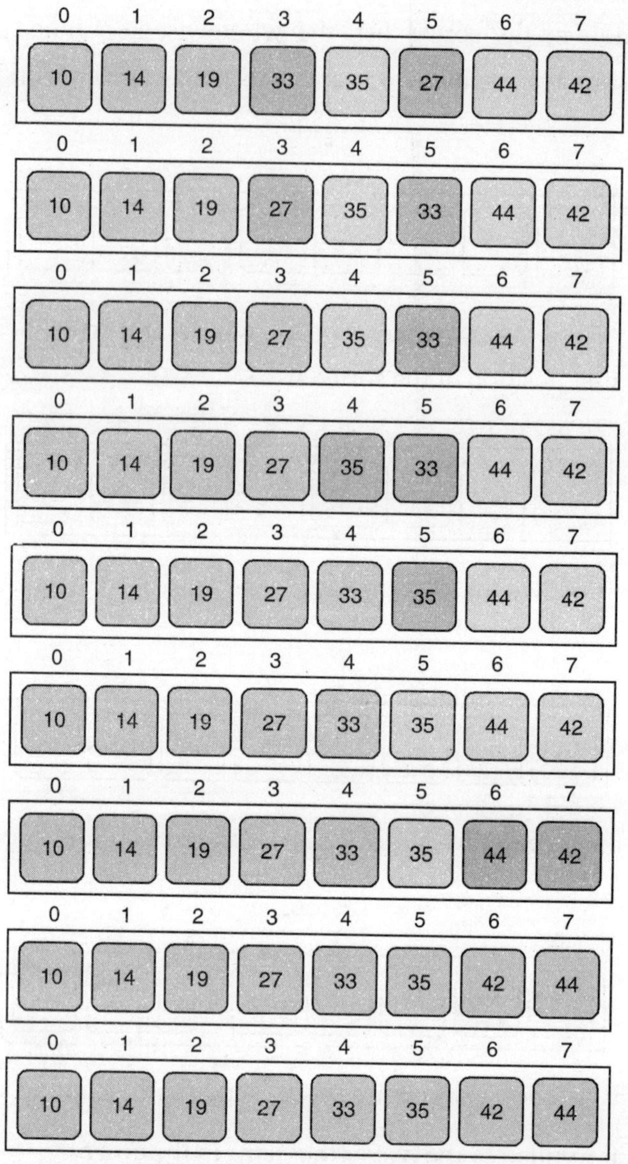

EXAMPLE : The selection sort algorithm is implemented in C programming languages. The given program selects the minimum number of the array and swaps it with the element in the first index. The second minimum number is swapped with the element present in the second index. The process goes on until the end of the array is reached.

```
#include <stdio.h>
void selectionSort(int array[], int size){
  int i, j, imin;
for(i = 0; i<size–1; i++) {
imin = i; //get index of minimum data
```

```
for(j = i+1; j<size; j++)
      if(array[j] < array[imin])
imin = j;

    //placing in correct position
    int temp;
    temp = array[i];
    array[i] = array[imin];
    array[imin] = temp;
  }
}
int main(){
  int n;
  n = 5;
  int arr[5] = {12, 19, 55, 2, 16}; // initialize the array
printf("Array before Sorting: ");
for(int i = 0; i<n; i++)
printf("%d ",arr[i]);
printf("\n");
selectionSort(arr, n);
printf("Array after Sorting: ");
for(int i = 0; i<n; i++)
printf("%d ", arr[i]);
printf("\n");
}
```

Output:

Array before Sorting: 12 19 55 2 16

Array after Sorting: 2 12 16 19 55

BUBBLE SORT (SINKING SORT)

Bubble sort is a simple sorting algorithm. This sorting algorithm is comparison–based algorithm in which each pair of adjacent elements is compared and the elements are swapped if they are not in order. This algorithm is not suitable for large data sets as its average and worst case complexity are of $O(n^2)$ where **n** is the number of items.

Bubble Sort Algorithm

Bubble Sort is an elementary sorting algorithm, which works by repeatedly exchanging adjacent elements, if necessary. When no exchanges are required, the file is sorted.

We assume **list** is an array of *n* elements. We further assume that **swap** function swaps the values of the given array elements.

Step 1 – Check if the first element in the input array is greater than the next element in the array.

Step 2 – If it is greater, swap the two elements; otherwise move the pointer forward in the array.

Step 3 – Repeat Step 2 until we reach the end of the array.

Step 4 – Check if the elements are sorted; if not, repeat the same process (Step 1 to Step 3) from the last element of the array to the first.

Step 5 – The final output achieved is the sorted array.

Algorithm: Sequential–Bubble–Sort (A)

```
fori ← 1 to length [A] do
for j ← length [A] down–to i +1 do
  if A[A] < A[j–1] then
    Exchange A[j] ↔A[j–1]
```

Pseudocode

We observe in algorithm that Bubble Sort compares each pair of array element unless the whole array is completely sorted in an ascending order. This may cause a few complexity issues like what if the array needs no more swapping as all the elements are already ascending.

To ease–out the issue, we use one flag variable **swapped** which will help us see if any swap has happened or not. If no swap has occurred, i.e. the array requires no more processing to be sorted, it will come out of the loop.

Pseudocode of bubble sort algorithm can be written as follows –

```
voidbubbleSort(int numbers[], intarray_size){
  inti, j, temp;
  for (i = (array_size – 1); i>= 0; i—)
  for (j = 1; j <= i; j++)
  if (numbers[j–1] > numbers[j]){
    temp = numbers[j–1];
```

```
    numbers[j–1] = numbers[j];
    numbers[j] = temp;
  }
}
```

Analysis

Here, the number of comparisons are

$$1 + 2 + 3 + \ldots + (n - 1) = n(n - 1)/2 = O(n^2)$$

Clearly, the graph shows the n^2 nature of the bubble sort.

In this algorithm, the number of comparison is irrespective of the data set, i.e. whether the provided input elements are in sorted order or in reverse order or at random.

Memory Requirement

From the algorithm stated above, it is clear that bubble sort does not require extra memory.

EXAMPLE : We take an unsorted array for our example. Bubble sort takes $O(n^2)$ time so we're keeping it short and precise.

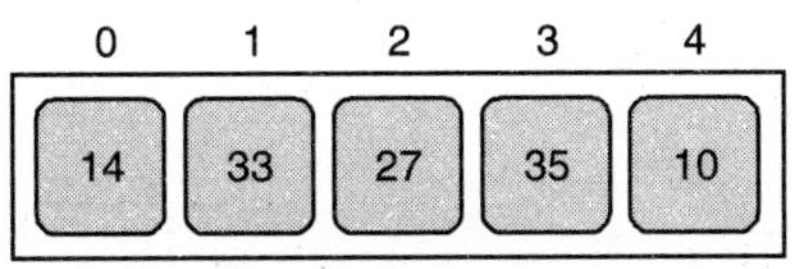

Bubble sort starts with very first two elements, comparing them to check which one is greater.

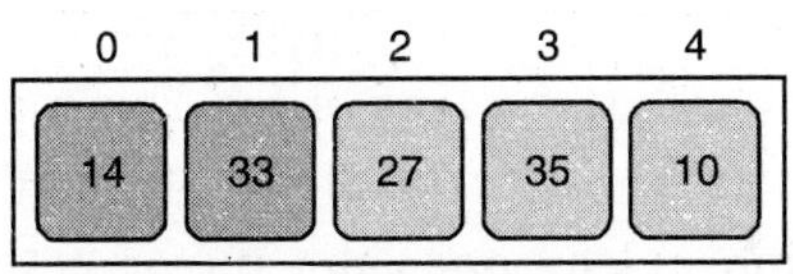

In this case, value 33 is greater than 14, so it is already in sorted locations. Next, we compare 33 with 27.

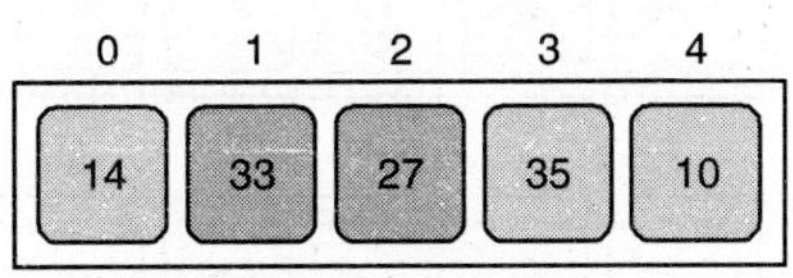

We find that 27 is smaller than 33 and these two values must be swapped.

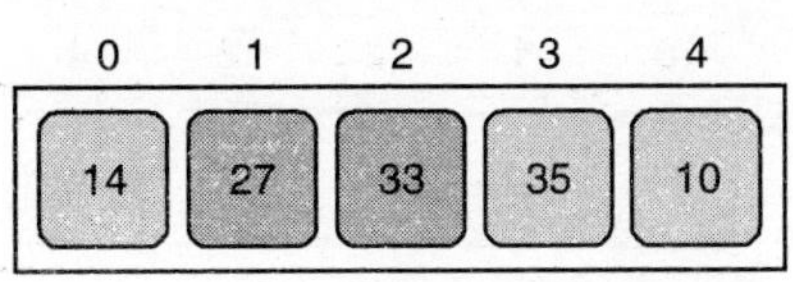

Next we compare 33 and 35. We find that both are in already sorted positions.

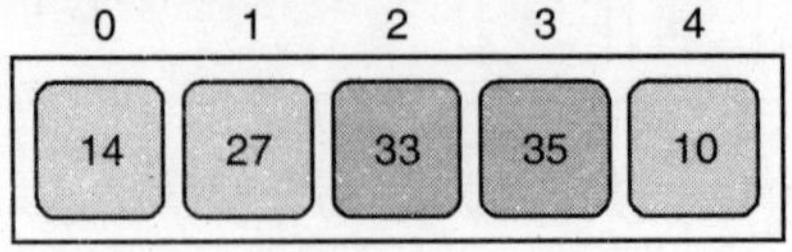

Then we move to the next two values, 35 and 10.

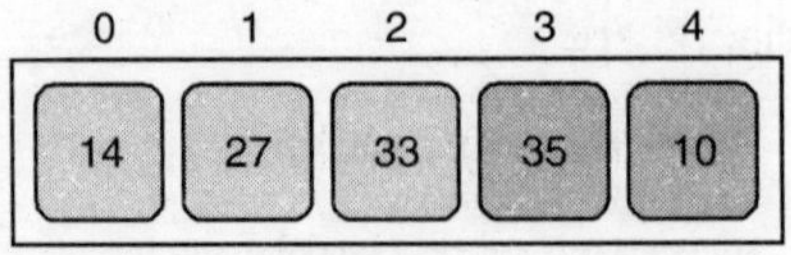

We know then that 10 is smaller 35. Hence they are not sorted. We swap these values. We find that we have reached the end of the array. After one iteration, the array should look like this –

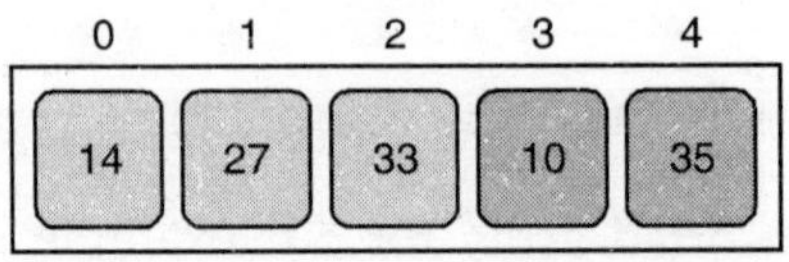

To be precise, we are now showing how an array should look like after each iteration. After the second iteration, it should look like this –

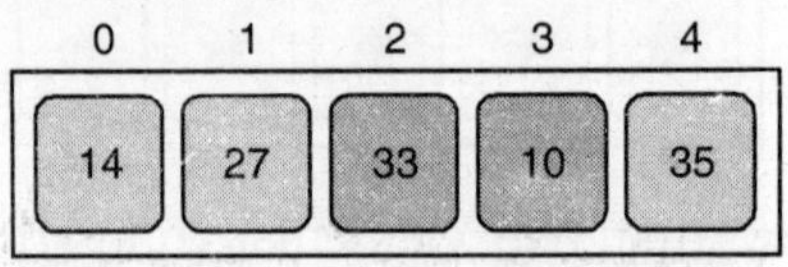

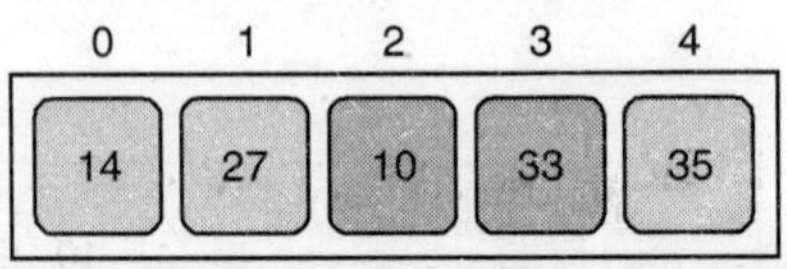

Notice that after each iteration, at least one value moves at the end.

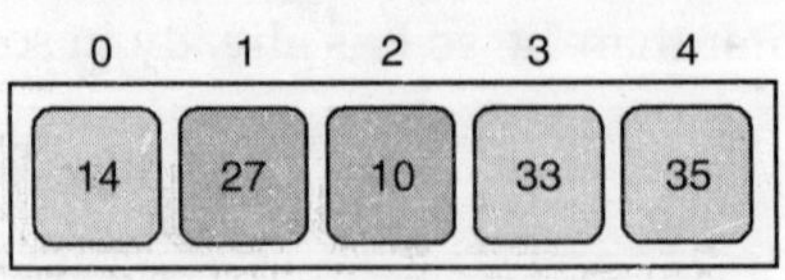

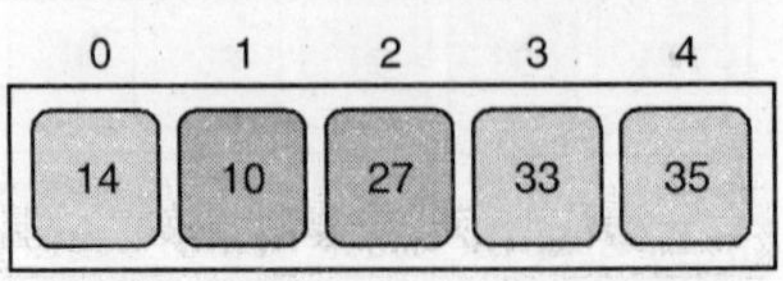

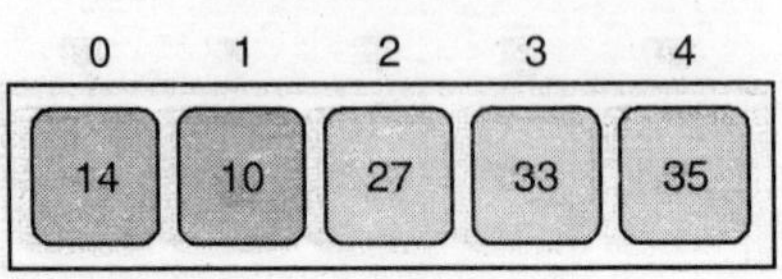

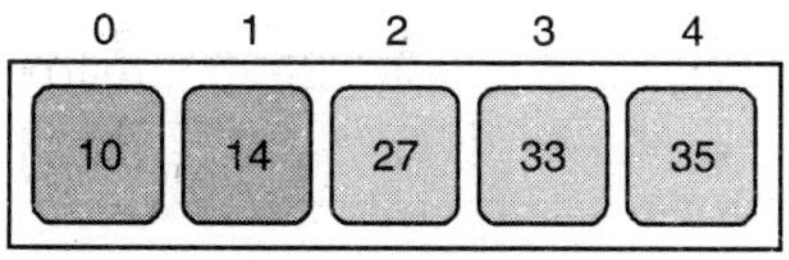

And when there's no swap required, bubble sort learns that an array is completely sorted.

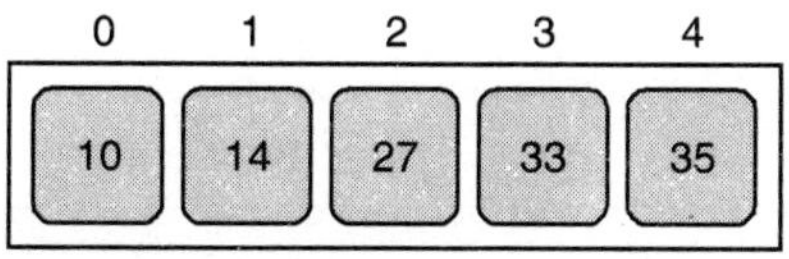

Now we should look into some practical aspects of bubble sort.

EXAMPLE : One more issue we did not address in our original algorithm and its improvised pseudocode, is that, after every iteration the highest values settles down at the end of the array. Hence, the next iteration need not include already sorted elements. For this purpose, in our implementation, we restrict the inner loop to avoid already sorted values.

```
#include <stdio.h>
void bubbleSort(int array[], int size){
for(int i = 0; i<size; i++) {
   int swaps = 0; //flag to detect any swap is there or not
for(int j = 0; j<size–i–1; j++) {
     if(array[j] > array[j+1]) { //when the current item is bigger than next
       int temp;
       temp = array[j];
       array[j] = array[j+1];
       array[j+1] = temp;
       swaps = 1; //set swap flag
     }

   }
   if(!swaps)
break; // No swap in this pass, so array is sorted
  }
}
int main(){
  int n;
  n = 5;
```

```
int arr[5] = {67, 44, 82, 17, 20}; //initialize an array
printf("Array before Sorting: ");
for(int i = 0; i<n; i++)
printf("%d ",arr[i]);
printf("\n");
bubbleSort(arr, n);
printf("Array after Sorting: ");
for(int i = 0; i<n; i++)
printf("%d ", arr[i]);
printf("\n");
}
```

Output

Array before Sorting: 67 44 82 17 20

Array after Sorting: 17 20 44 67 82

Sequential Search (Linear Search):

Linear search is a type of sequential searching algorithm. In this method, every element within the input array is traversed and compared with the key element to be found. If a match is found in the array the search is said to be successful; if there is no match found the search is said to be unsuccessful and gives the worst–case time complexity.

For instance, in the given animated diagram, we are searching for an element 33. Therefore, the linear search method searches for it sequentially from the very first element until it finds a match. This returns a successful search.

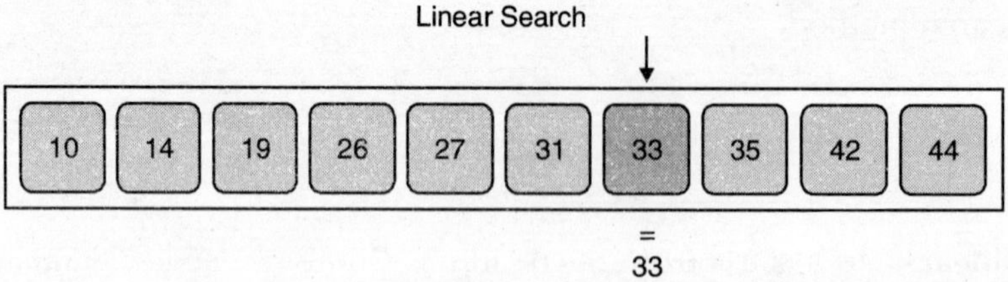

In the same diagram, if we have to search for an element 46, then it returns an unsuccessful search since 46 is not present in the input.

Linear Search Algorithm

The algorithm for linear search is relatively simple. The procedure starts at the very first index of the input array to be searched.

Step 1 – Start from the 0th index of the input array, compare the key value with the value present in the 0th index.

Step 2 – If the value matches with the key, return the position at which the value was found.

Step 3 – If the value does not match with the key, compare the next element in the array.

Step 4 – Repeat Step 3 until there is a match found. Return the position at which the match was found.

Step 5 – If it is an unsuccessful search, print that the element is not present in the array and exit the program.

```
procedure linear_search (list, value)
  for each item in the list
    if match item == value
      return the item's location
    end if
  end for
end procedure
```

Analysis

Linear search traverses through every element sequentially therefore, the best case is when the element is found in the very first iteration. The best–case time complexity would be **O(1)**.

However, the worst case of the linear search method would be an unsuccessful search that does not find the key value in the array, it performs n iterations. Therefore, the worst–case time complexity of the linear search algorithm would be **O(n)**.

EXAMPLE : Let us look at the step–by–step searching of the key element (say 47) in an array using the linear search method.

0	1	2	3	4	5	6	7
34	10	66	27	47	8	55	78

Step 1 : The linear search starts from the 0th index. Compare the key element with the value in the 0th index, 34.

0	1	2	3	4	5	6	7
34	10	66	27	47	8	55	78
=							
47							

However, 47 ≠ 34. So it moves to the next element.

Step 2 : Now, the key is compared with value in the 1st index of the array.

0	1	2	3	4	5	6	7
34	10	66	27	47	8	55	78
	= 47						

Still, 47 ≠ 10, making the algorithm move for another iteration.

Step 3 : The next element 66 is compared with 47. They are both not a match so the algorithm compares the further elements.

0	1	2	3	4	5	6	7
34	10	66	27	47	8	55	78
		= 47					

Step 4 : Now the element in 3rd index, 27, is compared with the key value, 47. They are not equal so the algorithm is pushed forward to check the next element.

0	1	2	3	4	5	6	7
34	10	66	27	47	8	55	78
			= 47				

Step 5 : Comparing the element in the 4th index of the array, 47, to the key 47. It is figured that both the elements match. Now, the position in which 47 is present, i.e., 4 is returned.

0	1	2	3	4	5	6	7
34	10	66	27	47	8	55	78
				= 47			

The output achieved is "Element found at 4th index".

Implementation

The Linear Search program can be seen implemented in four programming languages. The function compares the elements of input with the key value and returns the position of the key in the array or an unsuccessful search prompt if the key is not present in the array.

```
#include <stdio.h>
void linear_search(int a[], int n, int key){
  int i, count = 0;
for(i = 0; i< n; i++) {
   if(a[i] == key) { // compares each element of the array
```

```
printf("The element is found at %d position\n", i+1);
      count = count + 1;
    }
  }
if(count == 0) // for unsuccessful search
printf("The element is not present in the array\n");
}
int main(){
  int i, n, key;
  n = 6;
  int a[10] = {12, 44, 32, 18, 4, 10};
  key = 18;
linear_search(a, n, key);
  key = 23;
linear_search(a, n, key);
  return 0;
}
```

Output:

The element is found at 4 position

The element is not present in the array

Exhaustive Search :

A Search problem involves some set of possibilities and we are looking for one or more of the possibilities and we are looking for one or more of the possibilities that satisfy some property.

Example : Travelling Salesperson Problem

Method :

1. Generate a list of all potential solutions to the problem.
2. Evaluate potential solutions one by one disqualifying infeasible ones and for an optimization problem, keeping track of the best one found so far.

Travelling Salesman Problem :

The Travelling Salesman Problem (TSP) is an optimization problem used to find the shortest path to travel through the given number of cities.

Travelling salesman problem states that given a number of cities N and the distance between the cities, the traveller has to travel through all the given cities exactly once and return to the same city from where he started and also the length of the path is minimized.

The Travelling Salesman Problem (TSP) can be formulated as follows: to choose a pathway optimal by the given criterion. In this, optimal criterion is usually the minimal distance between towns or minimal travel expenses. Travelling salesman should visit a certain number of towns and return to the place of departure, so that they visit each town only once.

TSP can be solved as shown below:

1. Get all the routes from one city to another city by taking various permutations.
2. Compute the route length for each permutation and select the shortest among them.

TSP can be modeled as an undirected weighted graph, such that cities are the graph's vertices, paths are the graph's edges, and a path's distance is the edge's weight. It is a minimization problem starting and finishing at a specified vertex after having visited each other vertex exactly once. Often, the model is a complete graph (i.e. each pair of vertices is connected by an edge). If no path exists between two cities, adding an arbitrarily long edge will complete the graph without affecting the optimal tour.

EXAMPLE :

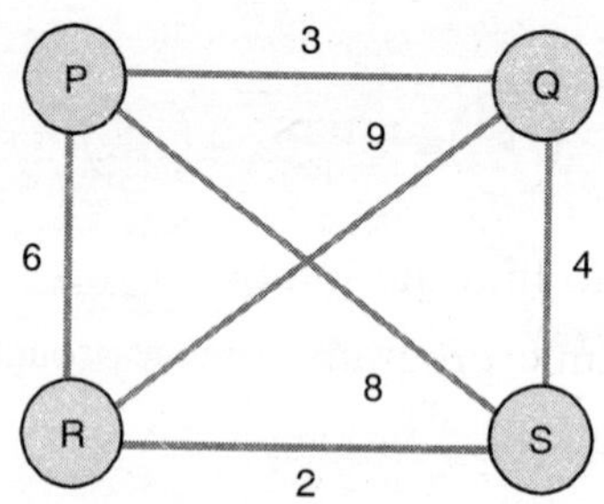

Here P Q R S are Cities.

Distance between various cities are represented as numbers in each of the edge.

Let assume, Salesperson starts from City P then the various routes using which he can visit each and every city exactly once and returns back to the start city P along with the cost is as shown below:

P Q R S P (COST = 22)

P Q S R P (COST = 15)

P R Q S P (COST = 27)

P R S Q P (COST = 15)

P S Q R P (COST = 27)

P S R Q P (COST = 22)

Finally considering routes with minimum cost to get the maximum profit, we will consider the below routes and cost:

P Q S R P (COST = 15)

P R S Q P (COST = 15)

Note : In general, for n cities number of routes = $(n - 1)!$ i.e., $f(n) = f(n - 1)!$ Hence the time complexity is given by , $F(n) = O(n!)$

If you look at the graph below, considering that the salesman starts from the vertex '*a*', they need to travel through all the remaining vertices *b, c, d, e, f* and get back to '*a*' while making sure that the cost taken is minimum.

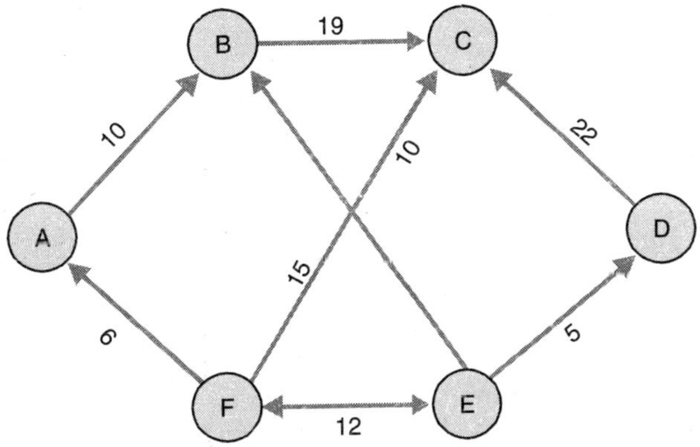

There are various approaches to find the solution to the travelling salesman problem: naïve approach, greedy approach, dynamic programming approach, etc. In this tutorial we will be learning about solving travelling salesman problem using greedy approach.

Travelling Salesperson Algorithm

As the definition for greedy approach states, we need to find the best optimal solution locally to figure out the global optimal solution. The inputs taken by the algorithm are the graph G {V, E}, where V is the set of vertices and E is the set of edges. The shortest path of graph G starting from one vertex returning to the same vertex is obtained as the output.

Algorithm

- Travelling salesman problem takes a graph G {V, E} as an input and declare another graph as the output (say G′) which will record the path the salesman is going to take from one node to another.
- The algorithm begins by sorting all the edges in the input graph G from the least distance to the largest distance.

- The first edge selected is the edge with least distance, and one of the two vertices (say A and B) being the origin node (say A).
- Then among the adjacent edges of the node other than the origin node (B), find the least cost edge and add it onto the output graph.
- Continue the process with further nodes making sure there are no cycles in the output graph and the path reaches back to the origin node A.
- However, if the origin is mentioned in the given problem, then the solution must always start from that node only. Let us look at some example problems to understand this better.

EXAMPLES : Consider the following graph with six cities and the distances between them –

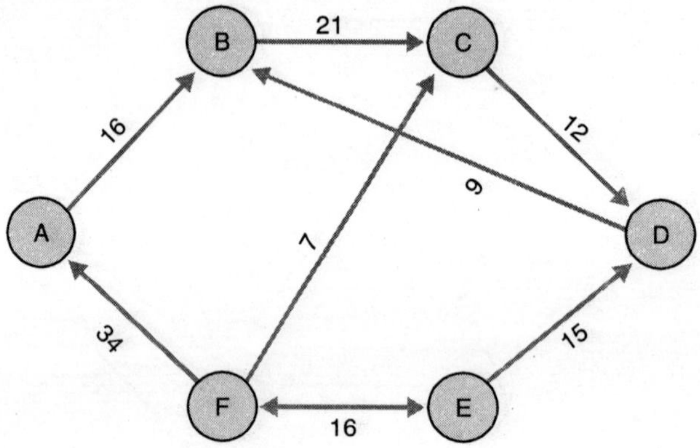

From the given graph, since the origin is already mentioned, the solution must always start from that node. Among the edges leading from A, A → B has the shortest distance.

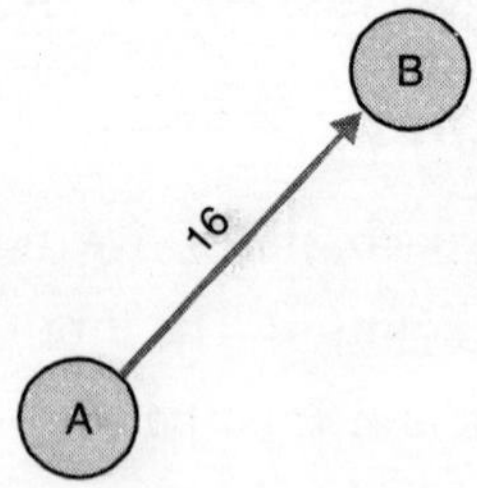

Then, B → C has the shortest and only edge between, therefore it is included in the output graph.

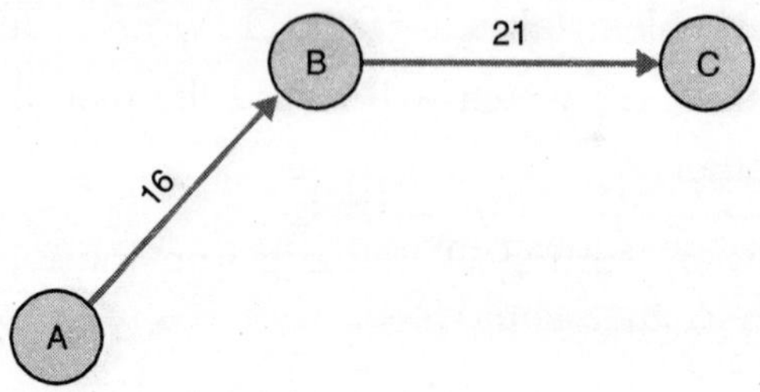

There's only one edge between C → D, therefore it is added to the output graph.

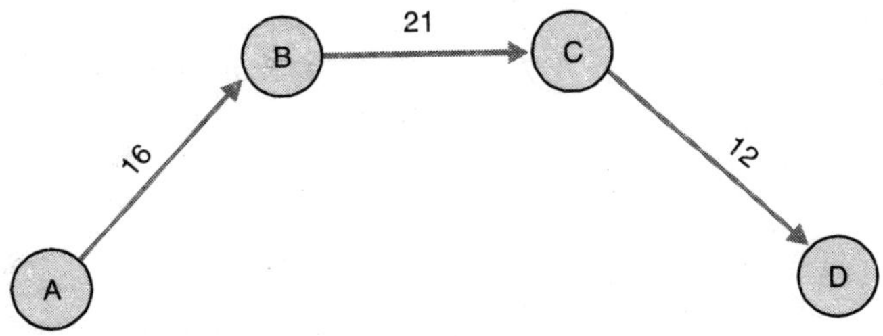

There's two outward edges from D. Even though, D → B has lower distance than D → E, B is already visited once and it would form a cycle if added to the output graph. Therefore, D→ E is added into the output graph.

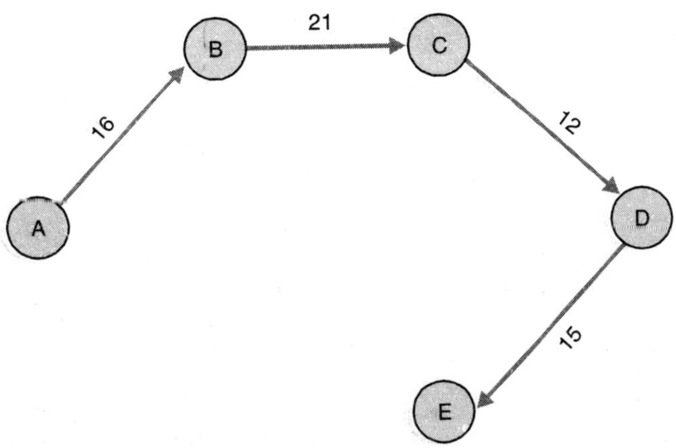

There's only one edge from e, that is E → F. Therefore, it is added into the output graph.

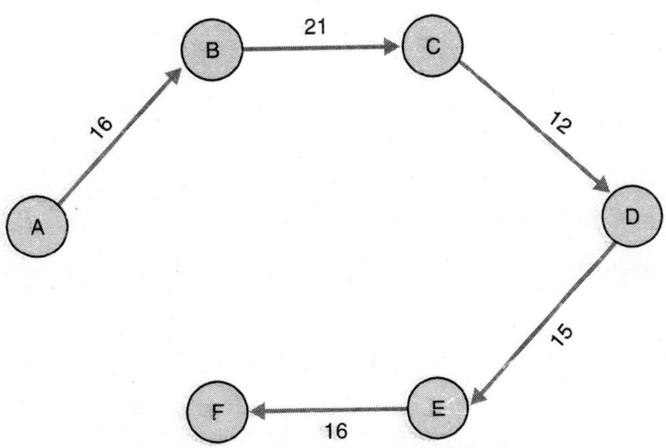

Again, even though F → C has lower distance than F → A, F → A is added into the output graph in order to avoid the cycle that would form and C is already visited once.

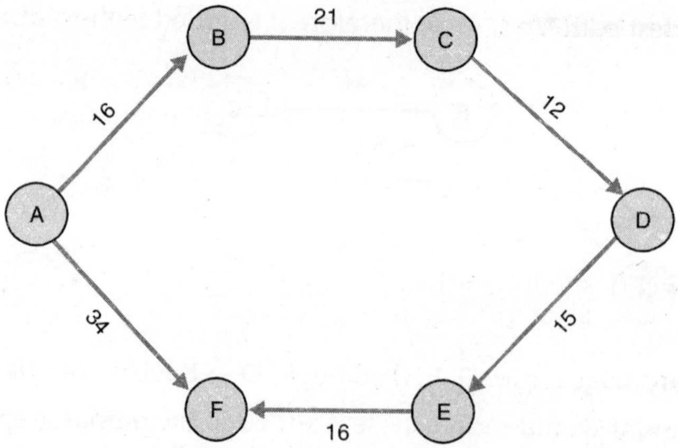

The shortest path that originates and ends at A is A → B → C → D → E → F → A

The cost of the path is: 16 + 21 + 12 + 15 + 16 + 34 = 114.

Even though, the cost of path could be decreased if it originates from other nodes but the question is not raised with respect to that.

Implementation of Travelling Salesman Problem using Greedy Approach is given below –

```
#include <stdio.h>
int tsp_g[10][10] = {
  {12, 30, 33, 10, 45},
  {56, 22, 9, 15, 18},
  {29, 13, 8, 5, 12},
  {33, 28, 16, 10, 3},
  {1, 4, 30, 24, 20}
};
int visited[10], n, cost = 0;

/* creating a function to generate the shortest path */
void travellingsalesman(int c){
  int k, adj_vertex = 999;
  int min = 999;

  /* marking the vertices visited in an assigned array */
  visited[c] = 1;
```

```
/* displaying the shortest path */
printf("%d ", c + 1);

/* checking the minimum cost edge in the graph */
for(k = 0; k < n; k++) {
    if((tsp_g[c][k] != 0) && (visited[k] == 0)) {
      if(tsp_g[c][k] < min) {
        min = tsp_g[c][k];
      }
adj_vertex = k;
    }
  }
if(min != 999) {
    cost = cost + min;
  }
if(adj_vertex == 999) {
adj_vertex = 0;
printf("%d", adj_vertex + 1);
    cost = cost + tsp_g[c][adj_vertex];
return;
  }
travellingsalesman(adj_vertex);
}

/* main function */
int main(){
  int i, j;
  n = 5;
for(i = 0; i< n; i++) {
    visited[i] = 0;
  }
printf("\nShortest Path: ");
```

```
travellingsalesman(0);
printf("\nMinimum Cost: ");
printf("%d\n", cost);
  return 0;
}
```

Output:

Shortest Path: 1 5 4 3 2 1

Minimum Cost: 99

Greedy Method

The greedy method is applied to optimization problems, that is problems that maximizes an objective function defined on this configurations. The general formula of the greedy method could not be simpler. In order to solve a given optimization problem we proceed by a sequence of choice. The sequence starts from some well understood starting configuration and then iteratively makes the decision that seems best from all of those that are currently possible.

A greedy algorithm always makes the choice that looks best at the moment that is it makes a local optimal choice that looks best at the moment in the hope that this choice will lead to a globally optimal solution.

Greedy choice property:

The first key ingredient is the greedy – choice property: a globally optimal solution can be arrived at by making a locally optimal choice. Here is where greedy algorithm differs from dynamic programming. In dynamic programming we make a choice at each step but the choice may depend on the solution to sub problems. In a greedy algorithm we make whatever choice seems best at the moment and then solves the subproblem arising after the choice is made. The choice made by a greedy algorithm may depend on choice so far but it could not depend on any further choices or on the solution to sub problems. Thus unlike dynamic programming which solves the sub problems bottom up greedy started G usually progress in a top down fashion making one greedy choice after another iteratively reducing each given problem instance to a smaller one.

Optimal substructure:

A problem exhibits optimal substructure in an optimal solution to the problem contains within it optimal solutions to the sub problems. This property is a key ingredient of accessing the applicability of dynamic programming as well as greedy algorithms.

0/1 Knapsack problem

Here knapsack is like a container or a bag. Suppose we have given some items which have some weights or profits. We have to put some items in the knapsack in such a way total value produces a maximum profit.

For example, the weight of the container is 20 kg. We have to select the items in such a way that the sum of the weight of items should be either smaller than or equal to the weight of the container, and the profit should be maximum.

There are two types of knapsack problems:

- 0/1 knapsack problem
- Fractional knapsack problem

We will discuss both the problems one by one. First, we will learn about the 0/1 knapsack problem.

What is the 0/1 knapsack problem?

The 0/1 knapsack problem means that the items are either completely or no items are filled in a knapsack. For example, we have two items having weights 2kg and 3kg, respectively. If we pick the 2kg item then we cannot pick 1kg item from the 2kg item (item is not divisible); we have to pick the 2kg item completely. This is a 0/1 knapsack problem in which either we pick the item completely or we will pick that item. The 0/1 knapsack problem is solved by the dynamic programming.

What is the fractional knapsack problem?

The fractional knapsack problem means that we can divide the item. For example, we have an item of 3 kg then we can pick the item of 2 kg and leave the item of 1 kg. The fractional knapsack problem is solved by the Greedy approach.

Example of 0/1 knapsack problem.

Consider the problem having weights and profits are:

Weights: {3, 4, 6, 5}

Profits: {2, 3, 1, 4}

The weight of the knapsack is 8 kg

The number of items is 4

The above problem can be solved by using the following method:

$x_i = \{1, 0, 0, 1\}$

$= \{0, 0, 0, 1\}$

$= \{0, 1, 0, 1\}$

The above are the possible combinations. 1 denotes that the item is completely picked and 0 means that no item is picked. Since there are 4 items so possible combinations will be: **2^4 = 16;** So. There are 16 possible combinations that can be made by using the above problem. Once all the combinations are made, we have to select the combination that provides the maximum profit.

0–1 Knapsack Algorithm

Problem Statement – A thief is robbing a store and can carry a maximal weight of ***W*** into his knapsack. There are ***n*** items and weight of ith item is wi and the profit of selecting this item is ***pi***. What items should the thief take?

Let i be the highest–numbered item in an optimal solution **S** for **W** dollars. Then **S′ = S – {*i*}** is an optimal solution for **W** – w_i dollars and the value to the solution S is V_i plus the value of the sub–problem.

We can express this fact in the following formula: define ***c*[*i*, *w*]** to be the solution for items **1, 2, … ,** ***i*** and the maximum weight *w*.

The algorithm takes the following inputs

- The maximum weight **W**
- The number of items ***n***
- The two sequences $v = <v_1, v_2, \ldots, v_n>$ **and** $w = < w_1, w_2, \ldots, w_n>$

The set of items to take can be deduced from the table, starting at ***c*[*n*, *w*]** and tracing backwards where the optimal values came from.

If ***c*[*i*, *w*] = *c*[*i*–1, *w*]**, then item i is not part of the solution, and we continue tracing with ***c*[*i*–1, *w*]**. Otherwise, item *i* is part of the solution, and we continue tracing with ***c* [*i* –1, *w* –W]**.

```
Dynamic–0–1–knapsack (v, w, n, W)
for w = 0 to W do
c[0, w] = 0
for i = 1 to n do
c[i, 0] = 0
 for w = 1 to W do
  if wi ≤ w then
   if vi + c[i–1, w–wi] then
c[i, w] = vi + c[i–1, w–wi]
   else c[i, w] = c[i–1, w]
  else
c[i, w] = c[i–1, w]
```

The following examples will establish our statement.

EXAMPLE : Let us consider that the capacity of the knapsack is W = 8 and the items are as shown in the following table.

Item	**A**	**B**	**C**	**D**
Profit	2	4	7	10
Weight	1	3	5	7

Solution

Using the greedy approach of 0–1 knapsack, the weight that's stored in the knapsack would be A+B = 4 with the maximum profit 2 + 4 = 6. But, that solution would not be the optimal solution.

Therefore, dynamic programming must be adopted to solve 0–1 knapsack problems.

Step 1 : Construct an adjacency table with maximum weight of knapsack as rows and items with respective weights and profits as columns.

Values to be stored in the table are cumulative profits of the items whose weights do not exceed the maximum weight of the knapsack (designated values of each row)

So we add zeroes to the 0th row and 0th column because if the weight of item is 0, then it weighs nothing; if the maximum weight of knapsack is 0, then no item can be added into the knapsack.

← Maximum Weights →

Items with Weights and Profits (rows)

	0	1	2	3	4	5	6	7	8
0	0	0	0	0	0	0	0	0	0
1 (1, 2)	0								
2 (3, 4)	0								
2 (5, 7)	0								
4 (7, 10)	0								

The remaining values are filled with the maximum profit achievable with respect to the items and weight per column that can be stored in the knapsack.

The formula to store the profit values is –

$c[i, w] = \max \{c[i-1, w - w[i]]+P[i]\}$□[□,□]=□□□{□[□−1,□−□[□]]+□[□]}

By computing all the values using the formula, the table obtained would be –

← Maximum Weights →

Items with Weights and Profits

	0	1	2	3	4	5	6	7	8
0	0	0	0	0	0	0	0	0	0
1 (1, 2)	0	1	1	1	1	1	1	1	1
2 (3, 4)	0	1	1	4	6	6	6	6	6
2 (5, 7)	0	1	1	4	6	7	9	9	11
4 (7, 10)	0	1	1	4	6	7	9	10	12

To find the items to be added in the knapsack, recognize the maximum profit from the table and identify the items that make up the profit, in this example, its {1, 7}.

← Maximum Weights →

Items with Weights and Profits

	0	1	2	3	4	5	6	7	8
0	0	0	0	0	0	0	0	0	0
1 (1, 2)	0	1	1	1	1	1	1	1	1
2 (3, 4)	0	1	1	4	6	6	6	6	6
2 (5, 7)	0	1	1	4	6	7	9	9	11
4 (7, 10)	0	1	1	4	6	7	9	10	12

The optimal solution is {1, 7} with the maximum profit is 12.

Analysis

This algorithm takes θ $(n.w)$ times as table c has $(n + 1)$. $(w + 1)$ entries, where each entry requires $\theta(1)$ time to compute.

Depth First Search

Depth First Search (DFS) algorithm traverses a graph in a depthward motion and uses a stack to remember to get the next vertex to start a search, when a dead end occurs in any iteration.

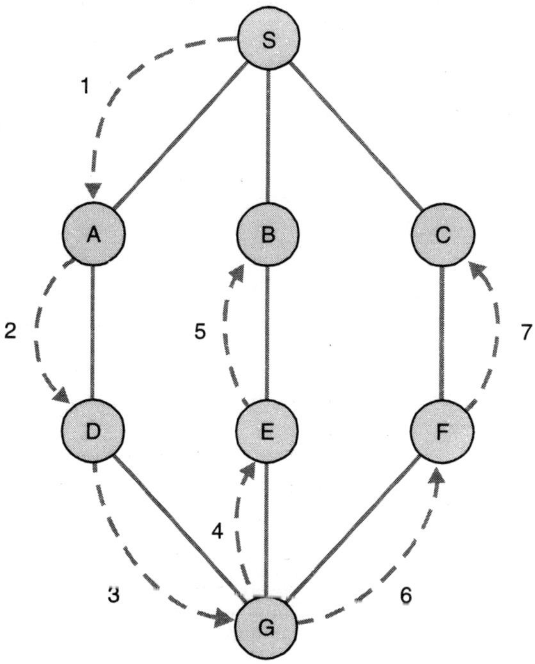

As in the example given above, DFS algorithm traverses from S to A to D to G to E to B first, then to F and lastly to C. It employs the following rules.

- **Rule 1** – Visit the adjacent unvisited vertex. Mark it as visited. Display it. Push it in a stack.
- **Rule 2** – If no adjacent vertex is found, pop up a vertex from the stack. (It will pop up all the vertices from the stack, which do not have adjacent vertices.)
- **Rule 3** – Repeat Rule 1 and Rule 2 until the stack is empty.

Step	Traversal	Description
1	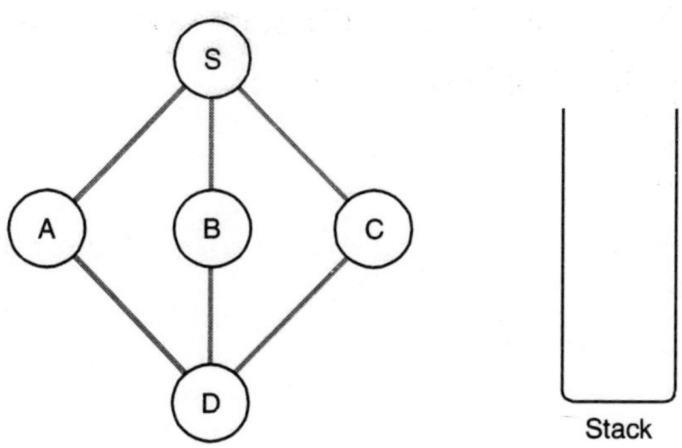	Initialize the stack.

2

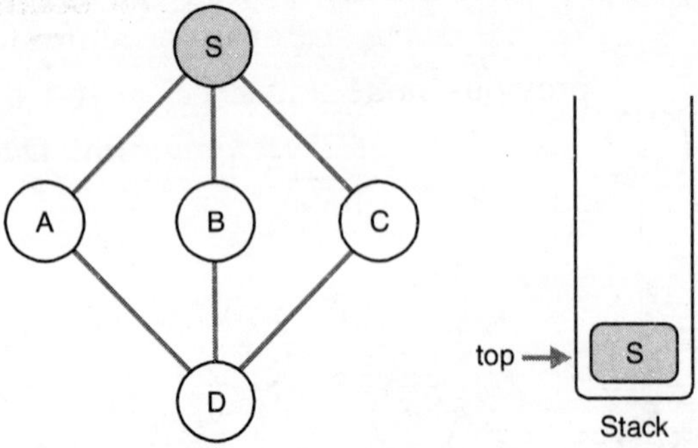

Mark **S** as visited and put it onto the stack. Explore any unvisited adjacent node from **S**. We have three nodes and we can pick any of them. For this example, we shall take the node in an alphabetical order.

3

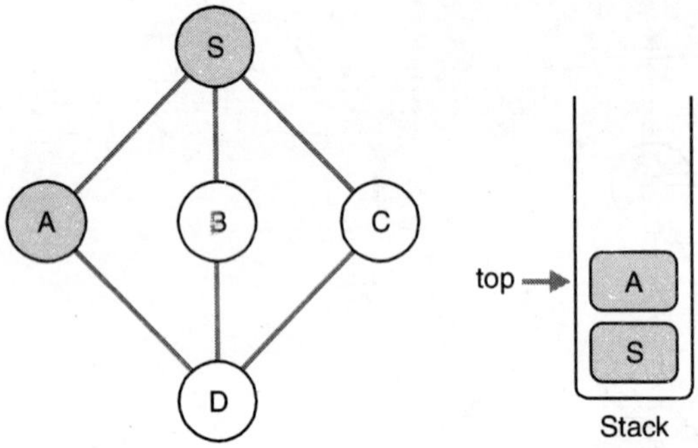

Mark **A** as visited and put it onto the stack. Explore any unvisited adjacent node from A. Both **S** and **D** are adjacent to **A** but we are concerned for unvisited nodes only.

4

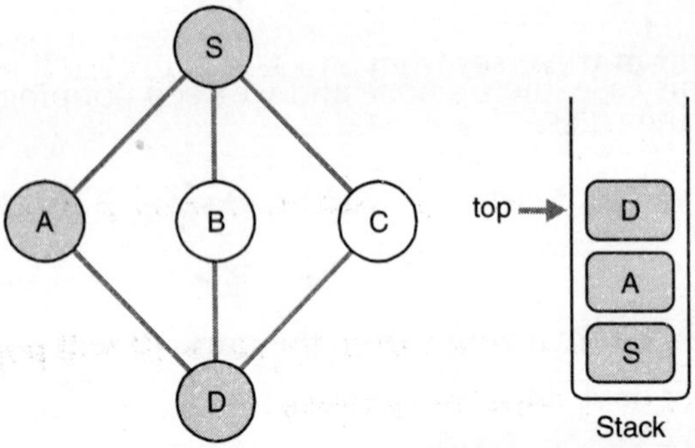

Visit **D** and mark it as visited and put onto the stack. Here, we have **B** and **C** nodes, which are adjacent to **D** and both are unvisited. However, we shall again choose in an alphabetical order.

5

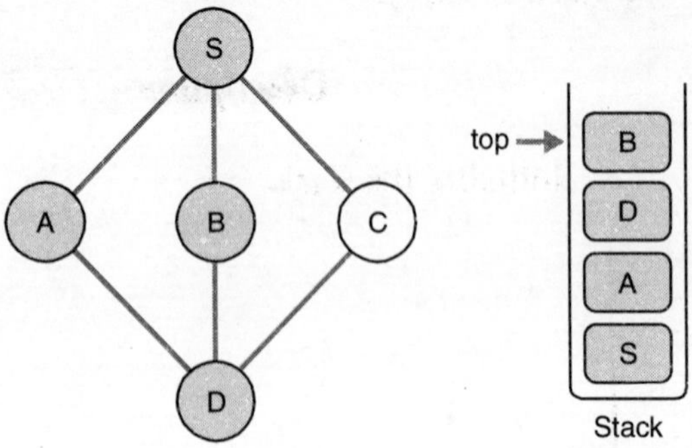

We choose **B**, mark it as visited and put onto the stack. Here **B** does not have any unvisited adjacent node. So, we pop **B** from the stack.

6

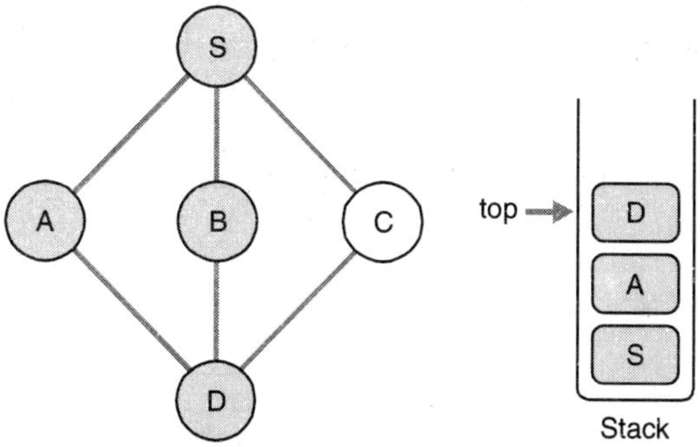

We check the stack top for return to the previous node and check if it has any unvisited nodes. Here, we find **D** to be on the top of the stack.

7

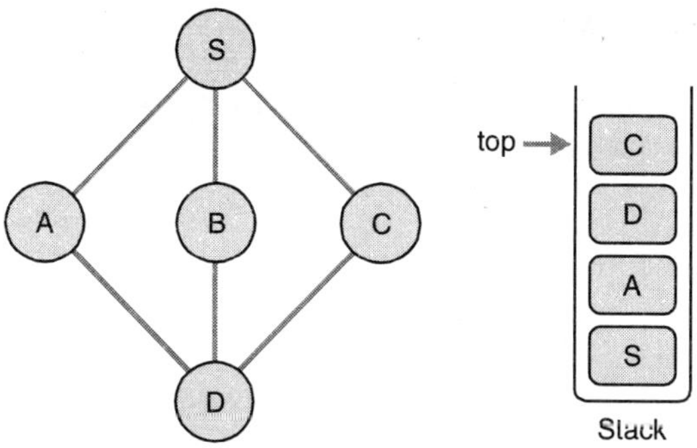

Only unvisited adjacent node is from **D** is **C** now. So we visit **C**, mark it as visited and put it onto the stack.

As **C** does not have any unvisited adjacent node so we keep popping the stack until we find a node that has an unvisited adjacent node. In this case, there's none and we keep popping until the stack is empty.

Breadth First Search (BFS)

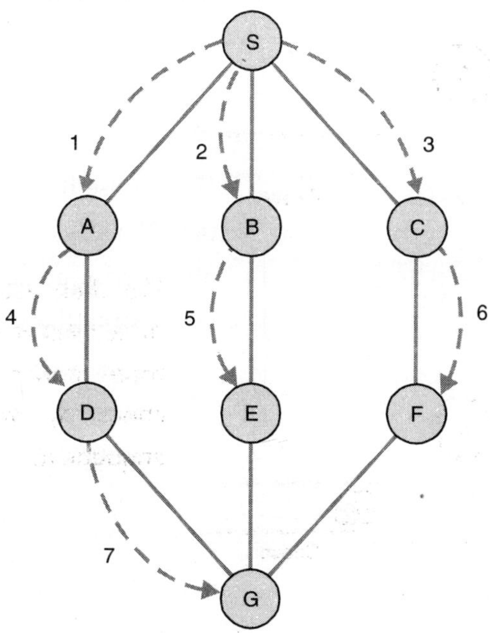

Breadth First Search (BFS) algorithm traverses a graph in a breadthward motion and uses a queue to remember to get the next vertex to start a search, when a dead end occurs in any iteration.

As in the example given above, BFS algorithm traverses from A to B to E to F first then to C and G lastly to D. It employs the following rules.

- **Rule 1** – Visit the adjacent unvisited vertex. Mark it as visited. Display it. Insert it in a queue.
- **Rule 2** – If no adjacent vertex is found, remove the first vertex from the queue.
- **Rule 3** – Repeat Rule 1 and Rule 2 until the queue is empty.

Step	Traversal	Description
1	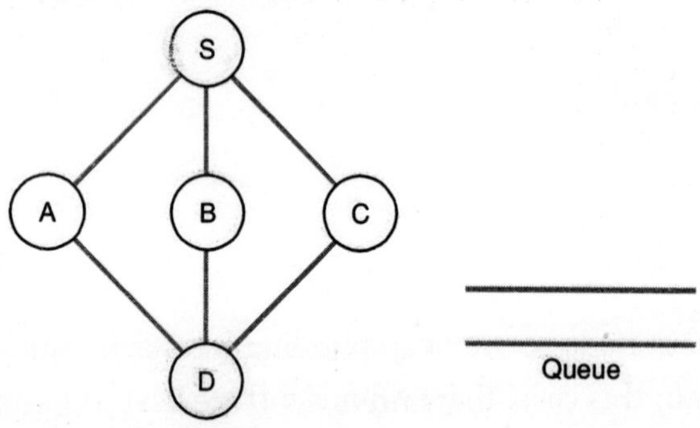	Initialize the queue.
2	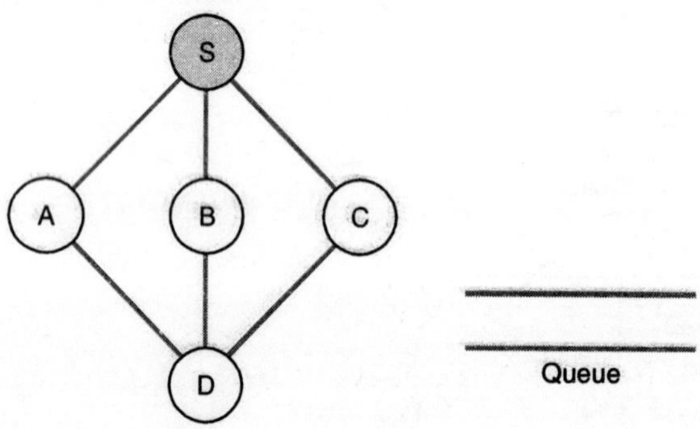	We start from visiting **S** (starting node), and mark it as visited.
3	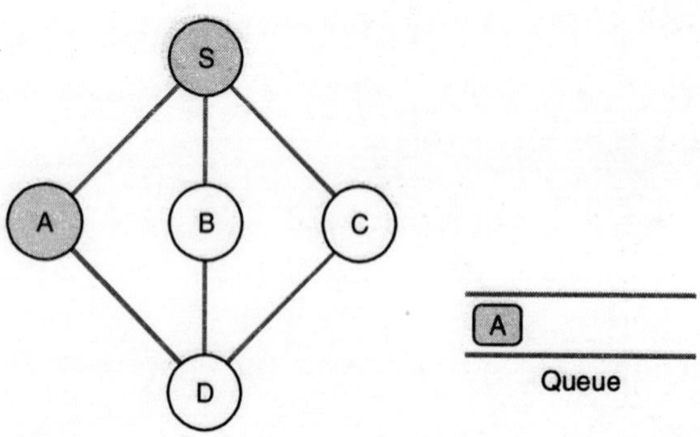	We then see an unvisited adjacent node from **S**. In this example, we have three nodes but alphabetically we choose **A**, mark it as visited and enqueue it.

4

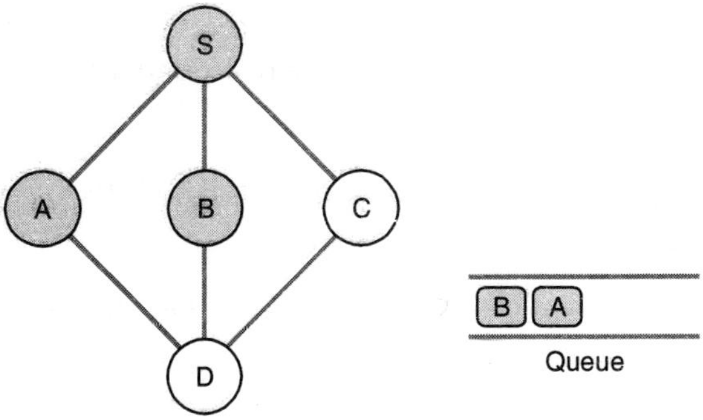

Next, the unvisited adjacent node from **S** is **B**. We mark it as visited and enqueue it.

5

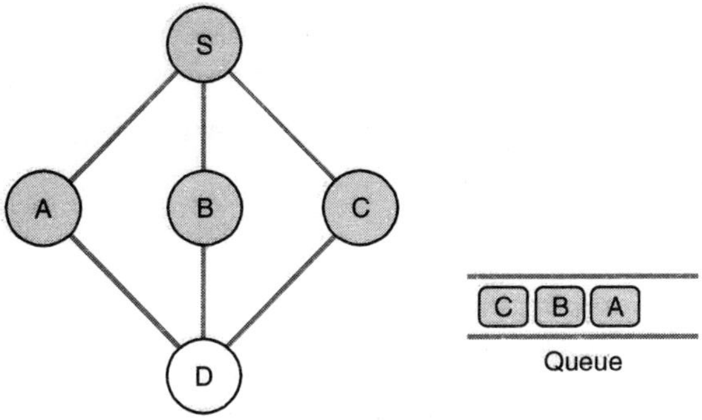

Next, the unvisited adjacent node from **S** is **C**. We mark it as visited and enqueue it.

6

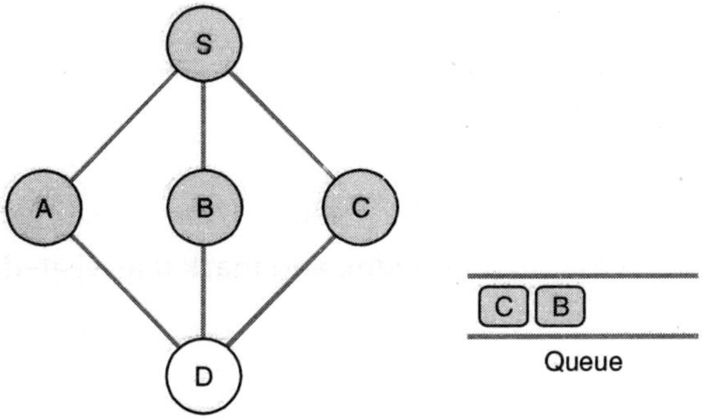

Now, **S** is left with no unvisited adjacent nodes. So, we dequeue and find **A**.

7

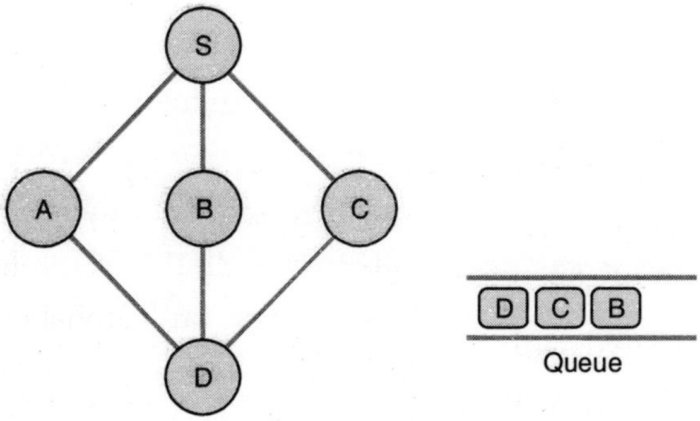

From **A** we have **D** as unvisited adjacent node. We mark it as visited and enqueue it.

At this stage, we are left with no unmarked (unvisited) nodes. But as per the algorithm we keep on dequeuing in order to get all unvisited nodes. When the queue gets emptied, the program is over.

Minimum Spanning tree

A spanning tree for a connected, undirected graph, G = (V, E) is a subgroup of G that is an undirected tree and contains all the vertices of 'G'. We can also define a spanning tree as "A subgraph T = (V, E) of G is a spanning tree of G if T is tree. A spanning tree of a graph should include all the vertices and a subset of edges (E^{I})"

Minimum–cost spanning Tree:

Consider a network of computers connected through bi–directional links. There is a positive cost associated with sending a message on each of the links. We assume that the cost of sending a message on a specific link does not depend in the direction. We want to board cast a message to all the computers starting from an arbitrary computer. We assume that the cost of the broadcast is the sum of the costs of the links used to forward the message. The network can be represented by an undirected graph with positive costs on the edges.

The problem is to find a fixed connected subgraph (corresponding to the links used in the broad cast), containing all vertices such that the sum of the costs of the edges in the subgraph is minimum. It is not difficult to see that this subgraph must be a tree. If any cycle had been present, then we could have broken it by deleting one of its edges, the graph still be connected, but the cost would be smaller since all costs are positive. This subgraph is called the minimum–cost spanning tree (MCST) and it has many uses besides broadcasts.

Definition:

In a weighted graph G = (V, E, W), the weight of a subgraph is the sum of the weights of the edges in the subgraph. A minimum spanning tree for a weighted graph is a spanning tree with minimum weight.

In minimum spanning tree problem, we are given a connected undirected graph G = (V, E) and a length function 'W' such that W€ is the (positive) length of edges '*e*' we are asked to find a subset of the edges that connects all the vertices together and has minimum total length.

We can also define minimum cost spanning tree in simple terms as follows. "A graph can have more than one spanning trees. The spanning tree which results in the lowest cost for visiting all nodes in the graph is called "Minimum spanning Tree".

The cost here is considered as that associated with the edges. The edges in the graph will have weights assigned to them which might represent to construct a set of links that would connect all the nodes and have minimum total cost or to be of minimum total length. In either case, the links have to form a tree. In case that is not so, the selected of links contains a cycle. Removal of any one of the linksin such case will result a tree called as "minimum cost spanning tree" or "minimum spanning tree".

EXAMPLE: A connected graph G with $n = 4$ is as shown below.

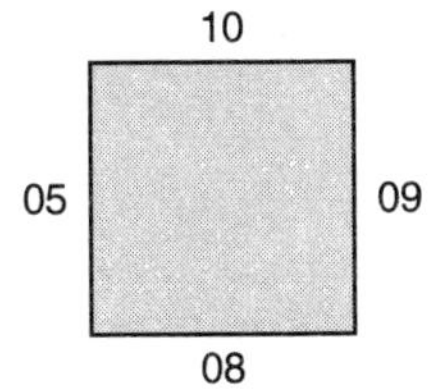

The spanning trees are as shown below.

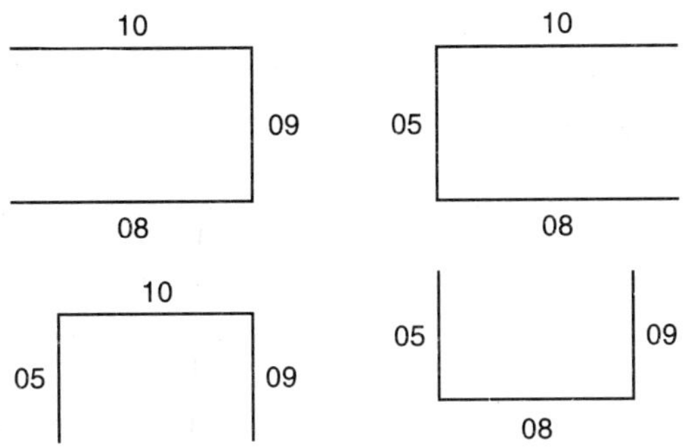

The spanning tree with the cost are as follows

W(T1) = 27, W(T2) – 23, W(T3) = 24 and W(T4) = 22

The cost of fourth tree is minimum.

Therefore, that spanning tree is called as minimum spanning tree.

Properties of a Spanning Tree:

The spanning tree holds the **below–mentioned principles**:

- The number of vertices (**V**) in the graph and the spanning tree is the same.
- There is a fixed number of edges in the spanning tree which is equal to one less than the total number of vertices (**E** = **V–1**).
- The spanning tree should not be **disconnected**, as in there should only be a single source of component, not more than that.
- The spanning tree should be **acyclic,** which means there would not be any cycle in the tree.
- The total cost (or weight) of the spanning tree is defined as the sum of the edge weights of all the edges of the spanning tree.
- There can be many possible spanning trees for a graph.

The following are two algorithm that are popularly used for finding minimum spanning tree.

(1) Kruskal's algorithm (2) Prim's algorithm

Kruskal's algorithm

Kruskal's algorithm is a minimum spanning tree algorithm that takes a graph as input and finds the subset of the edges of that graph which

- form a tree that includes every vertex
- has the minimum sum of weights among all the trees that can be formed from the graph

How Kruskal's algorithm works

It falls under a class of algorithms called greedy algorithm that find the local optimum in the hopes of finding a global optimum.

We start from the edges with the lowest weight and keep adding edges until we reach our goal.

The steps for implementing Kruskal's algorithm are as follows:

Sort all the edges from low weight to high

Take the edge with the lowest weight and add it to the spanning tree. If adding the edge created a cycle, then reject this edge.

Keep adding edges until we reach all vertices.

Note: algorithm in details will be explained in unit 5

Example of Kruskal's algorithm

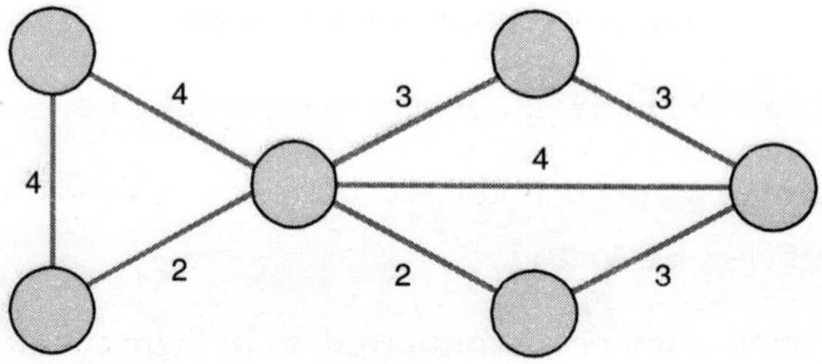

Step: 1

Start with a weighted graph

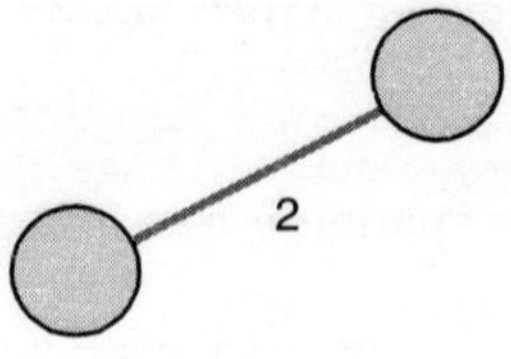

Step: 2

Choose the edge with the least weight, if there are more than 1, choose anyone

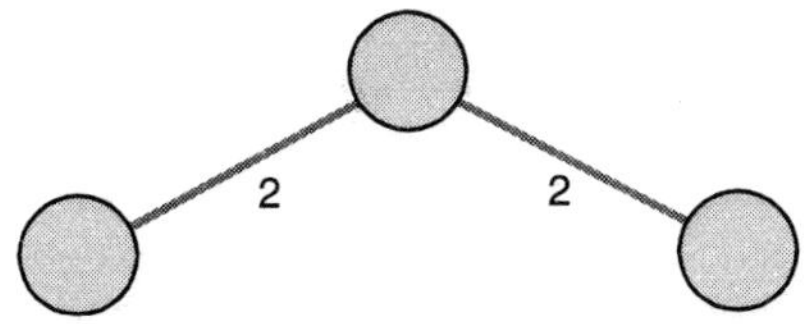

Step: 3

Choose the next shortest edge and add it

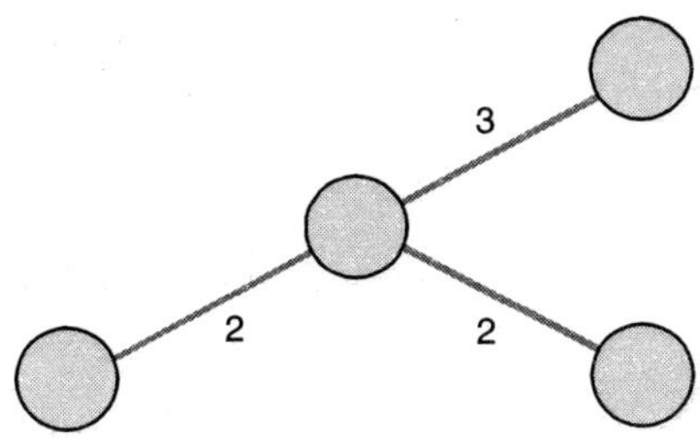

Step: 4

Choose the next shortest edge that doesn't create a cycle and add it.

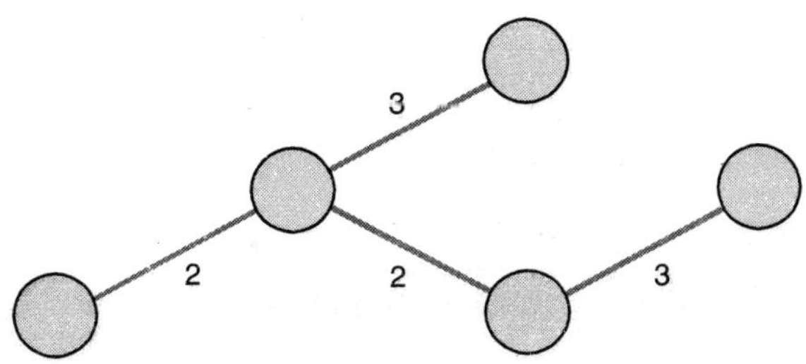

Step: 5

Choose the next shortest edge that doesn't create a cycle and add it

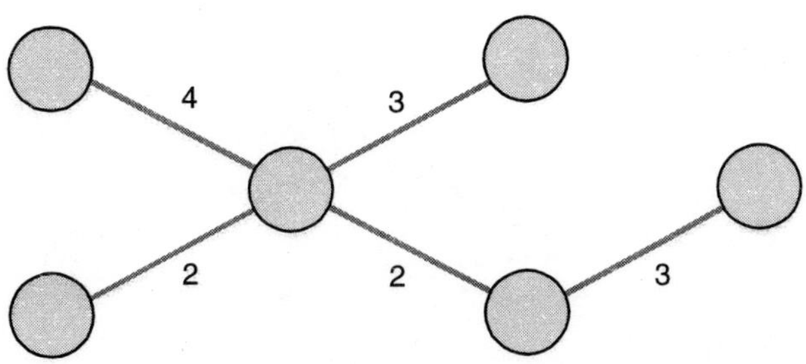

Step: 6

Repeat until you have a spanning tree. Here no more spanning tree is there, so we stop the process and accept it.

Total cost = 4+2+3+2+3

= 14

Kruskal's Algorithm Complexity

The time complexity Of Kruskal's Algorithm is: O (E log E).

Kruskal's Algorithm Applications

- To layout electrical wiring
- In computer network (LAN connection)

Prim's algorithm

Prim's algorithm is a minimum spanning tree algorithm that takes a graph as input and finds the subset of the edges of that graph which

- form a tree that includes every vertex
- has the minimum sum of weights among all the trees that can be formed from the graph

How Prim's algorithm works

It falls under a class of algorithms called greedy algorithm that find the local optimum in the hopes of finding a global optimum.

We start from one vertex and keep adding edges with the lowest weight until we reach our goal.

The steps for implementing Prim's algorithm are as follows:

1. Initialize the minimum spanning tree with a vertex chosen at random.
2. Find all the edges that connect the tree to new vertices, find the minimum and add it to the tree
3. Keep repeating step 2 until we get a minimum spanning tree

Note: algorithm in details will be explained in unit 5.

Example of Prim's algorithm

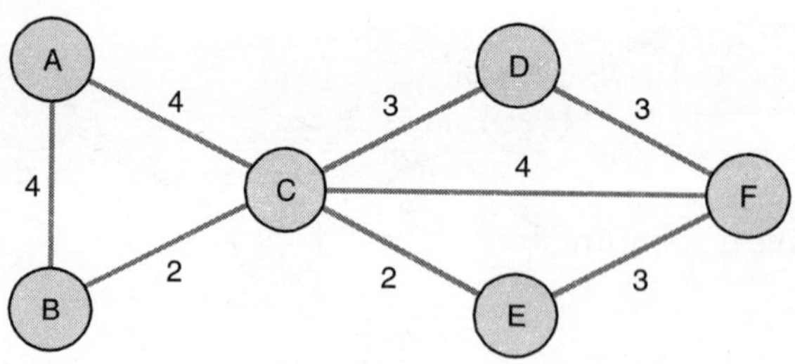

Step: 1

Start with a weighted graph

Step: 2

Choose a vertex

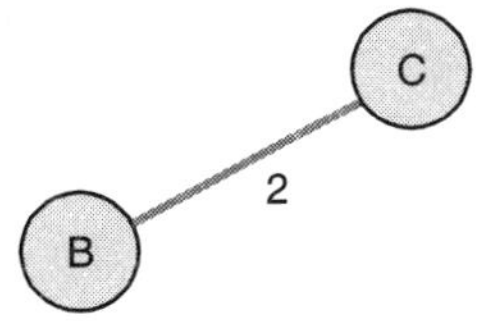

Step: 3

Choose the shortest edge from this vertex and add it

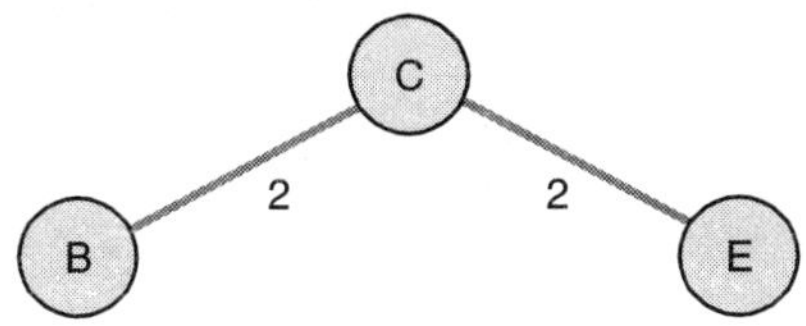

Step: 4

Choose the nearest vertex not yet in the solution

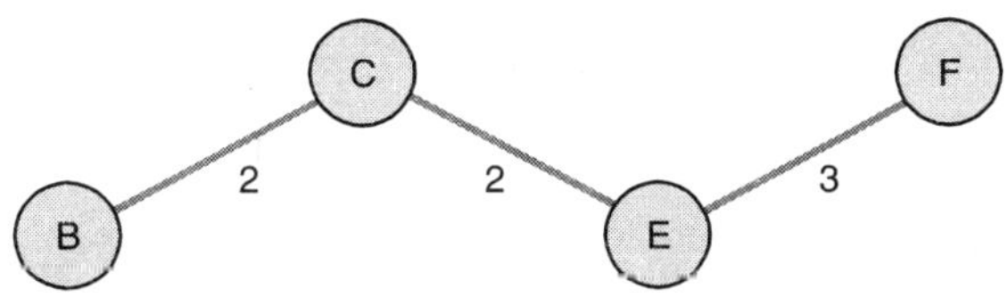

Step: 5

Choose the nearest edge not yet in the solution, if there are multiple choices, choose one at random

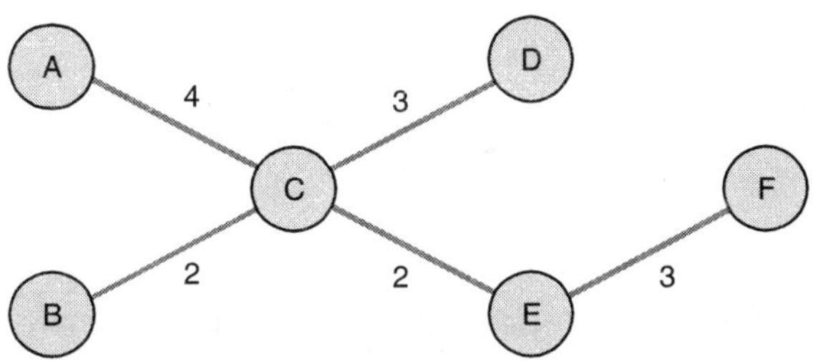

Step: 6

Repeat until you have a spanning tree.

Total cost = 4+2+3+2+3

= 14

Prim's Algorithm Complexity

The time complexity of Prim's algorithm is O(E log V).

Prim's Algorithm Application

- Laying cables of electrical wiring
- In network designed
- To make protocols in network cycles

QUESTIONS

Short Answers:

1. What is brute force?
2. Define exhaustive search.
3. Write the advantage of selection sort.
4. Write the advantage of bubble sort.
5. Disadvantage and advantage of sequential search.
6. What is linear search ?
7. What is travelling salesman problem? Give an example.
8. What is knapsack problem?
9. What is depth first search?
10. What is breadth first search?
11. What is spanning tree?
12. Why we need spanning tree.
13. List the two types of minimum spanning tree.
14. List the Application of Prim's Algorithm.
15. List the application of Kruskal's Algorithm.
16. Differences between selection sort and bubble sort.
17. Difference between bubble sort and sequential search.
18. List the properties of exhaustive search.
19. Define greedy method.
20. What is the 0/1 knapsack problem?

Long Answers:

1. Explain the K knapsack problem using greedy solution with an example.
2. Explain the implementation of DFS and BFS algorithm for a graph.

3. Write a program to sort a list of N elements using selection sort technique.
4. Explain the approach that is used for brute force.
5. Write an algorithm for selection sort and explain with an example.
6. Write an algorithm for bubble sort and explain the bubble sort with an example.
7. Write an algorithm for linear search and explain the search using an example.
8. What does travelling salesman problem ? Give an example and explain the steps using it.
9. Explain the algorithm of depth first search using an example.
10. Explain the algorithm of breadth first search using an example.
11. Define K knapsack problem with an example. Explain the procedure of it.
12. Explain the advantage and disadvantage of brute force.
13. Explain the methods for brute force with an example.

❍ ❍ ❍

UNIT

4

DECREASE–AND–CONQUER

Imagine yourself in a situation where you are having trouble coming up with a solution to your initial issue. What if I told you that a small part of the problem is simpler to solve and that you can use this answer to find the answer to the larger one? Interesting? The decrease and conquer strategy achieves just this.

A problem–solving strategy known as "Decrease and Conquer" involves slicing the size of the input at every stage of the solution procedure. Identical to divide–and–conquer as it breaks the problem down into smaller sub–problems, decrease–and–conquer reduces the size of the input data at each stage rather than increasing it.

Finding the maximum or smallest element in an array, finding the nearest pair of points in a group of points, and binary search are a few cases that can be resolved using the decrease–and–conquer strategy.

Since the quantity of input data is decreased at each stage, decreasing the space and time complexities of the solution, the decrease–and–conquer benefit is that it frequently produces efficient algorithms. A poor decision could result in an algorithm that is ineffective, thus it's critical to pick the best technique for minimizing the quantity of the input data.

VARIATIONS IN THE METHOD OF DECREASE AND CONQUER

The decrease–and–conquer strategy can take one of three main forms:

The first one is, "decrease by a specific value or a constant".

In this variant, each repetition or recursive step of said algorithm decreases the total size of the instance by the same constant. While other constant size decreases can occur, this constant often equals one. Many algorithms, including the following, use this variant.

Topological sorting, Graph search algorithms DFS and BFS, Insertion sort and various algorithms for producing subsets or permutations are examples of these.

The second one is, "decrease by a constant factor".

For each iteration or recursive step of an algorithm, this strategy decreases a problem instance by a constant amount. This constant factor usually equals two in applications. Very uncommon is a reduction by such a factor apart from two. Especially when the factor is bigger than 2, as in the fake–coin situation, decrease by a constant factor techniques are particularly effective. Examples of applications for this strategy are

Russian peasant multiplication, challenges with fake coins, and binary search.

The third or the last one is "decrease variable size".

In this modification, the algorithm's steps or iterations' size–reduction patterns change. Although the value for the second parameter in the problem of calculating the gcd of two numbers is always less on the right than on the left, it does not decrease by a constant or even a constant factor. Here are some examples of this strategy in action, and these are : Euclid's technique, interpolation search, and computing the median and selection problems.

EXAMPLE 1 : An example of how we create permutations using the decrease and conquer method

How can we get all $n!$ permutations with a set of n items, such as a_1, a_2, a_3, ... a_n? To find a solution, produce all $(n–1)!$ permutations. If this is resolved, we can solve the broader problem by placing n into each location within each permutation of the $(n - 1)$ elements.

If there is a single element, there's just one permutation, which is the recursive base case.

EXAMPLE 2 : Let's take an example of a binary search method where we apply the decrease–and–conquer technique. Finding an element's location inside a sorted array can be done using the searching method known as binary search.

With this method, an array's middle is always searched for the element.

Consider a sorted integer array, a = {5, 10, 15, 20, 25}. We want to find the index of element 10.

Approach

For instance, to obtain the permutations of {1,2,3}

First, we find the solution to permutations of {1, 2}

Start by finding the solution to permutations of {1} that is just {1}

Now we Insert 2 into {1}, giving: {2 1} and {1 2}

Insert 3 into {2 1} and {1 2} giving: {3 2 1} {2 3 1} {2 1 3} {3 1 2} {1 3 2} {1 2 3}

The total number of permutations we produce, n!, results in a runtime of *n*!. This is painfully slow for all but the smallest values of *n*, which isn't the algorithm's fault. The issue is simply that there are too few objects to generate.

Finding all paths for the traveling salesman problem is such a problem in which this might be applied.

Algorithm

Step 1: Start

Step 2: Set *p* (the element whose position to be found)

Step 3: Set the pointers first (at the first position) and last (at the last position)

Step 4: Find the middle element (mid)

Step 5: If *p*==mid, then print the middle element

Step 6: If *p*>mid, check *p* with elements right to mid

Step 7: If *p*<mid, check *p* with elements left to mid

Step 8: Repeat steps 4 to 7 till first meets last

Step 9: Return the result

Step 10: Stop

Advantages

Some of the benefits of "decrease and conquer" include;

Simplicity: When compared to other strategies including dynamic programming or divide–and–conquer, decrease–and–conquer is frequently easier to put into practise.

Effective Algorithms: The technique frequently produces efficient algorithms since each step reduces the size of the input data, which lowers both time and space complexity of the result.

Problem–Specific: The approach works effectively for particular issues where a simplified version of the issue can be resolved more quickly.

Disadvantages

Some of the setbacks of Decrease and Conquer include;

Problem–Specific: The method may not be appropriate for problems that are more complicated or to all difficulties.

Implementation Complexity: Compared to other strategies like divide–and–conquer, the strategy may be more difficult to put into practice and may necessitate more thorough planning.

INSERTION SORT

Insertion sort is one of the simplest sorting algorithms for the reason that it sorts a single element at a particular instance. It is not the best sorting algorithm in terms of performance, but it's slightly more efficient than selection sort and bubble sort in practical scenarios. It is an intuitive sorting technique.

Let's consider the example of cards to have a better understanding of the logic behind the insertion sort.

Suppose we have a set of cards in our hand, such that we want to arrange these cards in ascending order. To sort these cards, we have a number of intuitive ways.

One such thing we can do is initially we can hold all of the cards in our left hand, and we can start taking cards one after other from the left hand, followed by building a sorted arrangement in the right hand.

Assuming the first card to be already sorted, we will select the next unsorted card. If the unsorted card is found to be greater than the selected card, we will simply place it on the right side, else to the left side. At any stage during this whole process, the left hand will be unsorted, and the right hand will be sorted.

In the same way, we will sort the rest of the unsorted cards by placing them in the correct position. At each iteration, the insertion algorithm places an unsorted element at its right place.

ALGORITHM: INSERTION SORT (A)

```
for j = 2 to A.length
key = A[j]
// Insert A[j] into the sorted sequence A[1.. j – 1]
i = j – 1
while i > 0 and A[i] > key
A[i + 1] = A[i]
ii = i –1
A[i + 1] = key
```

How Insertion Sort Works

1. We will start by assuming the very first element of the array is already sorted. Inside the **key**, we will store the second element.

   Next, we will compare our first element with the **key**, such that if **the key** is found to be smaller than the first element, we will interchange their indexes or place the key at the first index. After doing this, we will notice that the first two elements are sorted.

2. Now, we will move on to the third element and compare it with the left–hand side elements. If it is the smallest element, then we will place the third element at the first index.

   Else if it is greater than the first element and smaller than the second element, then we will interchange its position with the third element and place it after the first element. After doing this, we will have our first three elements in a sorted manner.

3. Similarly, we will sort the rest of the elements and place them in their correct position.

   Consider the following example of an unsorted array that we will sort with the help of the Insertion Sort algorithm.

   A = (41, 22, 63, 14, 55, 36)

   Initially,

41	22	63	14	55	36

1st Iteration:

Set key = 22

Compare a_1 with a_0

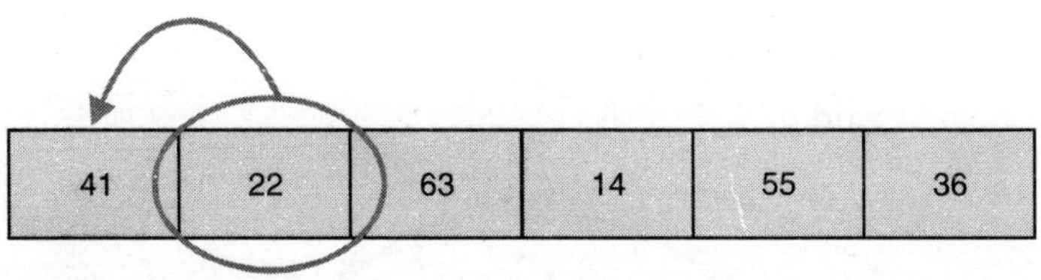

Since $a_0 > a_1$, swap both of them.

22	41	63	14	55	36

2nd Iteration:

Set key = 63

Compare a_2 with a_1 and a_0

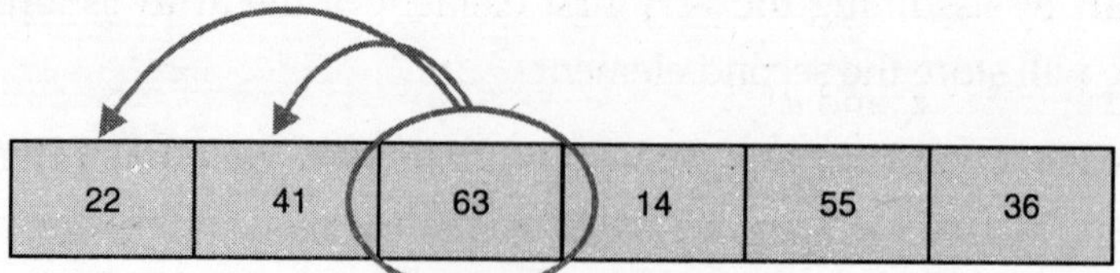

Since $a_2 > a_1 > a_0$, keep the array as it is.

22	41	63	14	55	36

3rd Iteration:

Set key = 14

Compare a_3 with a_2, a_1 and a_0

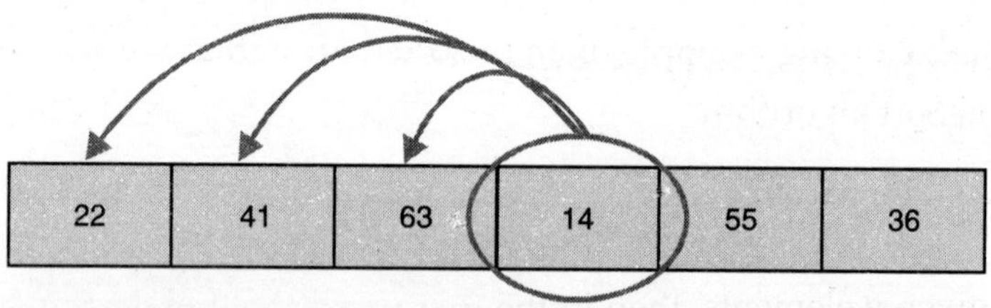

Since a_3 is the smallest among all the elements on the left–hand side, place a_3 at the beginning of the array.

14	22	41	63	55	36

4th Iteration:

Set key = 55

Compare a_4 with a_3, a_2, a_1 and a_0.

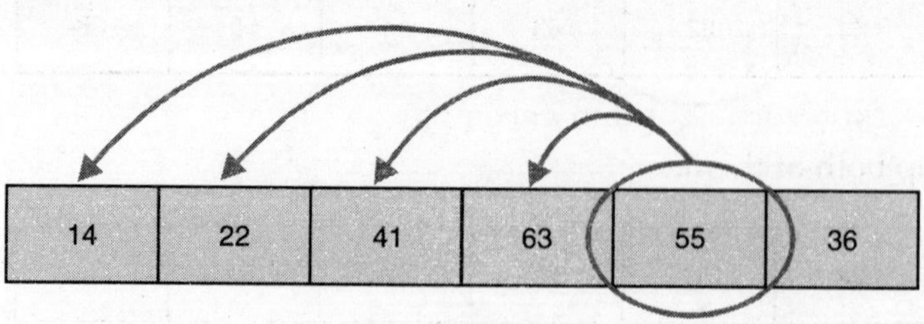

As $a_4 < a_3$, swap both of them.

14	22	41	55	63	36

5th Iteration:

Set key = 36

Compare a_5 with a_4, a_3, a_2, a_1 and a_0.

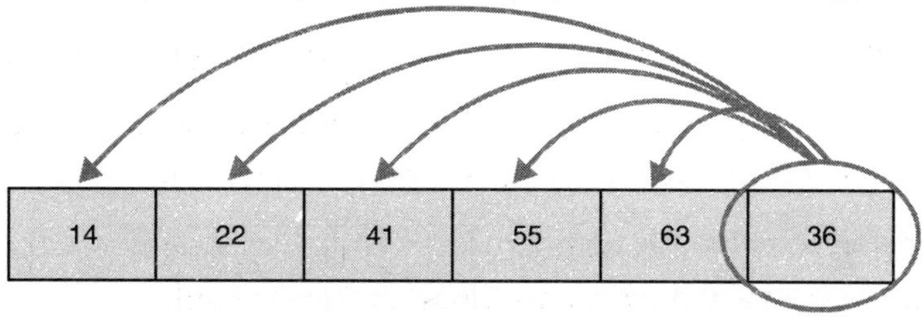

Since $a_5 < a_2$, so we will place the elements in their correct positions.

14	22	36	41	55	63

Hence the array is arranged in ascending order, so no more swapping is required.

Complexity Analysis of Insertion Sort

Input: Given n input elements.

Output: Number of steps incurred to sort a list.

Logic: If we are given $\boldsymbol{n}$ elements, then in the first pass, it will make $\boldsymbol{n-1}$ comparisons; in the second pass, it will do $\boldsymbol{n-2}$; in the third pass, it will do $\boldsymbol{n-3}$ and so on. Thus, the total number of comparisons can be found by;

Output;

$(n-1) + (n-2) + (n-3) + (n-4) + \ldots\ldots + 1$

41	22	63	14	55	36

Sum=

i.e., $O(n^2)$

Therefore, the insertion sort algorithm encompasses a time complexity of $\mathbf{O(n^2)}$ and a space complexity of **O(1)** because it necessitates some extra memory space for a **key** variable to perform swaps.

Time Complexities:

- **Best Case Complexity:** The insertion sort algorithm has a best–case time complexity of $\mathbf{O(n)}$ for the already sorted array because here, only the outer loop is running n times, and the inner loop is kept still.

- **Average Case Complexity:** The average–case time complexity for the insertion sort algorithm is **O(n^2)**, which is incurred when the existing elements are in jumbled order, i.e., neither in the ascending order nor in the descending order.
- **Worst Case Complexity:** The worst–case time complexity is also **O(n^2)**, which occurs when we sort the ascending order of an array into the descending order.

  In this algorithm, every individual element is compared with the rest of the elements, due to which n–1 comparisons are made for every n^{th} element.

  The insertion sort algorithm is highly recommended, especially when a few elements are left for sorting or in case the array encompasses few elements.

Space Complexity

The insertion sort encompasses a space complexity of **O(1) due** to the usage of an extra variable **key**.

Insertion Sort Applications

The insertion sort algorithm is used in the following cases:

- When the array contains only a few elements.
- When there exist few elements to sort.

Advantages of Insertion Sort

1. It is simple to implement.
2. It is efficient on small datasets.
3. It is stable (does not change the relative order of elements with equal keys)
4. It is in–place (only requires a constant amount O (1) of extra memory space).
5. It is an online algorithm, which can sort a list when it is received.

TOPOLOGICAL SORT

Definition:

Topological sort is a technique used in graph theory to order the vertices of a directed acyclic graph (DAG). It ensures that for every directed edge from vertex A to vertex B, vertex A comes before vertex B in the ordering. This is useful in scheduling problems, where tasks depend on the completion of other tasks. The algorithm begins by selecting a vertex with no incoming edges, adding it to the ordering, and removing all outgoing edges from the vertex. This process is repeated until all vertices are visited, and the resulting ordering is a topological sort of the DAG.

The **topological sort** algorithm takes a directed graph and returns an array of the nodes where each node appears *before* all the nodes it points to.

The ordering of the nodes in the array is called a *topological ordering*.

Here's an example:

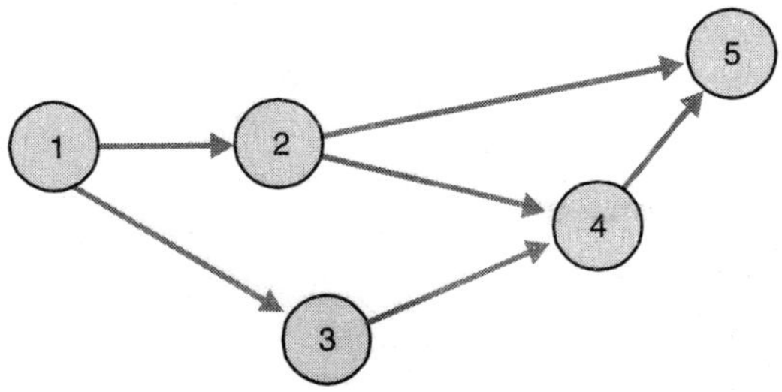

Since node 1 points to nodes 2 and 3, node 1 appears before them in the ordering. And, since nodes 2 and 3 both point to node 4, they appear before it in the ordering.

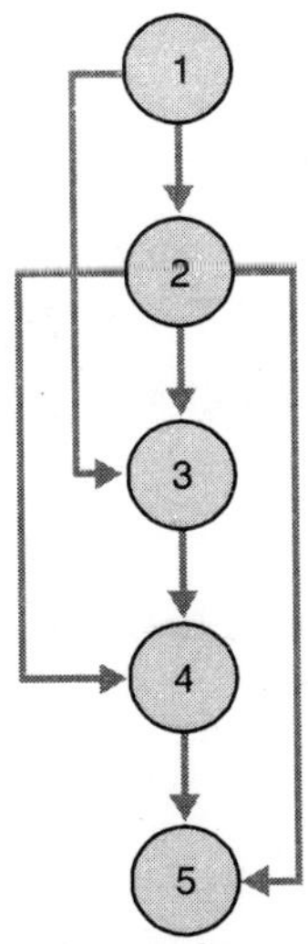

So [1, 2, 3, 4, 5] would be a topological ordering of the graph.

Can a graph have more than one valid topological ordering? Yes! In the example above, [1, 3, 2, 4, 5] works too.

Cyclic Graphs

Look at this directed graph with a cycle:

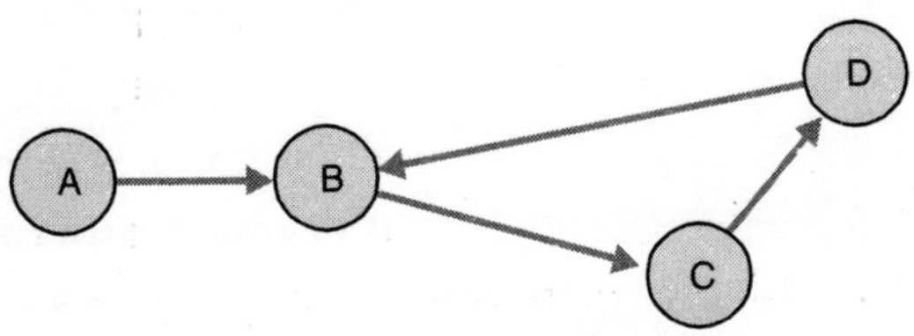

The cycle creates an impossible set of constraints—B has to be before *and* after D in the ordering.

As a rule, **cyclic graphs don't have valid topological orderings.**

The Algorithm

How can we produce a topological ordering for this directed graph?

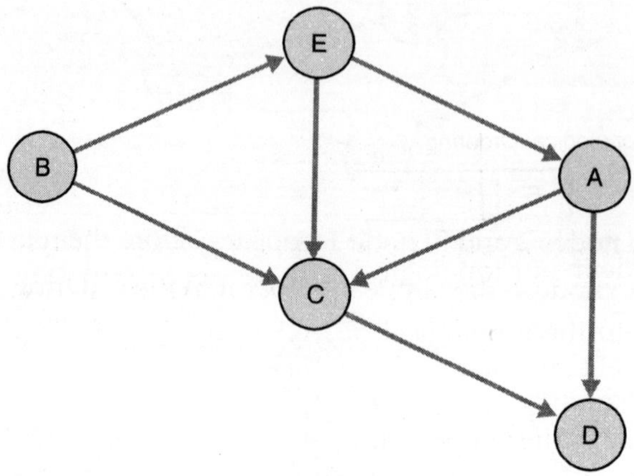

Well, let's focus on the *first* node in the topological ordering. That node can't have any incoming directed edges; it must have an indegree ↴ of zero.

Why?

Because if it had incoming directed edges, then the nodes pointing to it would have to come first.

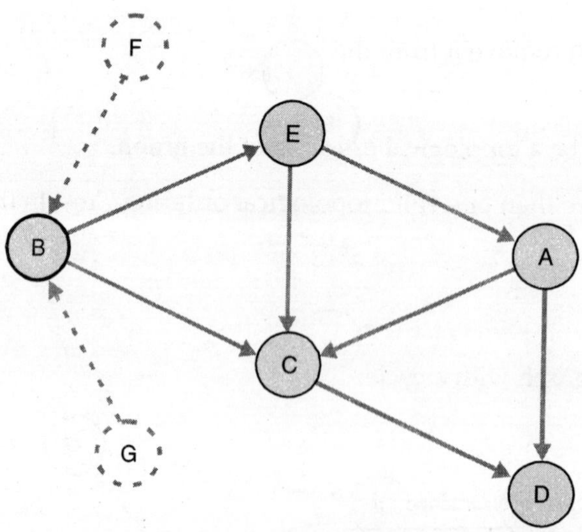

So, we'll find a node with an indegree of zero and add it to the topological ordering.

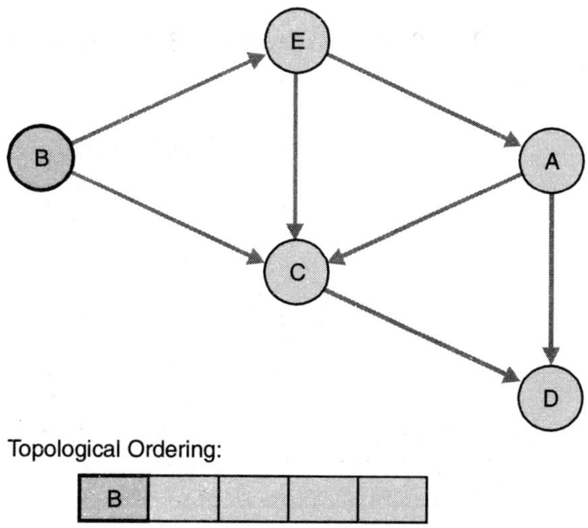

That covers the first node in our topological ordering. What about the next one?

Once a node is added to the topological ordering, we can take the node, and its outgoing edges, out of the graph.

Then, we can repeat our earlier approach: look for any node with an indegree of zero and add it to the ordering.

This is a common algorithm design pattern:

1. Figure out how to get the *first* thing.
2. Remove the first thing from the problem.
3. Repeat.

Here's what this looks like on our graph. We'll grab a node with an indegree of 0, add it to our topological ordering and remove it from the graph:

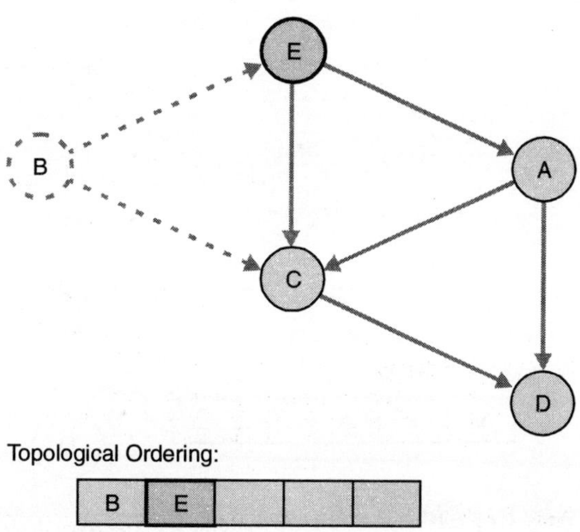

and repeat

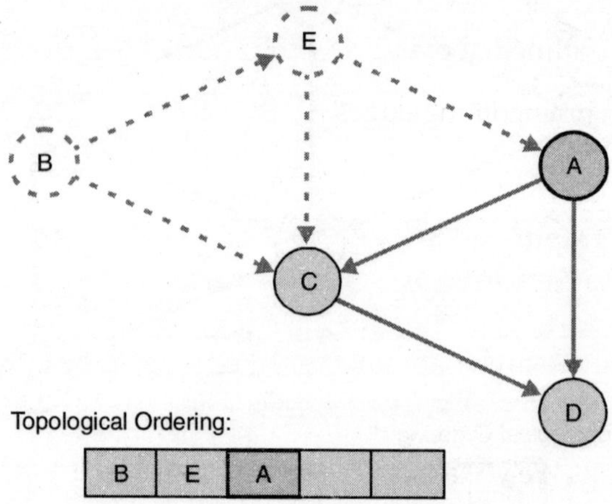

and repeat

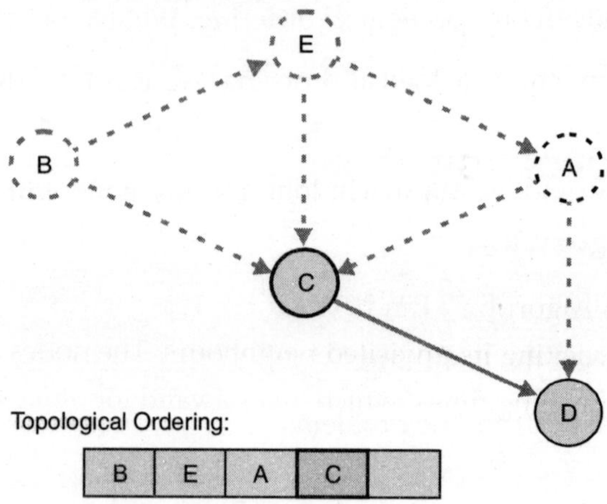

until we're

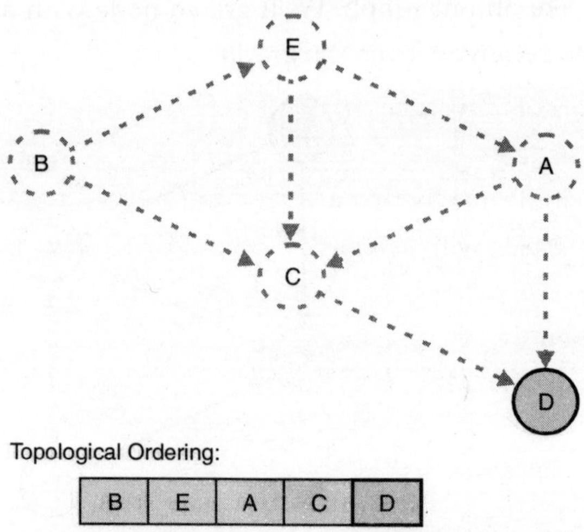

out of nodes.

Note: this isn't the *only* way to produce a topological ordering.

Implementation

We'll use the strategy we outlined above:

1. Identify a node with no incoming edges.
2. Add that node to the ordering.
3. Remove it from the graph.
4. Repeat.

We'll keep looping until there aren't any more nodes with indegree zero. This could happen for two reasons:

- There are no nodes left. We've taken all of them out of the graph and added them to the topological ordering.
- There are some nodes left, but they all have incoming edges. This means the graph has a cycle, and no topological ordering exists.

ALGORITHMS FOR TOPOLOGICAL SORTING

Depth–First Search Algorithm:

Depth–First Search (DFS Algorithm) can be used for Topological Sort by visiting each node in the graph and recursively visiting its unvisited neighbours. The nodes are added to the output list in reverse order of their finishing times, which gives a valid topological ordering.

Algorithm

Algorithm 3 : DFS Algorithm for Topological Sort

```
Data : A DAG G
Result : A topological sort of all vertices in G
Create an empty vertex list L;
Create a visited array to indicate whether a vertex has been visited;
Initialize all elements in visited with false;
foreach vertex u ∈ G do
    if visited[u] is false then
    | topologicalSortRecursive (u);
    end
end
return L;
Function topologicalSortRecursive (u) :
    visited[u] = ture;
```

```
    foreach u's neighboring vertex v do
        if visited[v] is false then
            topologicalSortRecursive (v);
        end
    end
    Add u to the front of list L;
```

Explanation:

- Create a temporary stack.
- Recursively call topological sorting for all its adjacent vertices, then push it to the stack (when all adjacent vertices are on stack). Note this step is same as Depth First Search in a recursive way.
- Atlast, print contents of stack.

EXAMPLE: Consider the following graph:

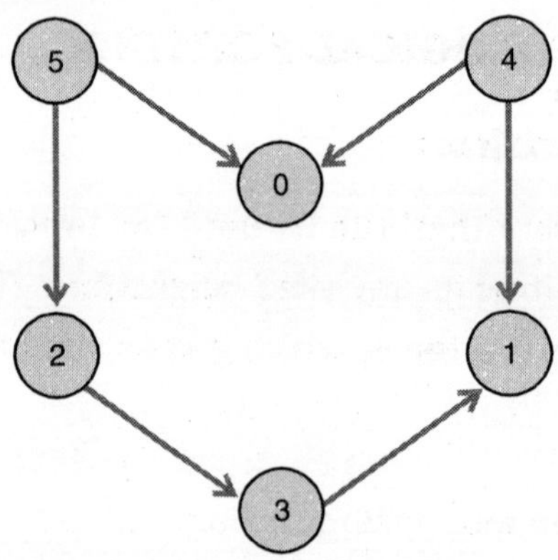

Following is the adjacency list of the given graph:

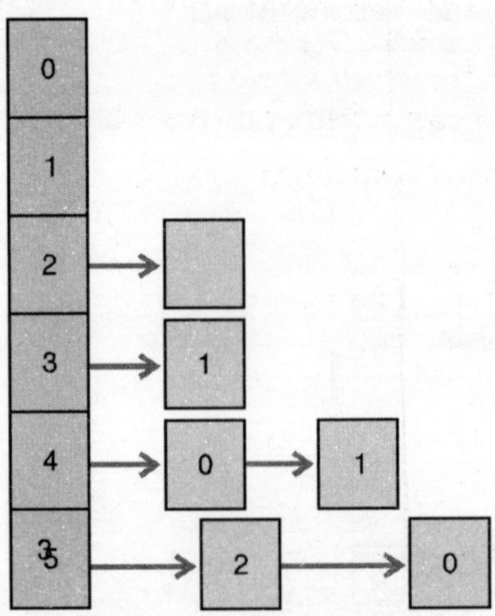

When topological() is called:

Visited[ ] =	F	F	F	F	F	F
	0	1	2	3	4	5

Stepwise demonstration of the stack after each iteration of the loop(topologicalSort()):

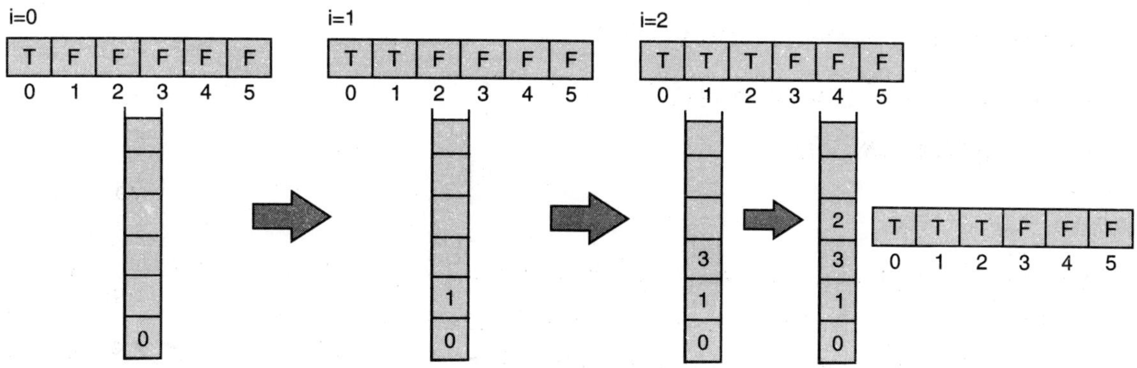

Go to node 0, it has no outgoing edges (i.e. no successors) so push node 0 into the stack and mark it visited.

Go to node 1, it has no outgoing edges (i.e. no successors) so push node 1 into the stack and mark it visited.

Go to node 2, process all the adjacent nodes (includes node) and mark node 2 visited.

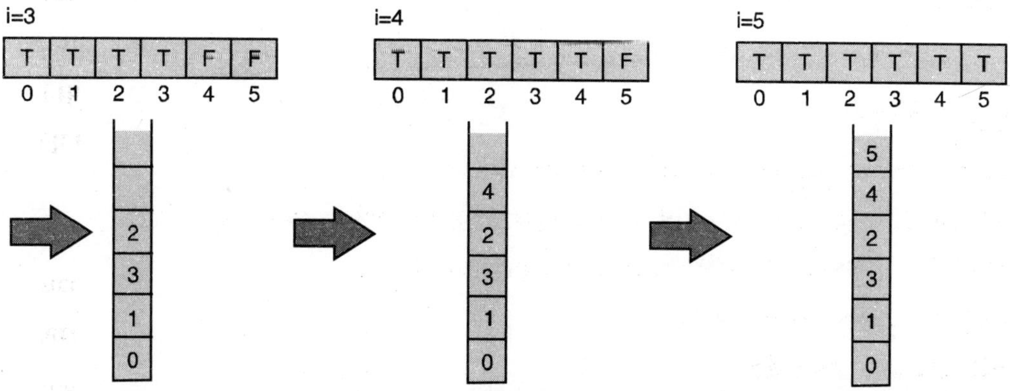

Node 3 is already visited so continue with next iteration

Go to node 4, all it's adjacent nodes are already visited so push node 4 into the stack and mark it visited.

Go to node 5, all it's adjacent nodes are already visited so push node 5 into the stack and mark it visited.

The contents of the stack are:

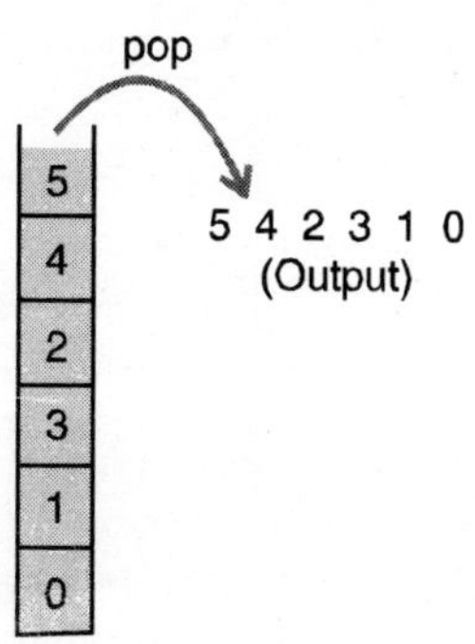

So the topological sorting of the above graph is "5 4 2 3 1 0". There can be more than one topological

Complexity

Worst case time complexity: **Θ(|V|+|E|)**

Average case time complexity: **Θ(|V|+|E|)**

Best case time complexity: **Θ(|V|+|E|)**

Space complexity: **Θ(|V|)**

Kahn's Algorithm

In a DAG, any path between two vertices has a finite length as the graph does not contain a cycle. Let be the longest path from (source vertex) to (destination vertex). Since is the longest path, there can be no incoming edge to. **Therefore, a DAG contains at least one vertex that has no incoming edge.**

Algorithm:

Algorithm 1: Kahn's Algorithm for Topological Sort

Data : A DAG G

Result : A topological sort of all vertices in *G*

Compute in-degree (number of incoming edges) for each vertex in *G*;

Put all the vertices with 0 in –degree into a queue *Q*;

Create an empty vertex list *L*;

while *Q is not empty* **do**

    Remove a vertex *u* from *Q*;

    Add *u* to the end of the *L*;

    foreach *u's neighboring node v* **do**

        Decrease *v*'s in-degree by 1;

        if *v's in-degree is 0* **then**

            Add *v* to *Q*;

        end

    end

end

return *L*;

Explanation:

- Compute the Indegree of all the vertices of the Graph and Initialize the variable count with zero(It maintains the Visited node count)
- All the nodes with the in–degree must have zero pick them and put them in a Queue
- Pick the node from the Queue mark it visited then, increment the count value and Decrement the Indegree value for all the nodes that are edges from the given node
- Keep Doing step 3 until the Queue is Empty
- Now compare the count value with the number of nodes of the graph, in–degree, and if they are not equal, then the Topological sort is not possible for the Graph.

EXAMPLE:

Input Format: V = 4, E = 3

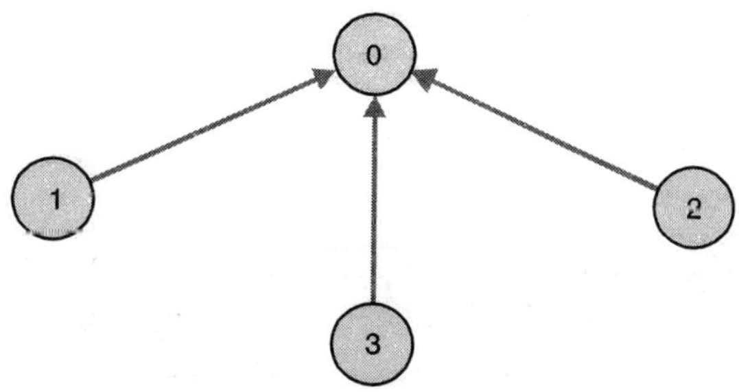

Result: 1, 2, 3, 0

Explanation: The necessary conditions for the ordering are:

- For edge **1 → 0** node 1 must appear before node 0.
- For edge **2 → 0** node 1 must appear before node 0.
- For edge **3 → 0** node 1 must appear before node 0.

Advantages of the Topological Sort:

- Efficient ordering.
- Easy implementation using adjacency lists.
- Wide range of applications.
- Low time and space complexity.
- Scalability for large–scale data processing.

Disadvantages of the Topological Sort:

- It only works on directed acyclic graphs (DAGs) and cannot handle cyclic graphs.

- This does not provide a unique solution if there are multiple valid orders for the nodes.
- It may not be the best algorithm for certain graph–related problems, depending on the specific requirements and constraints.
- These may require additional data structures and memory overhead for larger graphs, which can affect performance.

Applications of Topological Sort:

1. **Task Scheduling:** In project management and task scheduling, topological sort helps determine the optimal order of tasks with dependencies. Each node in the directed acyclic graph (DAG) represents a task, and directed edges represent dependencies between tasks. By performing a topological sort, you can schedule tasks in the correct sequence to ensure that dependent tasks are completed before their dependents.
2. **Software Dependency Resolution:** When managing software projects with multiple modules or libraries, topological sort assists in resolving dependencies between software components. The algorithm ensures that dependencies are resolved in the correct order during compilation or deployment, preventing issues arising from missing dependencies.
3. **Building Make files:** Make files in software development specify the sequence of commands required to build an application from its source code. Topological sort can be used to determine the correct order in which source files need to be compiled, taking into account their interdependencies.
4. **Compiler Optimizations:** In compilers, topological sort aids in optimizing the order in which code is generated for different program segments. This optimization ensures that variables are allocated in the correct order and that loops are compiled with appropriate loop unrolling techniques.
5. **Dependency Analysis:** In software engineering, topological sort is used to analyze dependencies between modules or components. This helps in understanding the relationships between different parts of a software system, enabling better maintenance and modification.
6. **Deadlock Detection:** Topological sort can be used in resource allocation systems to detect deadlocks, which occur when processes are waiting for resources that are blocked by other processes. By creating a resource allocation graph and performing a topological sort, you can identify cycles that indicate potential deadlocks.
7. **Course Scheduling:** In educational institutions, topological sort can help create efficient course schedules that ensure prerequisites are met. Each course is represented as a node, and prerequisites are represented by directed edges.

8. **Event Management:** In event scheduling systems, topological sort assists in determining the optimal order of events or tasks to ensure that no event starts before its prerequisites are completed.

Time and Space Complexity

Breaking the algorithm into chunks, we:

- *Determine the indegree for each node.* This is $O(M)$ time (where M is the number of edges), since this involves looking at each directed edge in the graph once.
- *Find nodes with no incoming edges.* This is a simple loop through all the nodes with some number of constant–time appends. $O(N)$ time (where N is the number of nodes).
- *Add nodes until we run out of nodes with no incoming edges.* This loop could run once for every node—$O(N)$ times. In the body, we:
  - o Do two constant–time operations on an array to add a node to the topological ordering.
  - o Decrement the indegree for each neighbour of the node we added. Over the entire algorithm, we'll end up doing exactly one decrement for each edge, making this step $O(M)$ time *overall*.
- *Check if we included all nodes or found a cycle.* This is a fast O(1) comparison.

Altogether, the time complexity is $O(M+N)$.

That's the fastest time we can expect, since we'll have to look at all the nodes and edges at least once.

What about space complexity? Here are the data structures we created:

- indegrees—this has one entry for each node in the graph, so it's $O(N)$ space.
- nodesWithNoIncomingEdges—in a graph with no edges, this would start out containing every node, so it's $O(N)$ space in the worst case.
- topological Ordering—in a graph with no cycles, this will eventually have every node. $O(N)$ space.

All in all, we have three structures and they're all $O(N)$ space. **Overall space complexity: $O(N)$.**

This is the best space complexity we can expect, since we *must* allocate a return array which costs $O(N)$ space itself.

Topological Sort vs Other Sorts:

Following is a comparison between topological sorting with other sorting algorithms.

Algorithm	Time Complexity	Space Complexity	Type of Sorting	Applications
Topological Sorting	O(V+E).	O(V).	Partial order sorting.	Dependency management, cycle detection, graph traversal, and task scheduling.
Bubble Sort	O(n^2).	O(1).	Comparison–based sorting.	Simple and easy to understand, useful for small datasets.
Insertion Sort	O(*n*^2).	O(1).	Comparison–based sorting.	Useful for small datasets, it can be efficient for partially sorted datasets.
Merge Sort	O(*n* log *n*).	O(*n*).	Comparison–based sorting.	Efficient for large datasets, stable sorting algorithm.
Quick Sort	O(*n* log *n*).	O(log *n*).	Comparison–based sorting.	Efficient for large datasets, unstable sorting algorithm.

ALGORITHM FOR GENERATING COMBINATORIAL OBJECTS

The algorithms for generating combinatorial objects vary depending on the specific type of object you want to generate—permutations, combinations, subsets, partitions, etc. Each type has its own set of rules and constraints. Here, I'll outline basic algorithms for generating permutations and combinations as examples:

Generating Permutations:

A permutation of a set is an arrangement of its elements. For example, for the set {1, 2, 3}, permutations include {1, 2, 3}, {1, 3, 2}, {2, 1, 3}, etc.

Algorithm for Generating Permutations (Recursive):

Recursive Backtracking:

Start with the entire set of elements.

Swap each element with every other element and recursively generate permutations for the remaining elements.

Backtrack by swapping elements back to their original positions for all possible combinations.

Generating Combinations:

A combination of a set refers to a selection of items without regard to the order. For example, combinations of 2 from the set {1, 2, 3} include {1, 2}, {1, 3}, {2, 3}, etc.

```
GeneratePermutations(sequence):
  if sequence is empty:
    Output the generated permutation
  else:
    for each element in the sequence:
      Add the element to the partial permutation
      GeneratePermutations(sequence – current_element)  # Recursive call
      Remove the element from the partial permutation (Backtracking)
```

Algorithm for Generating Combinations (Recursive):

Recursive Approach with Backtracking:

Generate combinations by selecting or not selecting each element, moving forward recursively.

Consider two cases: Include the current element in the combination or exclude it.

Explore all possible combinations by making recursive calls and backtracking to explore other options.

```
GenerateCombinations(sequence, chosen, start):
  if chosen is of the desired length:
    Output the generated combination
  else:
    for i from start to the length of the sequence:
      Add sequence[i] to chosen
      GenerateCombinations(sequence, chosen, i + 1)  # Recursive call
      Remove sequence[i] from chosen (Backtracking)
```

These pseudo–algorithms illustrate recursive approaches for generating permutations and combinations. They rely on recursive calls to explore all possible arrangements (permutations) or selections (combinations) while ensuring that each item is considered once and only once.

In practice, the actual implementation of these algorithms might involve additional optimizations, such as pruning unnecessary branches of the search tree, memoization to avoid recomputation of overlapping subproblems, or other strategies to enhance efficiency.

The selection of the most appropriate algorithm depends on the specific combinatorial object being generated and the constraints or requirements involved. Additionally, in the design and analysis of algorithms, the study often involves analyzing the time complexity and space complexity of these algorithms to understand their efficiency and scalability concerning input size.

DECREASE BY A CONSTANT FACTOR ALGORITHM

The "Decrease by a Constant Factor" algorithm is a strategy used in certain optimization problems, particularly in algorithms like binary search, quicksort, or merge sort. This strategy is employed when an algorithm aims to reduce the problem size by a constant factor at each step.

In many divide–and–conquer algorithms, including binary search or certain sorting algorithms, the problem size is often halved or reduced significantly in each iteration or recursive step. This reduction by a constant factor results in an algorithm that exhibits a logarithmic time complexity, such as O(log N) or O(N log N).

Let's take the example of binary search, which is a classic algorithm that uses the "decrease by a constant factor" approach:

```
#include <stdio.h>

int binary_search(int arr[], int target, int size) {
  int left = 0;
  int right = size – 1;

  while (left <= right) {
    int mid = left + (right – left) / 2; // Calculate the middle index

    if (arr[mid] == target) {
      return mid; // Element found at index mid
    } else if (arr[mid] < target) {
      left = mid + 1; // Search in the right half
    } else {
      right = mid – 1; // Search in the left half
    }
  }

  return –1; // Element not found
```

```
}

// Example usage:
int main() {
  int sorted_array[] = {2, 5, 8, 12, 16, 23, 38, 56, 72, 91};
  int target_element = 23;
  int array_size = sizeof(sorted_array) / sizeof(sorted_array[0]);

  int result_index = binary_search(sorted_array, target_element, array_size);

  if (result_index != -1) {
printf("Element %d found at index %d.\n", target_element, result_index);
  } else {
printf("Element not found.\n");
  }

  return 0;
}
```

❍ ❍ ❍

UNIT

5

DIVIDE-AND-CONQUER

INTRODUCTION

We know that many scientists identified a number of general techniques to solve a given problem. Here we will discuss that one more technique called divide and conquer. Divide and conquer is an algorithm designed technique most widely applicable and a technique for designing efficient algorithms.

The principle behind the divide and conquer algorithm design paradigm he's thought it is easier to solve several small instance of problem than one larger one.

The divide and conquer techniques involve solving particular problem by dividing it into one or more sub problems of smaller size, recursively solving each sub problem and then merging the solutions to a sub problem to proceed a solution to the original problem.

The divide and conquer paradigm involves three steps at each level of recursion.

1. **Divide:** Divide the problem into number of sub problems
2. **Conquer:** Conclude the sub problems by solving them recursively. If the sub problem sizes are small enough then solve the sub problem in a straightforward manner.
3. **Combine:** Combine the solution to the subproblems into the solution for the original problem.

EXAMPLE: In the classic merge sort algorithm, $S(n)$ denotes the problem of sorting a sequence of n numbers. Merge sort solving problem $S(n)$ by dividing it into two subproblems. $S[(n/2)]$ and $S[(n/2)]$. Recursively solving these two problems and then matching and resulting sorted sequence into a single sorted sequence that yields a solution to $S(n)$.

The marching steps takes $0(n)$ time thus the total running time of the merge sort algorithm is $0(n \log n)$.

Control abstraction for dividing and conquer method

The control abstraction is a procedure that reflects the way an actual program based on divide and conquer will look like. A control abstraction shows clearly the flow of control but the primary operation are specified by an another procedure. The control abstraction can be returned rather recursively or iteratively. However the basic functionality of rather method is one and same.

Consider an algorithm DandC given below. The algorithm is initially invoked as DandC(P) where P is the problem to be solved.

Small(P) is a boolean value function that determines whether the input size is small enough that the answer can be computed without splitting. If this is so the function S is invoked. Otherwisethe problem P is divided into smaller sub problems. These subproblems P_1, P_2 …… P_K are solved by recursive applications of D and C. Combine is a function that determines the solution of P using the solution to the K problems. If the size of P is n and the size of K sub problems are n_1, n_2,…..n_k, are solved by recursive applications of DandC.

Then the computing time of DandC is described by the recurrence relation.

```
Algorithm DandC
{
 If small(P) then return S(P);
Else
{
Divide P into smaller instances P1,P2,......Pk K>=1;
Apply D and C to each of these subproblems;
Return combine (DandC(P1), D and C(P2),...... DandC(Pk));
}
}
```

EXAMPLE:

Arrays as Input

There are various ways in which various algorithms can take input such that they can be solved using the divide and conquer technique. Arrays are one of them. In algorithms that require input to be in the form of a list, like various sorting algorithms, array data structures are most commonly used.

In the input for a sorting algorithm below, the array input is divided into subproblems until they cannot be divided further.

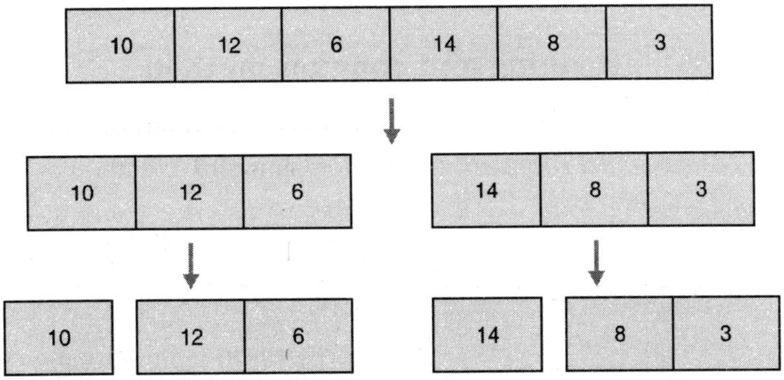

Then, the subproblems are sorted (the conquer step) and are merged to form the solution of the original array back (the combine step).

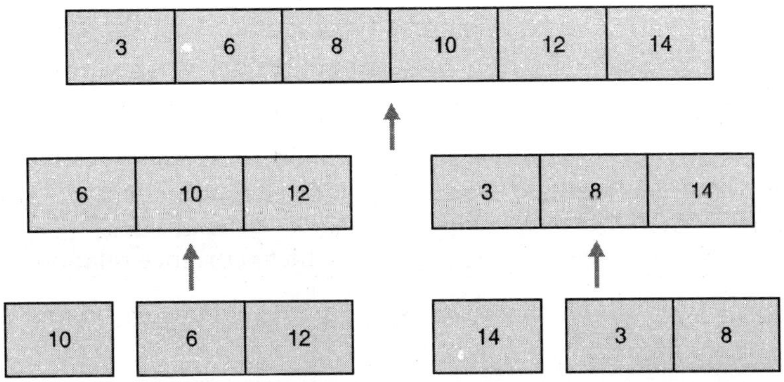

Since arrays are indexed and linear data structures, sorting algorithms most popularly use array data structures to receive input.

Pros and cons of Divide and Conquer Approach

Divide and conquer approach supports parallelism as sub-problems are independent. Hence, an algorithm, which is designed using this technique, can run on the multiprocessor system or in different machines simultaneously.

In this approach, most of the algorithms are designed using recursion, hence memory management is very high. For recursive function stack is used, where function state needs to be stored.

MERGE SORT

Merge sort is a sorting technique based on divide and conquer technique. With worst-case time complexity being $O(n \log n)$, it is one of the most used and approached algorithms.

Merge sort first divides the array into equal halves and then combines them in a sorted manner.

How Merge Sort Works?

To understand merge sort, we take an unsorted array as the following –

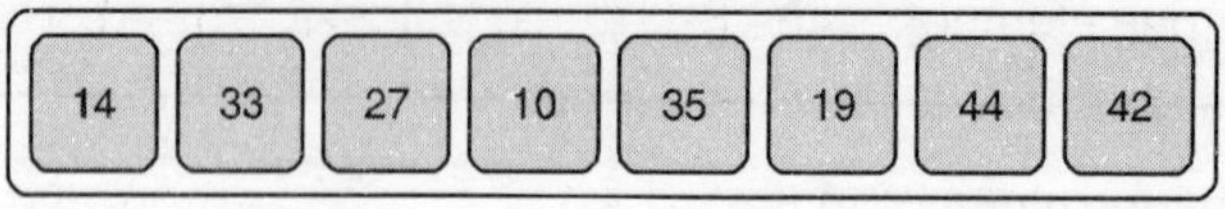

We know that merge sort first divides the whole array iteratively into equal halves unless the atomic values are achieved. We see here that an array of 8 items is divided into two arrays of size 4.

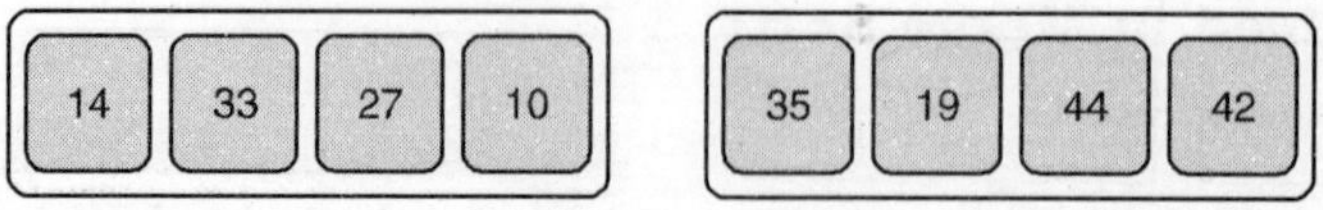

This does not change the sequence of appearance of items in the original. Now we divide these two arrays into halves.

We further divide these arrays and we achieve atomic value which can no more be divided.

Now, we combine them in exactly the same manner as they were broken down. Please note the color codes given to these lists.

We first compare the element for each list and then combine them into another list in a sorted manner. We see that 14 and 33 are in sorted positions. We compare 27 and 10 and in the target list of 2 values we put 10 first, followed by 27. We change the order of 19 and 35 whereas 42 and 44 are placed sequentially.

In the next iteration of the combining phase, we compare lists of two data values, and merge them into a list of found data values placing all in a sorted order.

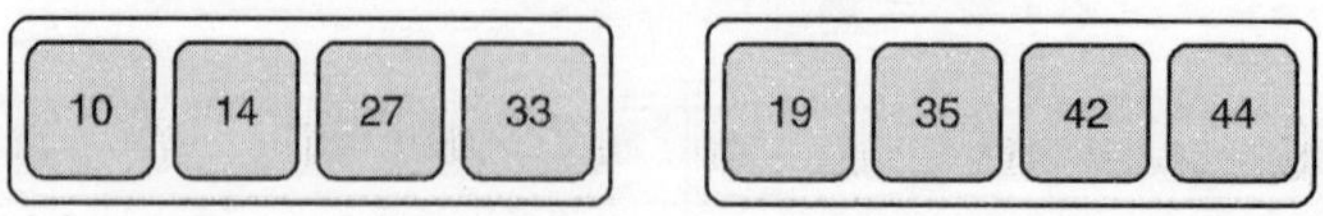

After the final merging, the list becomes sorted and is considered the final solution.

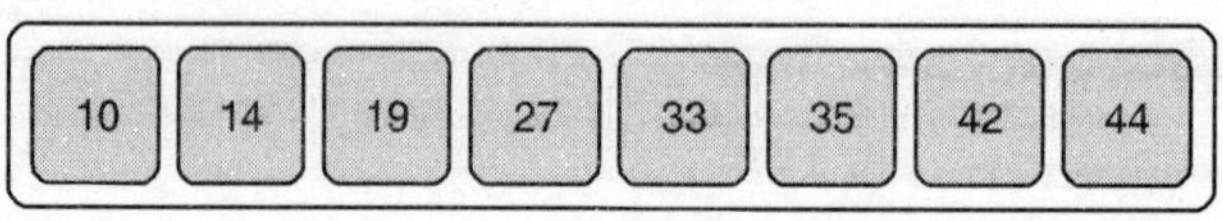

Merge Sort Algorithm

Merge sort keeps on dividing the list into equal halves until it can no more be divided. By definition, if it is only one element in the list, it is considered sorted. Then, merge sort combines the smaller sorted lists keeping the new list sorted too.

Step 1 – If it is only one element in the list, consider it already sorted, so return.

Step 2 – Divide the list recursively into two halves until it can no more be divided.

Step 3 – Merge the smaller lists into new list in sorted order.

The Steps involved in Merge Sort:

1. **Divide :** Divide the given array consisting of n elements into two parts of $n/2$ element seach.
2. **Conquer :** Sort the left part of the array and right part of the array recursively using merge sort.
3. **Combine/Merge :** Merge the sorted left part and sorted right part to get a single sorted array.

EXAMPLE:

N = 8

Elements: 5, 2, 4, 7, 1, 3, 2, 6

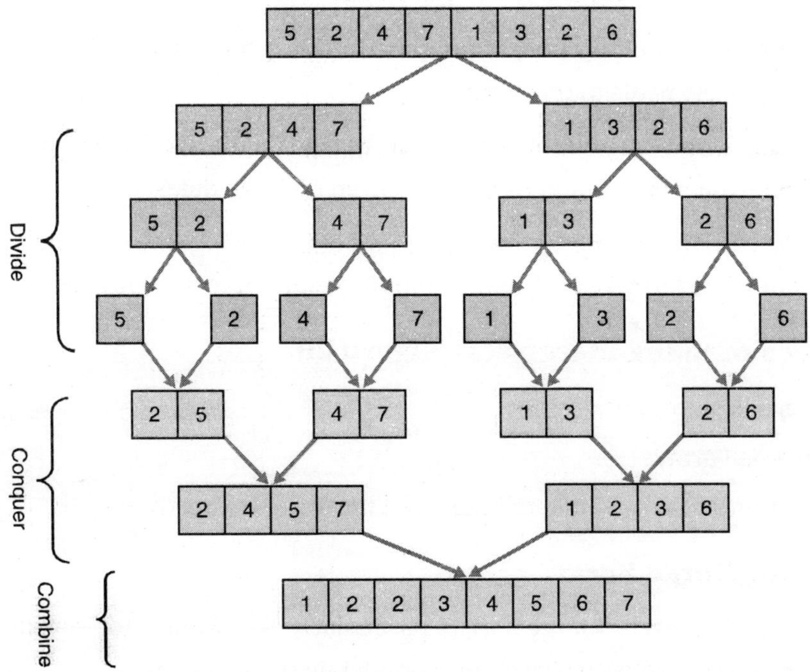

Algorithm MergeSort(a, low, high)

//Purpose: Sort the given array between lower bound and upper bound

//Inputs: a is an array consisting of unsorted elements with low and high as lower bound and upper bound

//Output a: It is an array consisting of sorted elements

if (low>high) **return** //No elements to partitionmid<-(low+high)/2//Divide the array into two parts

MergeSort (a, low, mid) //Sort the left part of the array MergeSort (a, mid+1, high) //Sort the right part of the array

SimpleMerge (a, low, mid, high) //Merge the left part and right part

//End of the algorithm MergeSort

Time complexity of merge sort:

Best-case	average case	worst-case
O(n log n)	O(n log n)	O(n log n)

Space complexity:

The space complexity of merge sort is O(n)

Advantages of using merge sort algorithm

- **Stability:** Merge sort is a stable sorting algorithm, which means it maintains the relative order of equal elements in the input array.
- **Guaranteed worst-case performance:** Merge sort has a worst-case time complexity of O(N logN), which means it performs well even on large datasets.
- **Parallelizable:** Merge sort is a naturally parallelizable algorithm, which means it can be easily parallelized to take advantage of multiple processors or threads.

Disadvantages of using merge sort algorithm

- extra space to store subarrays
- slow for small arrays
- the algorithm does the whole process even the array is already sorted

Applications of Merge Sort:

- **Sorting large datasets:** Merge sort is particularly well-suited for sorting large datasets due to its guaranteed worst-case time complexity of O(n log n).
- **External sorting:** Merge sort is commonly used in external sorting, where the data to be sorted is too large to fit into memory.

- **Custom sorting:** Merge sort can be adapted to handle different input distributions, such as partially sorted, nearly sorted, or completely unsorted data.

QUICK SORT

This is one of the best techniques for a large set of data. This technique also works on the method of partitioning. The process of divide and conquer is again recursively applied. In the merge sort method of sorting, the array was partitioned exactly at the midpoint, however in this method of sorting the partition is created at a position such that the elements to the left of the partition is less than the elements to the right of the partition. The entire process functions as follows. First we choose an element from a specific position in the array to be sorted (for example let the element "ele" be chosen as the first element of the array "*a*" so that ele = *a*[0]). Suppose that the elements of the array a are partitioned so that ele is placed into the position "*p*" and the following conditions are satisfied:

- Each of the elements in the positions 0 through *p*-1 is less than or equal to ele.
- Each of the elements in the positions *j*+1 through *n*-1 is greater than or equal to ele.

The purpose of quick sort is to move the data item in the correct direction jus enough for it to reach its final place. Thus the amount of swapping is greatly reduced and the required item moves a greater distance in a shorter duration of time.

EXAMPLE :

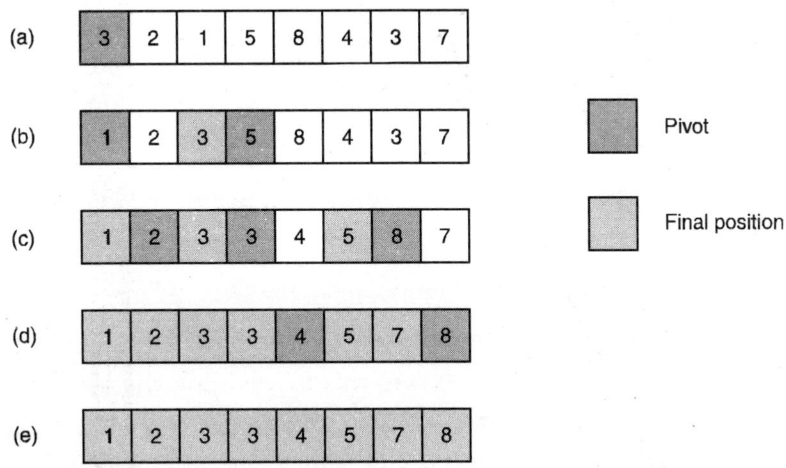

Algorithm : QuickSort (a, low, high)

//Purpose : Sort the given array using quicksort

//Inputs: low: The position of first element in array a

high: The position of the last element of array a

a: It is an array consisting of unsorted elements

```
//Output a: It is an array consisting of sorted elements
if (low>high) return //No elements to partition
k<--partition(a, low, high) //Divide the array into two parts
QuickSort(a, low, k-1) //Sort the left part of the array
QuickSort(a, k+1, high) //Sort the right part of the array
"algorithm QuickSort Ends here"
Algorithm : partition(a, low, high)
key<-a[low]
i<-low
j<-high+1
while(i<=j)
do i<-i+1 while(key>=a[i])
do j<-j-1 while(key<a[j])
end while
If (i<j) exchange(a[low], a[j])
return j //End of the algorithm Partition
```

Advantages of quick sort:

- **Efficiency:** Quick sort is known for its efficiency and has an average time complexity of $O(n \log n)$, where n represents the number of elements being sorted. In practice, it often outperforms other sorting algorithms like bubble sort or insertion sort, especially when dealing with large data sets.

- **In-place sorting:** Quick sort performs sorting in-place, meaning it doesn't require additional memory to store temporary data or intermediate results. This makes it memory-efficient and well-suited for situations where memory usage is a concern.

- **Fast average case:** Quick sort's average-case time complexity is significantly faster than many other sorting algorithms. It achieves this by dividing the input array into smaller sub-arrays based on a chosen pivot element and recursively sorting those sub-arrays. This "divide and conquer" approach allows quick sort to efficiently handle large data sets.

- **Good for parallelization:** Quick sort can be parallelized easily, taking advantage of multiple processors or computing resources. By splitting the input array into sub-arrays and sorting them concurrently, it can achieve faster sorting times on systems with parallel processing capabilities.

- **Efficient for large data sets:** Quick sort performs well on large data sets and exhibits good scalability. Its average and best-case time complexities make it suitable for sorting large arrays or lists efficiently.
- **Adaptive and stable:** Quick sort is adaptive, meaning it performs well on partially sorted or almost sorted arrays. Additionally, although the standard implementation of quick sort is not stable (i.e., it may change the relative order of equal elements), there are modifications, like the "three-way partitioning" approach, that can be used to make it stable.
- **Simple implementation:** Quick sort's algorithmic logic is relatively straightforward, making it easier to understand and implement compared to some other complex sorting algorithms

Disadvantages of quick sort:

1. **Unstable Sorting:** Quick sort is an unstable sorting algorithm, meaning that it does not guarantee the relative order of equal elements after the sorting process. If the order of equal elements is important, quick sort may not be suitable.
2. **Worst-case Performance:** Although quick sort has an average-case time complexity of $O(n \log n)$, its worst-case time complexity is $O(n^2)$. This worst-case scenario occurs when the pivot chosen is either the smallest or largest element in the array, causing unbalanced partitions. This can lead to poor performance on already sorted or nearly sorted data sets.
3. **Dependency on Pivot Selection:** The choice of pivot significantly affects the performance of quick sort. If a poorly chosen pivot divides the array into highly imbalanced partitions, the algorithm's efficiency may degrade. This issue is particularly prominent when dealing with already sorted or nearly sorted arrays.
4. **Recursive Overhead:** Quick sort heavily relies on recursion to divide the array into subarrays. Recursive function calls consume additional memory and can lead to stack overflow errors when dealing with large data sets. This makes quick sort less suitable for sorting extremely large arrays.
5. **Not Adaptive:** Quick sort's performance is not adaptive to the initial order of the elements. It does not take advantage of any pre-existing order or partially sorted input. This means that even if a portion of the array is already sorted, the quick sort will still perform partitioning operations on the entire array.
6. **Inefficient for Small Data Sets:** Quick sort has additional overhead in comparison to some simpler sorting algorithms, especially when dealing with small data sets. The recursive nature of quick sort and the constant splitting of the array can be inefficient for sorting small arrays or arrays with a small number of unique elements.

Applications of Quick Sort:

- **Sorting:** Quick sort is primarily used for sorting data. It is a very efficient algorithm and is faster than most other sorting algorithms in data structure.
- **Searching:** Quick sort can be used in searching algorithms. For example, if the user has an unsorted array and they want to find a specific value, can sort the array using quick sort and then perform a binary search on it.
- **Numerical analysis:** Quick sort can be used in numerical analysis, for example, to sort a large data set of numbers.
- **Parallel computing:** Quick sort is well-suited for parallel computing because it can be easily parallelized. This makes it an ideal choice for distributed computing systems.
- **Database management:** Quick sort can be used in database management systems to sort large amounts of data efficiently. It can also be used in indexing and searching algorithms.

Quicksort complexity

Time Complexity

Case	Time Complexity
Best Case	$O(n*\log n)$
Average Case	$O(n*\log n)$
Worst Case	$O(n^2)$

Space Complexity

Space Complexity	$O(n*\log n)$

BINARY SEARCH ALGORITHM

In this algorithm, we want to find whether element x belongs to a set of numbers stored in an array ***numbers***[]. Where ***l*** and ***r*** represent the left and right index of a sub-array in which searching operation should be performed.

Algorithm: Binary-Search(numbers[], x, l, r)

```
if l = r then
  return l
else
m := ⌊(l + r) / 2⌋
```

```
if x ≤ numbers[m] then
   return Binary-Search(numbers[], x, l, m)
else
   return Binary-Search(numbers[], x, m+1, r)
```

EXAMPLE : In this example, we are going to search element 63.

First *m* is determined and the element at index *m* is compared to *x*.

5	13	27	30	50	57	63	76
$i = 0$			$m = 3$				$r = 7$

As x > numbers [3], the element may reside in numbers [4…7]. Hence, the first half is discarded and the values of *l*, *m* and *r* are updated as shown below.

5	~~13~~	~~27~~	~~30~~	50	57	63	76
				L = 4	$m = 5$		$r = 7$

Now the element x needs to be searched in numbers [4…7]. As $x >$ numbers [5], new values of *l*, *m* and *r* are updated in a similar way.

~~5~~	~~13~~	~~27~~	~~30~~	~~50~~	~~57~~	63	76
						$l = m = 6$	$r = 7$

Now, comparing *x* with numbers[6], we get the match. Hence, the position of $x = 63$ have been determined.

Analysis

Linear search runs in ***O(n)*** time. Whereas binary search produces the result in ***O(log n)*** time.

Advantages of Binary Search

- Binary search is one of the quickest looking through calculations.
- It is utilized for tracking down the area of a component in a direct cluster.
- It chips away at the guideline of gap and overcomes strategy.
- It's a genuinely straightforward calculation, whenever comprehended properly
- It's notable and frequently executed for you as a library schedule
- It is preferred for large size data sets
- It is more efficient for large size data
- It is implemented on a multidimensional array

Disadvantages of Binary Search

- It's more confounded than straight inquiry and is over the top excess for tiny quantities of components.
- It works just on records that are arranged and kept arranged. That isn't generally feasible, particularly assuming components are continually being added to the rundown.
- It works just on component types for which there exists not as much relationship. A few kinds basically can't be arranged
- There is an extraordinary loss of effectiveness on the off chance that the rundown doesn't uphold irregular access. You want, for instance, to leap to the centre of the rundown right away. Assuming your rundown is a plain exhibit, that is perfect. On the off chance that it's a connected rundown, not really. Contingent upon the expense of your correlation activity, the expense of navigating a non-irregular access rundown could predominate the expense of the examinations.
- There are significantly quicker search techniques accessible, like hash queries. Anyway, a hash query requires the components to be coordinated in a substantially more confounded information structure.

Applications of Binary Search

1. This algorithm is used to search element in a given sorted array with more efficiency.
2. It could also be used for few other additional operations like- to find the smallest element in the array or to find the largest element in the array.

Binary Search Time Complexity

- In each iteration, the search space is getting divided by 2. That means that in the current iteration you have to deal with half of the previous iteration array.
- And the above steps continue till beg<end
- Best case could be the case where the first mid-value get matched to the element to be searched
- Best Time Complexity: O(1)
- Average Time Complexity: O(logn)
- Worst Time Complexity: O(logn)

Binary Search Space Complexity

1. No auxiliary space is required in Binary Search implementation

2. The binary search algorithm's space complexity depends on the way the algorithm has been implemented.
3. Two ways in which it can be implemented are:
   - **Iterative method:** In this method, the iterations are controlled through looping conditions. The space complexity of binary search in the iterative method is O(1).
   - **Recursive method:** In this method, there is no loop, and the new values are passed to the next recursion of the loop. Here, the max and min values are used as the boundary condition. The space complexity of binary search in the recursive method is O(log n).

BINARY TREE TRAVERSAL

The tree can be defined as a non-linear data structure that stores data in the form of nodes, and nodes are connected to each other with the help of edges. Among all the nodes, there is one main node called the ***root node***, and all other nodes are the children of these nodes.

In any data structure, traversal is an important operation. In the traversal operation, we walk through the data structure visiting each element of the data structure at least once. The traversal operation plays a very important role while doing various other operations on the data structure like some of the operations are searching, in which we need to visit each element of the data structure at least once so that we can compare each incoming element from the data structure to the key that we want to find in the data structure. So like any other data structure, the tree data also needs to be traversed to access each element, also known as a node of the tree data structure.

There are different ways of traversing a tree depending upon the order in which the tree's nodes are visited and the types of data structure used for traversing the tree. There are various data structures involved in traversing a tree, as traversing a tree involves iterating over all nodes in some manner.

As from a given node, there could be more than one way to traverse or visit the next node of the tree, so it becomes important to store one of the nodes traverses further and store the rest of the nodes having a possible path for backtracking the tree if needed. Backtracking is not a linear approach, so we need different data structures for traversing through the whole tree. The stack and queue are the major data structure that is used for traversing a tree.

Traversal is a technique for visiting all of a tree's nodes and printing their values. Traversing a tree involves iterating over all nodes in some manner. We always start from the root (head) node since all nodes are connected by edges (links). As the tree is not a linear data structure, there can be more than one possible next node from a given node, so some nodes must be deferred, i.e., stored in some way for later visiting.

Types of Traversal of Binary Tree

There are three types of traversal of a binary tree.

1. Inorder tree traversal
2. Preorder tree traversal
3. Postorder tree traversal

Note:

- **Inorder:** left, root, right
- **Preorder:** root, left, right
- **Postorder:** left, right, root

Inorder Traversal

- In Inorder traversal we traverse from left-root-right.
- In this traversal left subtree visited first then the root and later the right subtree.
- remember that every node may represent a subtree itself.

Algorithm

Until all nodes are traversed

1. Recursively Traverse the left subtree
2. Visit the Root.
3. Recursively Traverse the right subtree.

Example of inorder traversal

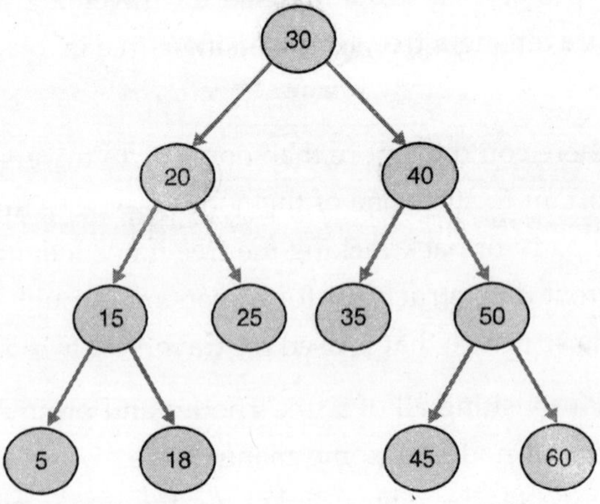

- we start recursive call from 30(root) then move to 20 (20 also have sub tree so apply in order on it), 15 and 5.

- 5 have no child .so print 5 then move to it's parent node which is 15 print and then move to 15's right node which is 18.
- 18 have no child print 18 and move to 20 .print 20 then move it right node which is 25 .25 have no subtree so print 25.
- print root node 30 .
- now recursively traverse to right subtree of root node .so move to 40. 40 have subtree so traverse to left subtree of 40.
- left subtree of 40 have only one node which is 35. 35 had no further subtree so print 35. move to 40 and print 40.
- traverse to right subtree of 40. so move to 50 now have subtree so traverse to left subtree of 50 .move to 45 , 45 have no further subtree so print 45.
- move to 50 and print 50. now traverse to right subtree of 50 hence move to 60 and print 60.
- **our final output is {5 , 15 , 18 , 20 , 25 , 30 , 35 , 40 , 45 , 50 , 60}**

Advantages of Inorder Traversal

There are many advantages to using inorder traversal when working with trees.

- One of the biggest advantages is that it allows for easy retrieval of data. This is because, in inorder traversal, the leftmost child is always visited first. As a result, all of the data is stored in order, making it easy to retrieve later on.
- Another advantage of the inorder traversal is that it can be used to easily find out whether or not a tree is balanced. This is because the inorder traversal algorithm always visits the leftmost child first. As a result, if the tree is balanced, the algorithm will always visit the same number of nodes on each side of the tree.

Disadvantages of Inorder Traversal

There are a few disadvantages to using inorder traversal that you should be aware of.

- First, it can be difficult to implement if you're not familiar with recursion.
- Second, it's not the most efficient algorithm possible – other algorithms, such as preorder or postorder traversal, can often traverse a tree more quickly.
- Finally, an inorder traversal isn't always the best choice for every type of tree – sometimes, another algorithm, such as breadth-first search, will be a better fit for the data structures involved.

Preorder Traversal

- In Preorder traversal we traverse from root-left-right.
- In this traversal root visited first then the left subtree and later the right subtree.
- Remember that every node may represent a subtree itself.

Algorithm of preorder traversal

Until all nodes are traversed

1. Visit the Root
2. Recursively Traverse the left subtree
3. Recursively Traverse the right subtree

Example of preorder traversal

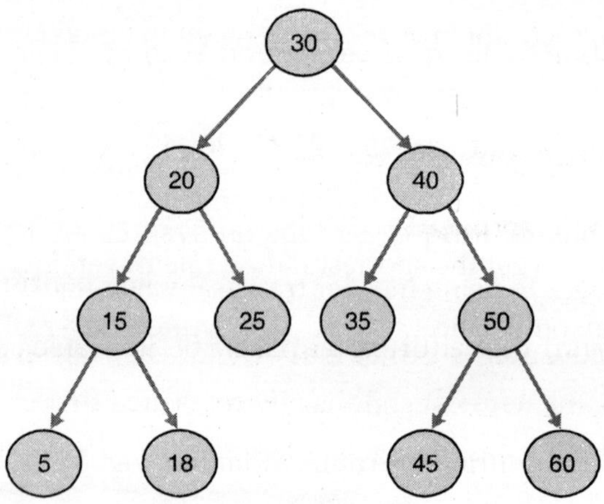

- Start with root node 30 .print 30 and recursively traverse the left subtree.
- next node is 20. now 20 have subtree so print 20 and traverse to left subtree of 20 .
- next node is 15 and 15 have subtree so print 15 and traverse to left subtree of 15.
- 5 is next node and 5 have no subtree so print 5 and traverse to right subtree of 15.
- next node is 18 and 18 have no child so print 18 and traverse to right subtree of 20.
- 25 is right subtree of 20 .25 have no child so print 25 and start traverse to right subtree of 30.
- next node is 40. node 40 have subtree so print 40 and then traverse to left subtree of 40.
- next node is 35. 35 have no subtree so print 35 and then traverse to right subtree of 40.
- next node is 50. 50 have subtree so print 50 and traverse to left subtree of 50.
- next node is 45. 45 have no subtree so print 45 and then print 60(right subtree) of 50.
- **our final output is {30 , 20 , 15 , 5 , 18 , 25 , 40 , 35 , 50 , 45 , 60}**

Advantages:

- Preorder traversal is used to create a copy of the binary tree.
- It is used to get the prefix of an expression.
- Binary tree traversals give quick searching, insertion, and deletion in cases where the tree is balanced.
- In Preorder traversal, the root node value is printed before visiting the left subtree and right subtree.
- It is also part of the Depth-First Algorithm, and order is root node > left sub tree > right sub tree; hence it is also known as the NLR algorithm.
- Preorder Traversal, part of the Depth first algorithm, will use less memory space as compared to the Breadth first algorithm.

Disadvantages:

- Preorder traversal works well while traversing trees. However, as it is a depth first algorithm, searching graphs can get you struck in an infinite loop as depth first algorithms travel around in a cyclic manner for graphs forever.
- There is no possibility to get the shortest path while traversing.
- In Preorder traversal, on duplicating nodes and values can make a complete duplicate of the tree.

Postorder Traversal

- In Preorder traversal we traverse from left-right-root.
- In this traversal left subtree visited first then the right subtree and later the root.
- Remember that every node may represent a subtree itself.

Algorithm of postorder traversal

Until all nodes are traversed

1. Recursively Traverse the left subtree
2. Recursively Traverse the right subtree.
3. Visit the Root.

Example of postorder traversal

- We start from 30, and following Post-order traversal, we first visit the left subtree 20. 20 is also traversed post-order.

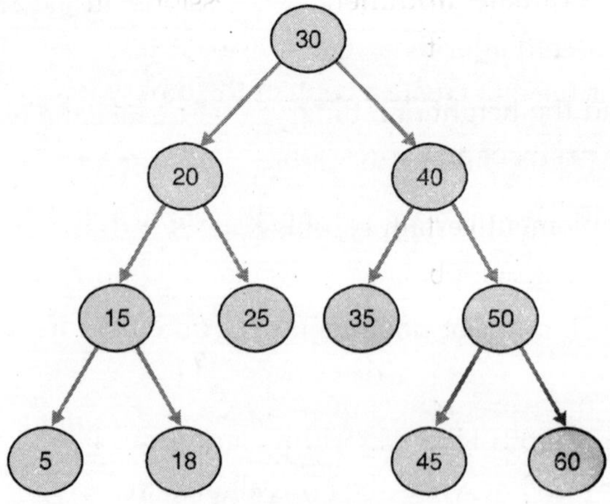

- 15 is left subtree of 20 .15 is also traversed post order.
- 5 is left subtree of 15. 5 have no subtree so print 5 and traverse to right subtree of 15 .
- 18 is right subtree of 15. 18 have no subtree so print 18 and then print 15. post order traversal for 15 is finished.
- next move to right subtree of 20.
- 25 is right subtree of 20. 25 have no subtree so print 25 and then print 20. post order traversal for 20 is finished.
- next visit the right subtree of 30 which is 40 .40 is also traversed post-order (40 have subtree).
- 35 is left subtree of 40. 35 have no more subtree so print 35 and traverse to right subtree of 40.
- 50 is right subtree of 40. 50 should also traversed post order.
- 45 is left subtree of 50. 45 have no more subtree so print 45 and then print 60 which is right subtree of 50.
- next print 50 . post order traversal for 50 is finished.
- now print 40, and post order traversal for 40 is finished.
- print 30. post order traversal for 30 is finished.
- **our final output is {5 , 18 , 15 , 25 , 20 , 35 , 45 , 60 , 50 , 40 , 30}**

Advantages

- It can be used to delete a binary tree from memory because it visits the child nodes before the parent nodes.

- It can be used to evaluate arithmetic expressions in postfix notation because the operators are encountered after their operands.
- It can be used to find the height of a binary tree because the height of a node is equal to the maximum height of its child nodes plus one.
- It can be used to implement certain types of binary tree balancing algorithms because it allows for easy computation of balance factors and subtree heights.

Disadvantages

- It is more complex than preorder and inorder traversals and can be more difficult to implement and understand.
- Postorder traversal requires additional memory to maintain the call stack, which can be a problem for very large trees.
- It may not be the most efficient traversal method for certain use cases, as it can result in a larger number of cache misses and branch mispredictions than other methods.
- In some cases, postorder traversal may not be necessary or desirable for a particular application or problem.

COMPLEXITY OF TREE TRAVERSAL TECHNIQUES

Time and Space Complexity of Tree Traversal Algorithms

Time complexity: In all the traversals, we visit every node once. It takes O(1) time to visit a node; hence, the time complexity of all the traversals will be $O(n)$. Thus, the time complexity is $O(n)$ for all traversals.

Auxiliary space:

- For preorder, postorder, and inorder tree traversals: If we consider the recursion stack, the space required is $O(h)$, where h is the tree's height. Else, it is O(1).
- For level-order traversal: Every node will be pushed in the queue exactly once. So, in the worst case, there can be $O(n)$ nodes in the queue at a single moment. Hence, the space complexity is $O(n)$.

Difference between Binary Tree and Binary Search Tree

Binary Tree	Binary Search Tree
A non-linear data structure having at most two child nodes.	A node based binary tree where the further subtrees are also binary search tree

It is unordered.	It is ordered.
Slower in the process of searching, insertion and deletion.	Faster in the process of searching, insertion and deletion.
No ordering is there in terms of how the nodes will be arranged.	The elements of the left subtree has values lesser than that of the right sub tree.

STRASSEN'S ALGORITHM MATRIX MULTIPLICATION

Strassen's Algorithm is an innovative method for matrix multiplication that aims to reduce the number of basic arithmetic operations compared to the standard matrix multiplication algorithm (known as the naïve method or the standard matrix multiplication method). This algorithm was introduced by Volker Strassen in 1969.

Standard matrix multiplication involves iterating through rows and columns of matrices to perform multiplication and addition operations for each resulting element of the product matrix. The time complexity for this method is $O(n^3)$, where n is the size of the matrices.

Strassen's Algorithm employs a divide-and-conquer strategy to reduce the number of multiplications required for matrix multiplication. It breaks down the matrix multiplication into a series of sub-matrix multiplications using a set of recursive formulas. Instead of performing 8 multiplications and 4 additions for each element as in the standard method, Strassen's Algorithm performs only 7 multiplications.

Strassen's Algorithm Steps:

Split the matrices: Divide the input matrices into smaller sub-matrices, typically into quarters.

Calculate intermediate matrices: Create 10 intermediate matrices using the sub-matrices generated from step 1.

Perform additions and subtractions: Use the intermediate matrices to calculate the product matrix using a set of formulas involving additions and subtractions.

Combine the results: Combine the calculated sub-matrices to form the final product matrix.

Mathematical Description (for 2 × 2 Matrices):

Suppose we have two matrices A and B:

$A = [[A_{11}, A_{12}], [A_{21}, A_{22}]]$

$B = [[B_{11}, B_{12}], [B_{21}, B_{22}]]$

The product matrix C = A * B can be calculated using Strassen's Algorithm with fewer multiplications:

$P_1 = A_{11} * (B_{12} - B_{22})$

$P_2 = (A_{11} + A_{12}) * B_{22}$

$P_3 = (A_{21} + A_{22}) * B_{11}$

$P_4 = A_{22} * (B_{21} - B_{11})$

$P_5 = (A_{11} + A_{22}) * (B_{11} + B_{22})$

$P_6 = (A_{12} - A_{22}) * (B_{21} + B_{22})$

$P_7 = (A_{11} - A_{21}) * (B_{11} + B_{12})$

$C_{11} = P_5 + P_4 - P_2 + P_6$

$C_{12} = P_1 + P_2$

$C_{21} = P_3 + P_4$

$C_{22} = P_5 + P_1 - P_3 - P_7$

Pseudo code:

```
FUNCTION StrassenMatrixMultiply(A, B):
  n = A.rows  // Assuming A and B are n x n matrices

  // Base case: If the matrices are small enough, perform standard matrix multiplication
  IF n == 1:
    RETURN A × B

  // Divide matrices A and B into submatrices
  // Submatrices A11, A12, A21, A22 and B11, B12, B21, B22 are n/2 x n/2 matrices
  Split A into submatrices A11, A12, A21, A22
  Split B into submatrices B11, B12, B21, B22

  // Intermediate matrices (P1 to P7) for recursive calculations
  P1 = StrassenMatrixMultiply(A11, B12 – B22)
  P2 = StrassenMatrixMultiply(A11 + A12, B22)
  P3 = StrassenMatrixMultiply(A21 + A22, B11)
  P4 = StrassenMatrixMultiply(A22, B21 - B11)
```

```
P5 = StrassenMatrixMultiply(A11 + A22, B11 + B22)
P6 = StrassenMatrixMultiply(A12 - A22, B21 + B22)
P7 = StrassenMatrixMultiply(A11 - A21, B11 + B12)

// Calculate submatrices of the result using the intermediate matrices
C11 = P5 + P4 - P2 + P6
C12 = P1 + P2
C21 = P3 + P4
C22 = P5 + P1 - P3 - P7

// Combine the submatrices to form the result matrix
Result Matrix = CombineSubmatrices(C11, C12, C21, C22)

RETURN ResultMatrix
```

Steps of the Algorithm:

Base Case Check:

If the size of the matrices reaches 1×1 ($n == 1$), perform standard matrix multiplication and return the result.

Matrix Division: Divide both input matrices A and B into four equal-sized submatrices:

$A_{11}, A_{12}, A_{21}, A_{22}$ for matrix A

$B_{11}, B_{12}, B_{21}, B_{22}$ for matrix B

Intermediate Matrix Calculations (P_1 to P_7): Calculate seven intermediate matrices (P_1 to P_7) recursively using the submatrices.

These intermediate matrices represent partial results needed to calculate the resulting product matrix.

Calculate Result Submatrices: Use the intermediate matrices to compute the submatrices C_{11}, C_{12}, C_{21}, and C_{22}.

Combine these submatrices to form the resulting matrix using specific addition and subtraction operations on the intermediate matrices.

Return ResultMatrix: Combine the calculated submatrices to form the final product matrix.

Return the ResultMatrix obtained from combining the submatrices.

Key Operations:

Matrix Splitting: Dividing the matrices A and B into submatrices A_{11}, A_{12}, A_{21}, A_{22}, B_{11}, B_{12}, B_{21}, B_{22}.

Intermediate Matrix Computations: Calculating intermediate matrices P_1 to P_7 using recursive calls to Strassen Matrix Multiply.

Combining Submatrices: Forming the result matrix by combining the calculated submatrices C_{11}, C_{12}, C_{21}, and C_{22}.

Strassen's Algorithm utilizes this divide-and-conquer approach to recursively break down the matrix multiplication problem into smaller sub-problems, reducing the number of multiplications needed compared to the standard matrix multiplication algorithm. Despite its theoretical improvement in asymptotic complexity, the practical performance gain might depend on various factors such as matrix size, hardware architecture, and implementation details.

```
#include <stdio.h>

// Function to add two matrices
void matrixAdd(int A[2][2], int B[2][2], int C[2][2]) {
  for (int i = 0; i< 2; i++) {
    for (int j = 0; j < 2; j++) {
      C[i][j] = A[i][j] + B[i][j];
    }
  }
}

// Function to subtract two matrices
void matrixSubtract(int A[2][2], int B[2][2], int C[2][2]) {
  for (int i = 0; i< 2; i++) {
    for (int j = 0; j < 2; j++) {
      C[i][j] = A[i][j] - B[i][j];
    }
  }
}

// Function to multiply two 2x2 matrices using Strassen's Algorithm
```

```
void strassenMatrixMultiply(int A[2][2], int B[2][2], int C[2][2]) {
  int P1, P2, P3, P4, P5, P6, P7;
  int temp1[2][2], temp2[2][2];

  // Calculate intermediate matrices P1 to P7
  P1 = (A[0][0] + A[1][1]) × (B[0][0] + B[1][1]);
  P2 = (A[1][0] + A[1][1]) × B[0][0];
  P3 = A[0][0] × (B[0][1] - B[1][1]);
  P4 = A[1][1] × (B[1][0] - B[0][0]);
  P5 = (A[0][0] + A[0][1]) × B[1][1];
  P6 = (A[1][0] - A[0][0]) × (B[0][0] + B[0][1]);
  P7 = (A[0][1] - A[1][1]) × (B[1][0] + B[1][1]);

  // Calculate the submatrices C11, C12, C22, C22
  temp1[0][0] = P5 + P4 – P2 + P6;
  temp1[0][1] = P1 + P2;
  temp1[1][0] = P3 + P4;
  temp1[1][1] = P5 + P1 – P3 – P7;

  // Copy the temporary matrix to the result matrix C
  for (int i = 0; i< 2; i++) {
    for (int j = 0; j < 2; j++) {
      C[i][j] = temp1[i][j];
    }
  }
}

// Function to display a 2x2 matrix
void displayMatrix(int matrix[2][2]) {
  for (int i = 0; i< 2; i++) {
    for (int j = 0; j < 2; j++) {
printf("%d ", matrix[i][j]);
    }
printf("\n");
```

```
  }
}

// Main function
int main() {
  int A[2][2] = {{1, 2}, {3, 4}};
  int B[2][2] = {{5, 6}, {7, 8}};
  int C[2][2];

printf("Matrix A:\n");
displayMatrix(A);
printf("\nMatrix B:\n");
displayMatrix(B);

printf("\nMatrix multiplication using Strassen's Algorithm:\n");
strassenMatrixMultiply(A, B, C);

displayMatrix(C);

  return 0;
}
```

Output

```
Matrix A:
1 2
3 4

Matrix B:
5 6
7 8

Matrix multiplication using Strassen's Algorithm:
19 100
6 121
```

❍❍❍

UNIT

6

SPACE TIME AND TRADE-OFF

The space-time trade-off is a crucial concept in the design and analysis of algorithms, focusing on the balance between the amount of memory space used and the time taken by an algorithm to execute.

Space Complexity:

Space complexity refers to the amount of memory space required by an algorithm to solve a computational problem based on its input size. It involves analyzing the additional space (apart from the input) used by the algorithm for variables, data structures, recursion, etc. Space complexity is generally expressed in terms of Big O notation, denoted as $O(f(n))$, where 'n' represents the input size and '$f(n)$' denotes the maximum space used relative to 'n'.

Time Complexity:

Time complexity measures the amount of time taken by an algorithm to run as a function of the input size. It evaluates the number of operations or steps an algorithm performs concerning the input. Time complexity is also expressed in Big O notation, denoted as $O(g(n))$, where 'n' represents the input size, and '$g(n)$' represents the worst-case time taken by the algorithm concerning 'n'.

Trade-off:

A trade-off refers to the situation where achieving gains in one aspect of a system, product, or process involves accepting disadvantages in another aspect. In the context of algorithm design and analysis, the space-time trade-off denotes the balance or compromise between space complexity (memory usage) and time complexity (execution speed). Optimizing one aspect may result in a compromise in the other; for instance, reducing memory consumption might lead to an increase in execution time and vice versa. The trade-off is crucial in decision-making during algorithm design, where choices are made to balance space and time complexities based on specific requirements, constraints, and priorities.

Trade-off between Space and Time Complexity:

Space-Time Dilemma: Often, reducing time complexity might result in increased space complexity, and vice versa. Algorithms designed for optimal time efficiency might consume more memory space, while those optimized for minimal space might take more time to execute.

Optimization Decisions: Designing an algorithm involves making decisions regarding the trade-off between space and time complexities. Sometimes, sacrifices in one area (space or time) are necessary to optimize the other. The optimal choice depends on the specific requirements of the problem, such as available memory resources, desired execution speed, input size, etc.

EXAMPLES:

- **Space-optimized algorithms:** Some sorting algorithms like in-place sorting (e.g., Quicksort), which rearrange elements without additional data structures, might have better space complexity but might not be as fast as other algorithms.
- **Time-optimized algorithms:** Hash tables or dynamic programming algorithms might consume more memory space to achieve faster execution time.

Importance in Algorithm Design:

Scalability: Understanding space-time trade-offs is crucial for developing algorithms that can scale efficiently with larger inputs.

Resource Utilization: Efficient utilization of computational resources (memory and processing power) is critical in modern computing systems.

Algorithm Selection: The choice of algorithms in applications often depends on the trade-off between space and time complexities, considering constraints and priorities.

Two varieties of space-for-time algorithms:

Input enhancement — preprocess the input (or its part) to store some info to be used later in solving the problem

- counting methods for sorting
- string searching algorithms

prestructuring — preprocess the input to make accessing its elements easier

- hashing
- indexing schemes (e.g., B-trees)

SORTING BY COUNTING

Sorting by counting is a non-comparison-based sorting algorithm that works particularly well when the range of numbers to be sorted is relatively small and known beforehand. It is efficient for sorting integers within a specific range.

Steps involved in Sorting by Counting:

1. Counting Occurrences:

- Determine the range of elements in the input array.
- Create an auxiliary array (often called the "count" array) to store the count of occurrences for each element within the range.
- Traverse the input array and count the occurrences of each element, incrementing the corresponding count in the auxiliary array.

Calculate Positions:

- Modify the count array to store the positions of elements in the sorted output.
- For instance, if count[i] represents the count of elements less than or equal to 'i', update count[i] to represent the position of 'i' in the sorted output.

Building the Sorted Array:

Iterate through the original array:

- Use the count array to determine the position of each element in the sorted array.
- Place the elements in their correct positions in the output array based on the information derived from the count array.
- Decrease the count of the corresponding element in the count array to accommodate duplicates.

```
ALGORITHM : ComparisonCountingSort(A[0..n –1])
//Sorts an array by comparison counting
//Input: An array A[0..n–1] of orderable elements
//Output:Array S[0..n–1] of A's elements sorted in nondecreasing order
for i ← 0 to n – 1 do Count [i] ← 0
for i ← 0 to n – 2 do
    for j ← i + 1 to n – 1 do
        if A[i] < A[j]
            Count [j] ← Count[j] + 1
```

```
        else Count [i] ← Count[i] + 1
    for i ← 0 to n – 1 do S[Count[i]] ← A[i]
    return S
```

EXAMPLE: Let's say you have an array of integers: [4, 2, 3, 4, 1, 1, 3]. The range of elements is from 1 to 4.

Counting occurrences:

- Create a count array with indices from 1 to 4 and initialize counts to zero.
- Count occurrences: count[1] = 2, count[2] = 1, count[3] = 2, count[4] = 2.

Calculate positions:

- Modify the count array to represent positions: count[i] += count[i - 1].
- Adjust the count array: count[1] = 2, count[2] = 3, count[3] = 5, count[4] = 7.

Building the sorted array:

- Iterate through the input array.
- Place elements in their correct positions based on the count array.
- Starting from the end of the original array helps in maintaining stability.
- Final sorted array: [1, 1, 2, 3, 3, 4, 4].

Complexity Analysis:

Time Complexity: $O(n + k)$, where 'n' is the number of elements in the input array and 'k' is the range of the elements.

Space Complexity: $O(n + k)$, requiring additional space for the count array.

STRING SEARCHING

String matching algorithms are techniques used to find occurrences or positions of a specific pattern (substring) within a larger text or string. These algorithms aim to efficiently identify where a particular pattern occurs within a given text.

Here are some commonly used string matching algorithms:

Brute Force Algorithm:

Description: It is the simplest method where the pattern is compared character by character with all possible positions in the text.

Time Complexity: $O(m * n)$ where 'm' is the length of the pattern and 'n' is the length of the text.

Advantages: Easy to implement.

Disadvantages: Inefficient for large texts or patterns.

Knuth-Morris-Pratt (KMP) Algorithm:

Description: Utilizes information from previous matches to avoid unnecessary comparisons by preprocessing the pattern to create a prefix table.

Time Complexity: $O(m + n)$ where 'm' is the length of the pattern and 'n' is the length of the text.

Advantages: More efficient than brute force. Handles larger patterns and texts better.

Disadvantages: Slightly more complex to implement than brute force.

Boyer-Moore Algorithm:

Description: Compares the pattern from right to left and uses heuristics to skip comparisons and shift the pattern efficiently.

Time Complexity: In the best-case scenario, it's $O(n/m)$, but in the worst case, it can be $O(m \times n)$.

Advantages: Very efficient in practice, especially for larger patterns.

Disadvantages: May have worst-case time complexity issues for certain patterns.

Rabin-Karp Algorithm:

Description: Utilizes hashing to compare the pattern with substrings of the text by computing hash values.

Time Complexity: Average-case time complexity is $O(n + m)$, but its worst-case time complexity can be $O(n * m)$.

Advantages: Useful for multiple pattern searches.

Disadvantages: Hash collisions can affect performance. May not be as efficient in certain scenarios.

Aho-Corasick Algorithm:

Description: Efficiently searches for multiple patterns in a single pass through the text. Constructs a finite state machine to match all patterns simultaneously.

Time Complexity: $O(n + z + m)$, where 'n' is the length of the text, 'm' is the total length of patterns, and 'z' is the number of matches.

Advantages: Great for multiple pattern searches.

Disadvantages: More complex data structure.

Applications of String Matching Algorithms:

Plagiarism Detection: The documents to be compared are decomposed into string tokens and compared using string matching algorithms. Thus, these algorithms are used to detect similarities between them and declare if the work is plagiarized or original.

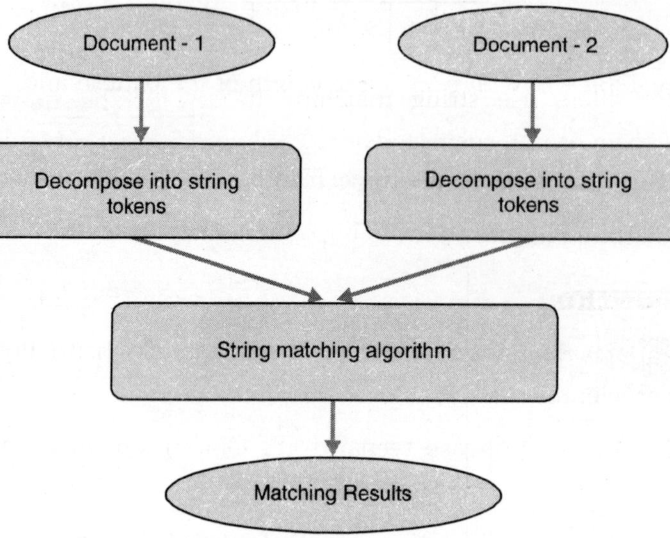

Bioinformatics and DNA Sequencing: Bioinformatics involves applying information technology and computer science to problems involving genetic sequences to find DNA patterns. String matching algorithms and DNA analysis are both collectively used for finding the occurrence of the pattern set.

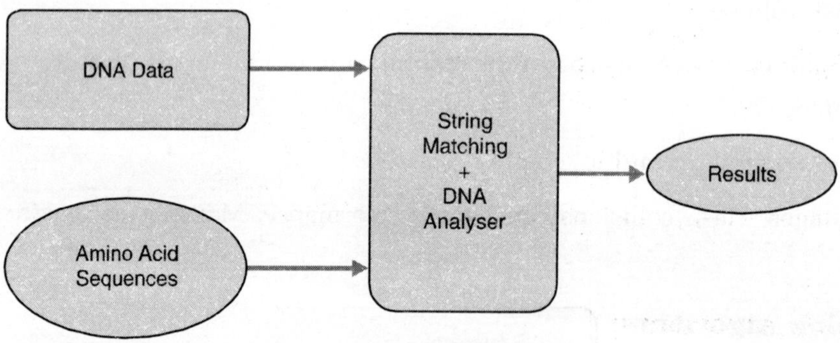

Digital Forensics: String matching algorithms are used to locate specific text strings of interest in the digital forensic text, which are useful for the investigation.

Spelling Checker: Trie is built based on a predefined set of patterns. Then, this trie is used for string matching. The text is taken as input, and if any such pattern occurs, it is shown by reaching the acceptance state.

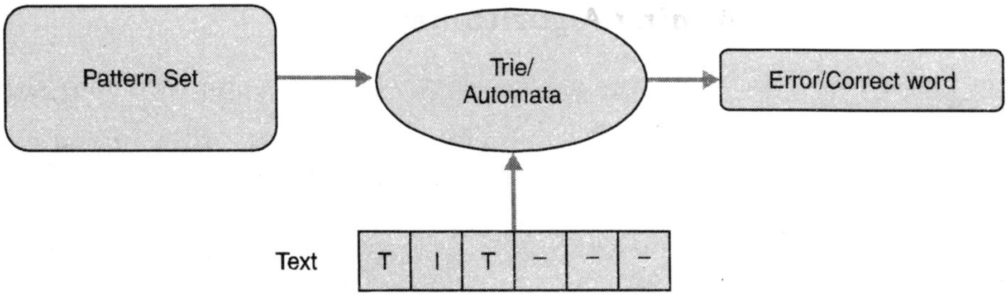

Spam filters: Spam filters use string matching to discard the spam. For example, to categorize an email as spam or not, suspected spam keywords are searched in the content of the email by string matching algorithms. Hence, the content is classified as spam or not.

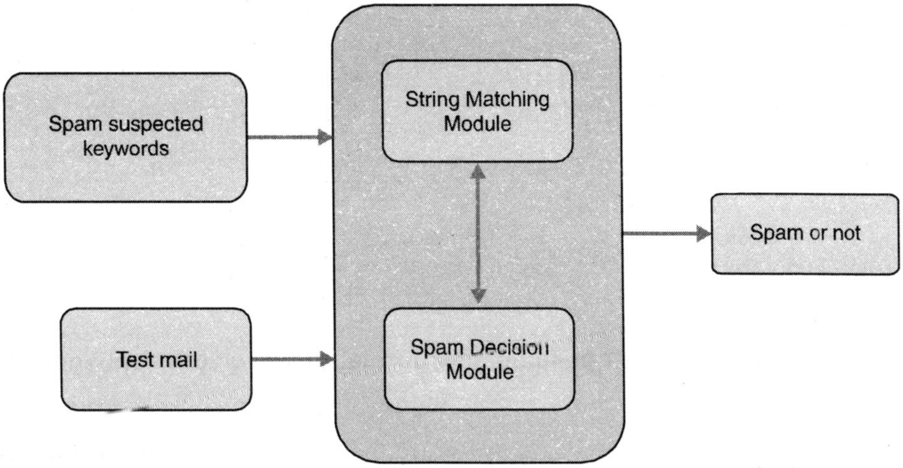

Search engines or content search in large databases: To categorize and organize data efficiently, string matching algorithms are used. Categorization is done based on the search keywords. Thus, string matching algorithms make it easier for one to find the information they are searching for.

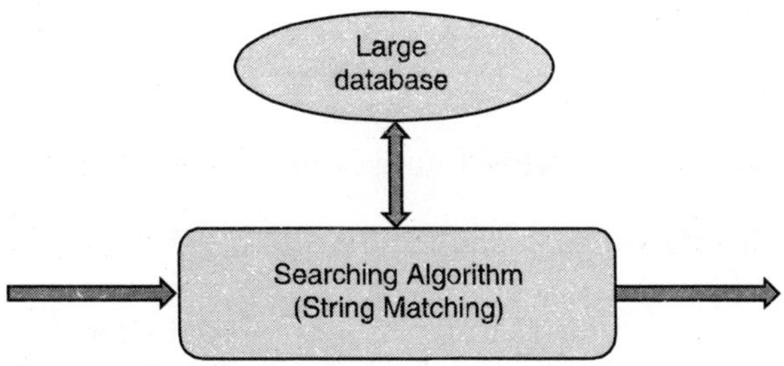

Intrusion Detection System: The data packets containing intrusion-related keywords are found by applying string matching algorithms. All the malicious code is stored in the database, and every incoming data is compared with stored data. If a match is found, then the alarm is generated. It is based on exact string matching algorithms where each intruded packet must be detected.

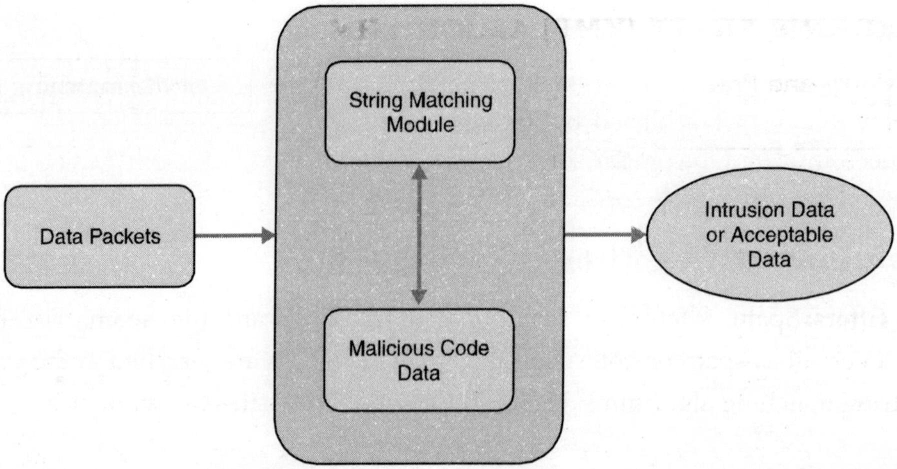

String matching operation is a core part in many text processing applications. The objective of this algorithm is to find pattern P from given text T. Typically |P|<< |T|. In the design of compilers and text editors, string matching operation is crucial. So locating P in T efficiently is very important.

The problem is defined as follows: "Given some text string T[1....*n*] of size *n*, find all occurrences of pattern P[1...*m*] of size *m* in T."

We say that P occurs in text T with number of shifts *s*, if $0 \le s \le n - m$ and T[$(s + 1) \ldots (s + m)$] = P[1...*m*].

Consider the following example

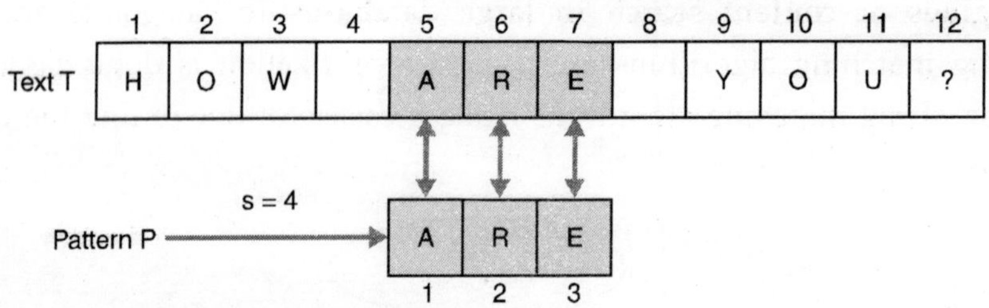

- In this example, pattern P = ARE is found in text T after four shifts.
- The classical application of such algorithms are to find particular protein pattern in DNA sequence.
- Strings may be encoded using set of character alphabets {*a*, *b*, ..., *z*}, binary alphabets {0, 1}, decimal alphabets {0, 1, 2, ..., 9}, DNA alphabets {A, C, G, T}. The encoding of the string directly affects the efficiency of searching.
- In the next sections, we will discuss and analyze a few string-matching algorithms.

KNUTH MORRIS PRATT (KMP) ALGORITHM

Knuth-Morris and Pratt introduce a linear time algorithm for the string-matching problem. A matching time of O (n) is achieved by avoiding comparison with an element of 'S' that have previously been involved in comparison with some element of the pattern 'p' to be matched. i.e., backtracking on the string 'S' never occurs.

Components of KMP Algorithm:

1. **The Prefix Function (Π):** The Prefix Function, Π for a pattern encapsulates knowledge about how the pattern matches against the shift of itself. This information can be used to avoid a useless shift of the pattern 'p.' In other words, this enables avoiding backtracking of the string 'S.'
2. **The KMP Matcher:** With string 'S,' pattern 'p' and prefix function 'Π' as inputs, find the occurrence of 'p' in 'S' and returns the number of shifts of 'p' after which occurrences are found.

The Prefix Function (Π)

Following pseudo code compute the prefix function, Π:

COMPUTE- PREFIX- FUNCTION (P)

```
1. m ←length [P]                //'p' pattern to be matched
2. Π [1] ← 0
3. k ← 0
4. for q ← 2 to m
5. do while k > 0 and P [k + 1] ≠ P [q]
6. do k ← Π [k]
7. If P [k + 1] = P [q]
8. then k ← k + 1
9. Π [q] ← k
10. Return Π
```

Running Time Analysis:

In the above pseudo code for calculating the prefix function, the for loop from step 4 to step 10 runs 'm' times. Step 1 to Step 3 take constant time. Hence the running time of computing prefix function is O (m).

EXAMPLE: Compute Π for the pattern 'p' below:

P:	a	b	a	b	a	c	A

Solution:

Initially: $m = \text{length}\ [p] = 7$

$\Pi[1] = 0$

$k = 0$

Step 1: $q = 2, k = 0$

$\Pi[2] = 0$

q	1	2	3	4	5	6	7
p	a	b	a	b	a	c	a
Π	0	0					

Step 2: $q = 3, k = 0$

$\Pi[3] = 1$

q	1	2	3	4	5	6	7
p	a	b	a	b	a	c	a
Π	0	0	1				

Step 3: $q = 4, k = 1$

$\Pi[4] = 2$

q	1	2	3	4	5	6	7
p	a	b	a	b	a	c	a
Π	0	0	1	2			

Step 4: $q = 5, k = 2$

$\Pi[5] = 3$

q	1	2	3	4	5	6	7
p	a	b	a	b	a	c	a
Π	0	0	1	2	3		

Step 5: $q = 6, k = 3$

$\Pi[6] = 0$

q	1	2	3	4	5	6	7
p	a	b	a	b	a	c	a
Π	0	0	1	2	3	0	

Step 6: $q = 7, k = 1$

$\Pi[7] = 1$

q	1	2	3	4	5	6	7
p	a	b	a	b	a	c	a
Π	0	0	1	2	3	0	1

After iteration 6 times, the prefix function computation is complete:

q	1	2	3	4	5	6	7
p	a	b	a	b	a	c	a
Π	0	0	1	2	3	0	1

The KMP Matcher:

The KMP Matcher with the pattern 'p,' the string 'S' and prefix function 'Π' as input, finds a match of p in S. Following pseudo code compute the matching component of KMP algorithm:

KMP-MATCHER (T, P)

```
1. n ← length [T]
2. m ← length [P]
3. Π ← COMPUTE-PREFIX-FUNCTION (P)
4. q ← 0                // numbers of characters matched
5. for i ← 1 to n       // scan S from left to right
6. do while q > 0 and P [q + 1] ≠ T [i]
7. do q ← Π [q]                  // next character does not match
8. If P [q + 1] = T [i]
9. then q ← q + 1                          // next character matches
10. If q = m                                  // is all of p matched?
11. then print "Pattern occurs with shift" i - m
12. q ← Π [q]                                     // look for the next match
```

Running Time Analysis:

The for loop beginning in step 5 runs '*n*' times, i.e., as long as the length of the string 'S.' Since step 1 to step 4 take constant times, the running time is dominated by this for the loop. Thus running time of the matching function is O (n).

EXAMPLE: Given a string 'T' and pattern 'P' as follows:

T:	b	a	c	b	a	b	a	b	a	b	a	c	a	c	a

P:	a	b	a	b	a	c	a

Let us execute the KMP Algorithm to find whether 'P' occurs in 'T.'

For 'p' the prefix function, ? was computed previously and is as follows:

q	1	2	3	4	5	6	7
p	a	b	a	b	a	c	a
Π	0	0	1	2	3	0	1

Solution:

Initially: n = size of T = 15

m = size of P = 7

Step 1: $i = 1$, $q = 0$

Comparing P[1] with T[1]

T:	b	a	c	b	a	b	a	b	a	b	a	c	a	a	b

↑

P:	a	b	a	b	a	c	a

P[1] does not match with T[1]. *'p'* will be shifted one position to be right.

Step 2: $i = 2$, $q = 0$

Comparing P[1] with T[2]

T:	b	a	c	b	a	b	a	b	a	b	a	c	a	a	b

↑

P:		a	b	a	b	a	c	a

P[1] mathches T[2]. Since there is a match, p is not shifted.

Step 3: $i = 3$, $q = 1$

Comparing P[2] with T[3] P[2] doesn't match with T[3]

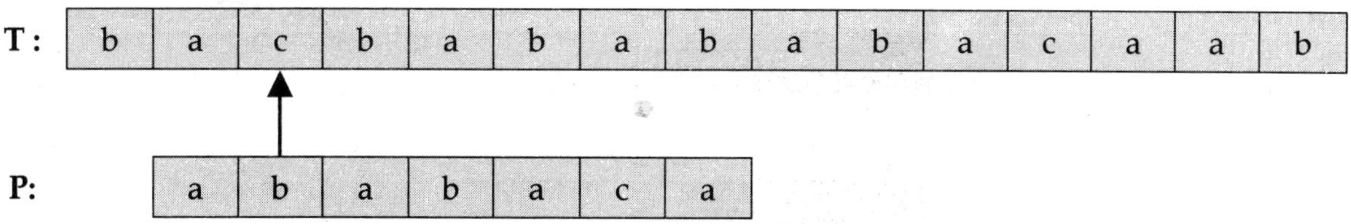

Backtracking on p, Comparing P[1] and T[3]

Step 4: $i = 4$, $q = 0$

Comparing P[1] with T[4] P[1] doesn't match with T[4]

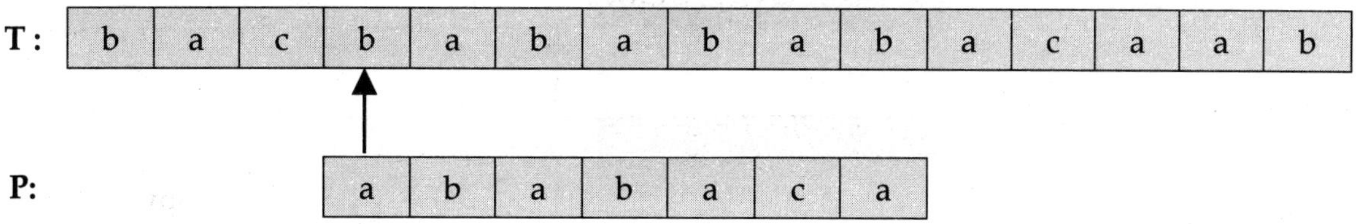

Step 5: $i = 5$, $q = 0$

Comparing P[1] with T[5] P[1] doesn't match with T[5]

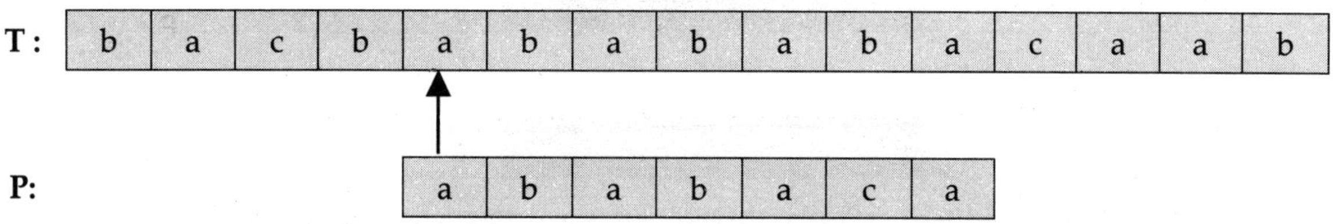

Step 6: $i = 6$, $q = 1$

Comparing P[2] with T[6] P[2] doesn't match with T[6]

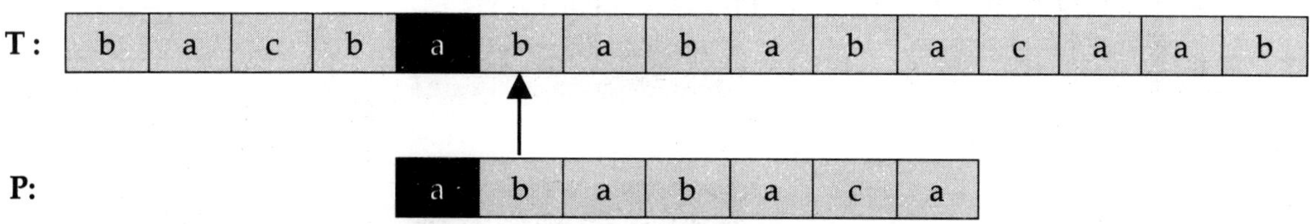

Step 7: $i = 7$, $q = 2$

Comparing P[3] with T[7] P[3] matches with T[7]

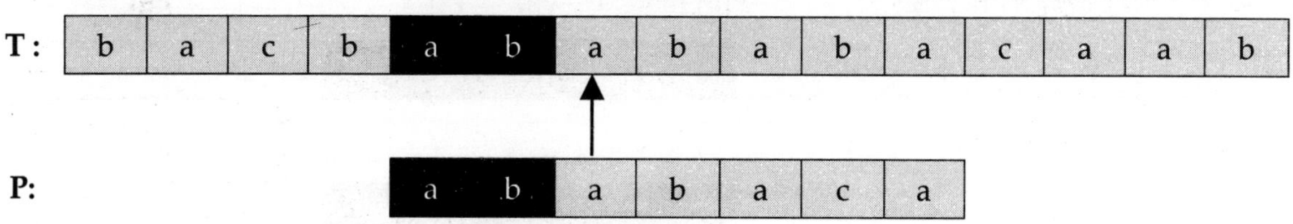

Step 8: $i = 8$, $q = 3$

Comparing P[4] with T[8] P[4] matches with T[8]

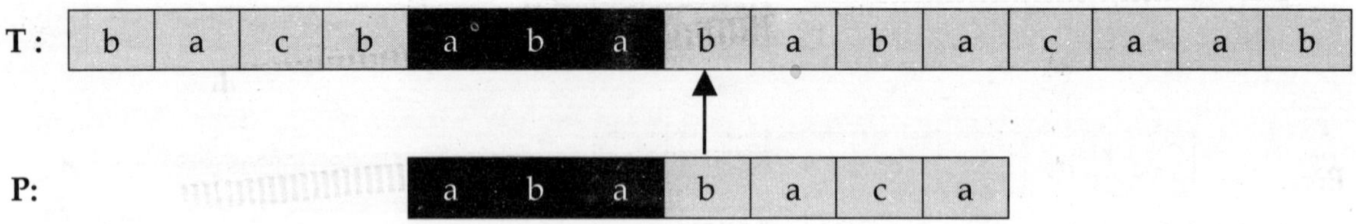

Step 9: $i = 9$, $q = 4$

Comparing P[5] with T[9] P[5] matches with T[9]

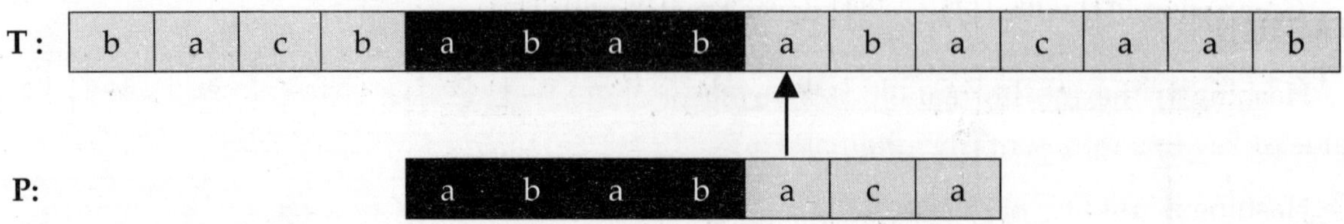

Step 10: $i = 10$, $q = 5$

Comparing P[6] with T[10] P[6] doesn't match with T[10]

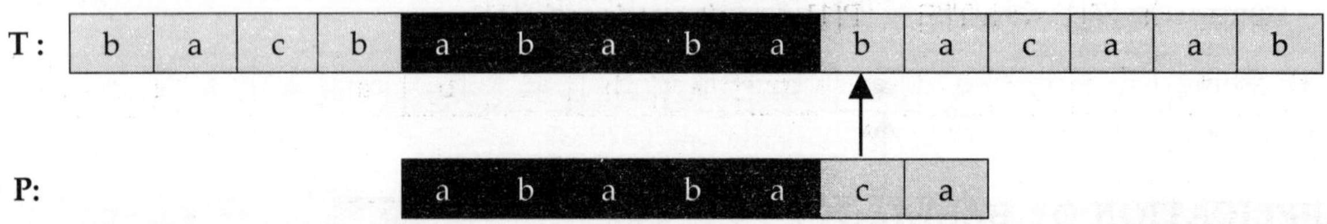

Backtracking on p, Comparing P[4] with T[10] because after mismatch $q = \Pi[5] = 3$.

Step 11: $i = 11$, $q = 4$

Comparing P[5] with T[11] P[5] match with T[11]

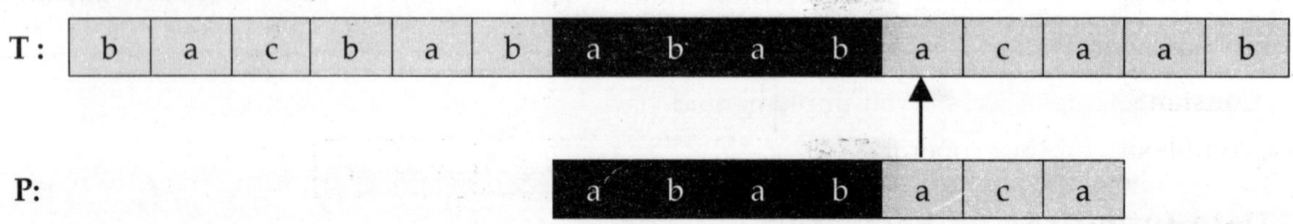

Step 12: $i = 12$, $q = 5$

Comparing P[6] with T[12] P[6] matches with T[12]

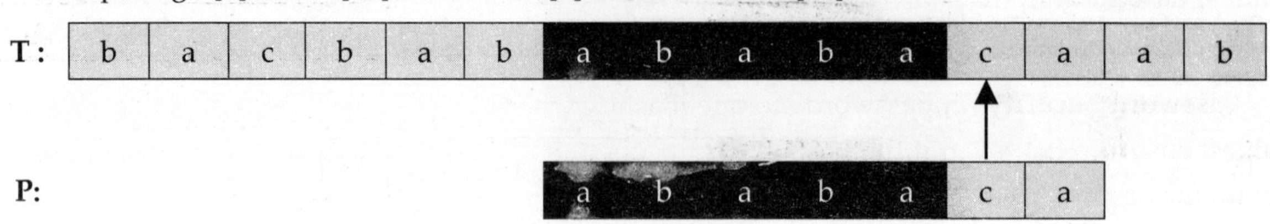

Step 13: $i = 13$, $q = 6$

Comparing P[7] with T[13] P[7] matches with T[13]

T:

b	a	c	b	a	b	a	b	a	b	a	c	a	a	b

P:

a	b	a	b	a	c	a

Pattern 'P' has been found to complexity occur in a string 'T.' The total number of shifts that took place for the match to be found is i-m = 13 - 7 = 6 shifts.

HASHING

Hashing is the transformation of a string of character into a usually shorter fixed-length value or key that represents the original string.

Hashing is used to index and retrieve items in a database because it is faster to find the item using the shortest hashed key than to find it using the original value. It is also used in many encryption algorithms.

A hash code is generated by using a key, which is a unique value.

Hashing is a technique in which given key field value is converted into the address of storage location of the record by applying the same operation on it.

APPLICATION OF HASHING

1. Data Retrieval Efficiency:

Data Indexing: Hashing allows for efficient data retrieval by mapping keys to indexes in data structures like hash tables. This enables quick lookup, insertion, and deletion of elements based on their keys.

Constant Time Access: Well-implemented hash functions provide constant-time average-case complexity for these operations.

2. Data Integrity and Security:

Checksums and Integrity Verification: Hash functions generate fixed-size outputs (hash values) based on input data. They're used to verify the integrity of transmitted or stored data. Even a small change in the input will produce a significantly different hash output.

Password Security: In password storage, hashing is used to convert passwords into hashed values, ensuring that even if the hashed data is obtained, it's challenging to reverse-engineer or obtain the original password.

3.Cryptography:

Message Digests: Cryptographic hash functions create unique, fixed-size digests for varying lengths of input data. They are fundamental in digital signatures, ensuring data integrity and non-repudiation.

Key Derivation: Hash functions are also used in key derivation functions to derive cryptographic keys from passwords or other shared secrets.

4. Data Structures and Algorithms:

Bloom Filters: Hash functions are integral to Bloom filters, a space-efficient probabilistic data structure used for membership queries.

Cuckoo Hashing: This hashing technique resolves collisions by moving items to alternative locations based on multiple hash functions.

5. Performance Optimization:

Caching: Hash functions aid in efficient caching mechanisms, where hashed keys determine the storage and retrieval of frequently accessed data.

Load Balancing: In distributed systems, hash functions help evenly distribute load across servers by mapping keys to nodes.

HASH TABLES

Hash tables, also known as hash maps or dictionaries, are data structures that store key-value pairs. They use a hashing function to map keys to indexes in an array, allowing for efficient insertion, deletion, and lookup of values associated with specific keys.

Components of a Hash Table:

Hash Function:

It takes a key as input and returns an index in the underlying array where the corresponding value is stored. This function aims to spread keys uniformly across the available indices.

Array or Bucket Array:

It's an array where the actual key-value pairs are stored. Each index in the array is often called a "bucket" or "slot" and can hold multiple elements due to potential collisions (two keys hashing to the same index).

Hash Table Representation:

Hash Function: You create a hash function that takes the book title as input and calculates an index where the book will be placed on the shelf. For instance, the hash function might sum the ASCII values of the characters in the title and use modulo division to determine the shelf index.

Shelves as Buckets:

The shelves in the library represent the array or buckets in the hash table. Each shelf (bucket) can hold multiple books.

Steps:

Insertion: When a new book arrives, you use the hash function to determine its shelf location based on its title.

For example, if the book title "Introduction to Algorithms" results in a hash index of 3, you place this book on shelf 3.

Retrieval: When someone asks for a book, you apply the hash function to the title to find its shelf location and directly go to that shelf to retrieve the book.

For instance, if someone wants "The Catcher in the Rye," the hash function indicates it's on shelf 5, so you quickly locate it there.

Handling Collisions:

In case two books have the same hash index due to the hash function (a collision), you might place them in the same shelf (bucket) and organize them in a secondary data structure, like a list or linked list, within that shelf.

Advantages:

Efficiency: Using the hash function, finding and placing books is fast on average.

Space Utilization: Books are distributed across shelves based on the hash, efficiently utilizing space.

Assume we have a set of integers 54, 26, 93, 17, 77, 31. Our first hash function required to be as "remainder method" simply takes the item and divide it by table size, returning remainder as its hash value i.e.

1. *h* item = item % (size of table)
2. Let us say the size of table = 11, then
3. 54 % 11 = 10   26 % 11 = 4   93 % 11 = 5
4. 17 % 11 = 6   77 % 11 = 0   31 % 11 = 9

ITEM	HASH VALUE
54	10
26	4
93	5
17	6
77	0
31	9

0	1	2	3	4	5	6	7	8	9	10
77				26	93	17			31	54

Fig. Hash Table

Now when we need to search any element, we just need to divide it by the table size, and we get the hash value. So we get the O (1) search time.

Now taking one more element 44 when we apply the hash function on 44, we get (44 % 11 = 0), But 0 hash value already has an element 77. This Problem is called as Collision.

Collision: According to the Hash Function, two or more item would need in the same slot. This is said to be called as Collision.

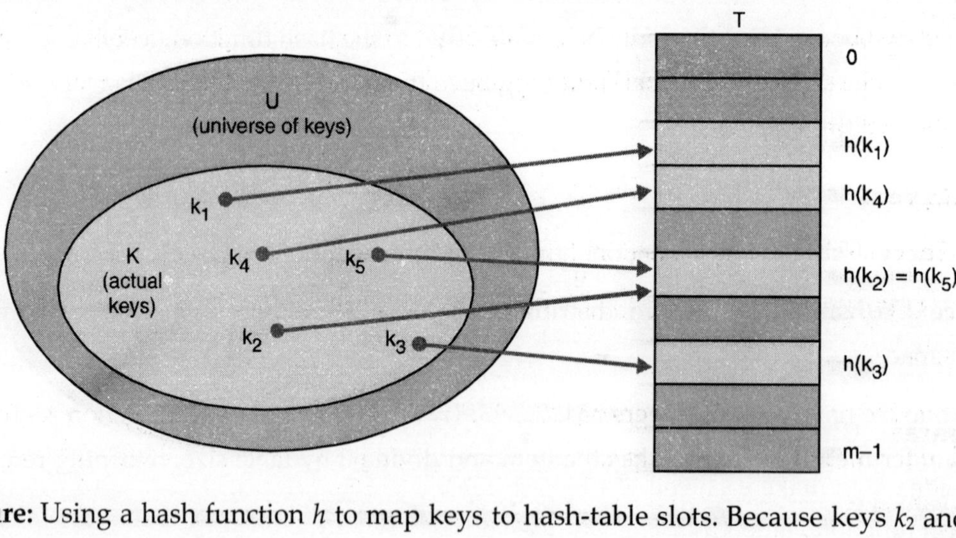

Figure: Using a hash function h to map keys to hash-table slots. Because keys k_2 and k_5 map to the same slot, they collide.

The hashing process generates a small number for a big key, so there is a possibility that two keys could produce the same value. The situation where the newly inserted key maps to an already occupied, and it must be handled using some collision handling technology.

Collision in Hashing

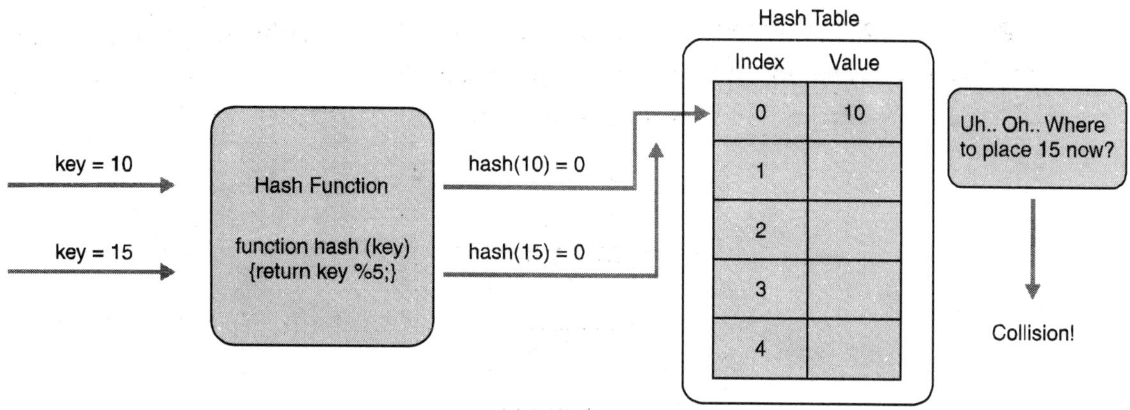

What is Collision in Hashing

How to handle Collisions?

There are mainly two methods to handle collision:

1. Separate Chaining:
2. Open Addressing:

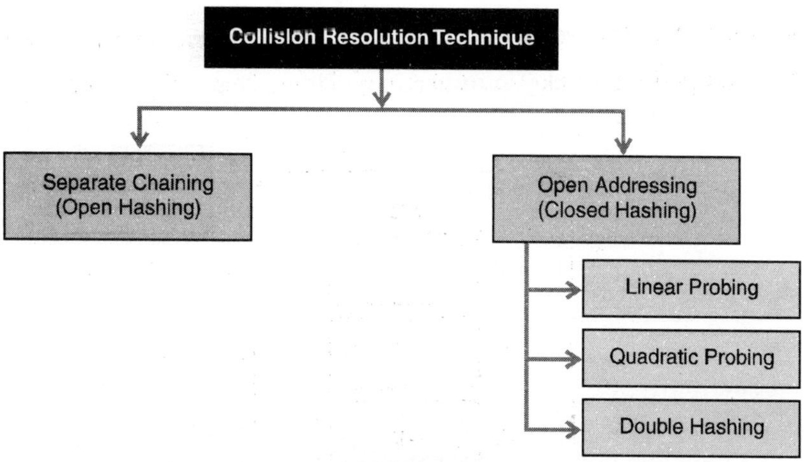

Collision resolution technique

(1) Separate Chaining

The idea is to make each cell of the hash table point to a linked list of records that have the same hash function value. Chaining is simple but requires additional memory outside the table.

Example: We have given a hash function and we have to insert some elements in the hash table using a separate chaining method for collision resolution technique.

Hash function = key % 5,

Elements = 12, 15, 22, 25 and 37.

Let's see step by step approach to how to solve the above problem:

- **Step 1:** First draw the empty hash table which will have a possible range of hash values from 0 to 4 according to the hash function provided.

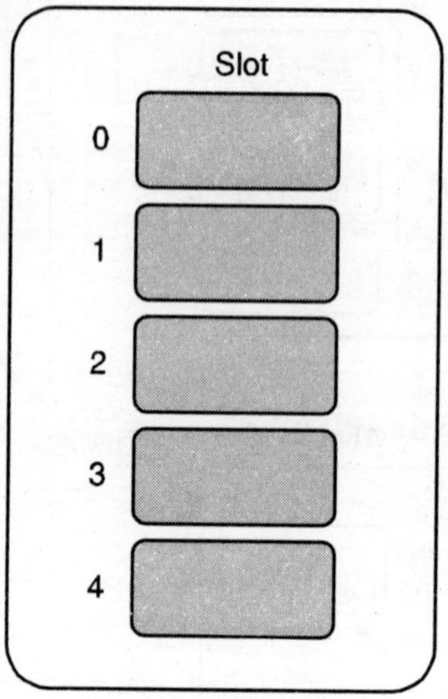

Hash table

- **Step 2:** Now insert all the keys in the hash table one by one. The first key to be inserted is 12 which is mapped to bucket number 2 which is calculated by using the hash function 12%5=2.

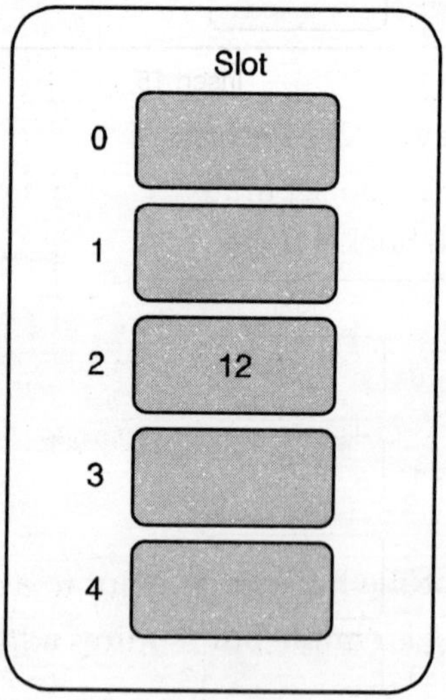

Insert 12

- **Step 3:** Now the next key is 22. It will map to bucket number 2 because 22%5=2. But bucket 2 is already occupied by key 12.

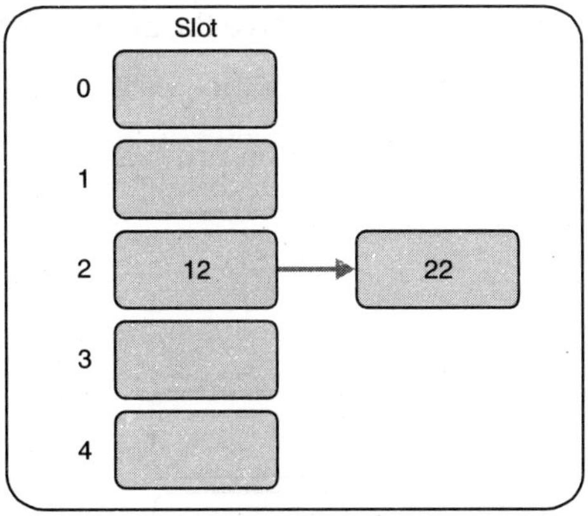

Insert 22

- **Step 4:** The next key is 15. It will map to slot number 0 because 15%5=0.

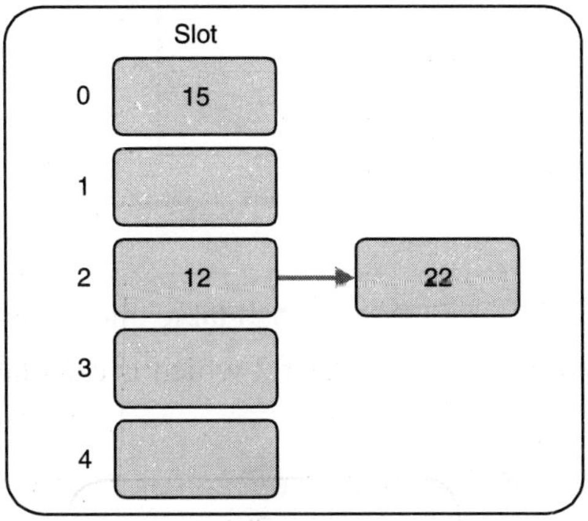

Insert 15

- **Step 5:** Now the next key is 25. Its bucket number will be 25%5 = 0. But bucket 0 is already occupied by key 25. So separate chaining method will again handle the collision by creating a linked list to bucket 0.

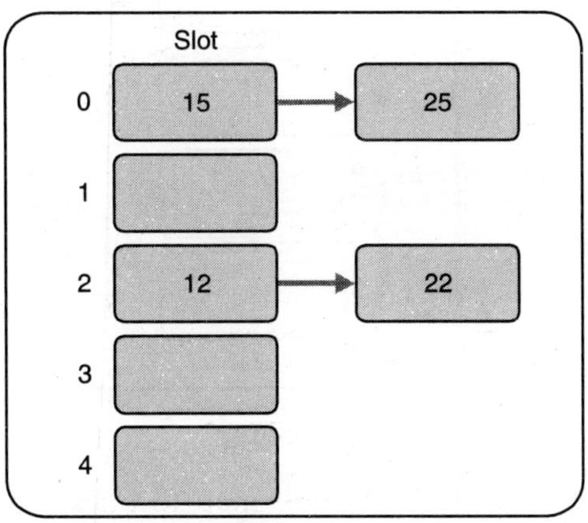

Insert 25

Hence In this way, the separate chaining method is used as the collision resolution technique.

(2) Open Addressing

In open addressing, all elements are stored in the hash table itself. Each table entry contains either a record or NIL. When searching for an element, we examine the table slots one by one until the desired element is found or it is clear that the element is not in the table.

2. (a) Linear Probing

In linear probing, the hash table is searched sequentially that starts from the original location of the hash. If in case the location that we get is already occupied, then we check for the next location.

Algorithm:

1. *Calculate the hash key. i.e. key = data % size*
2. *Check, if hashTable[key] is empty*
    - *store the value directly by hashTable[key] = data*
3. *If the hash index already has some value then*
    - *check for next index using key = (key+1) % size*
4. *Check, if the next index is available hashTable[key] then store the value. Otherwise try for next index.*
5. *Do the above process till we find the space.*

EXAMPLE: Let us consider a simple hash function as "key mod 5" and a sequence of keys that are to be inserted are 50, 70, 76, 85, 93.

- **Step 1:** First draw the empty hash table which will have a possible range of hash values from 0 to 4 according to the hash function provided.

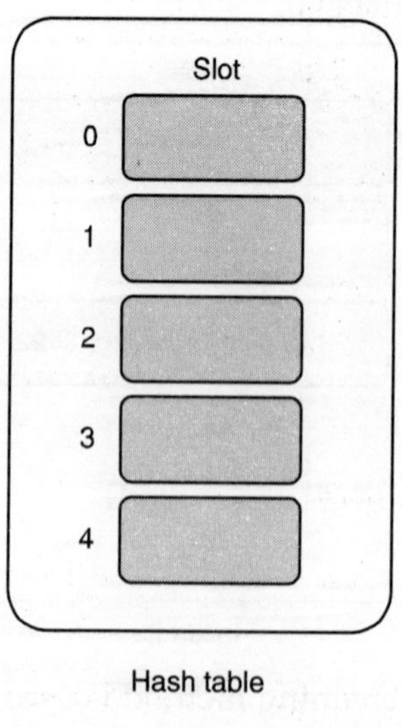

Hash table

- **Step 2:** Now insert all the keys in the hash table one by one. The first key is 50. It will map to slot number 0 because 50%5=0. So insert it into slot number 0.

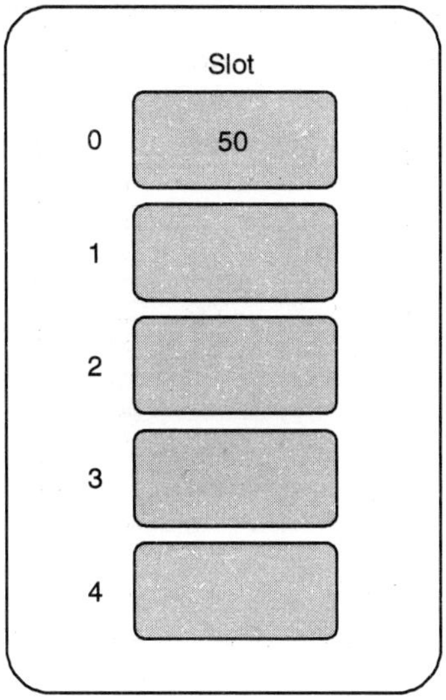

Insert 50 into hash table

- **Step 3:** The next key is 70. It will map to slot number 0 because 70%5=0 but 50 is already at slot number 0 so, search for the next empty slot and insert it.

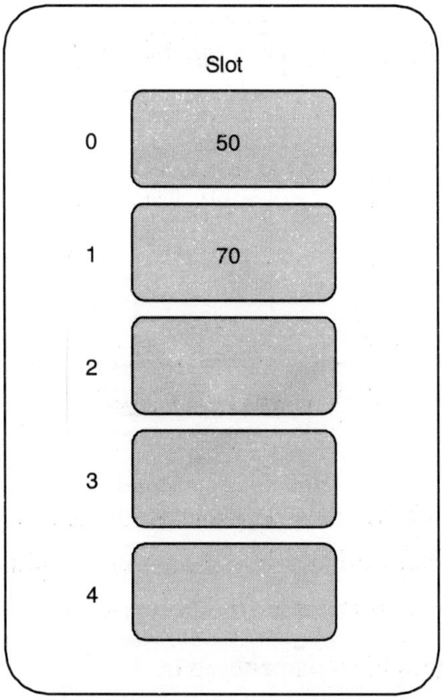

Insert 70 into hash table

- **Step 4:** The next key is 76. It will map to slot number 1 because 76%5=1 but 70 is already at slot number 1 so, search for the next empty slot and insert it.

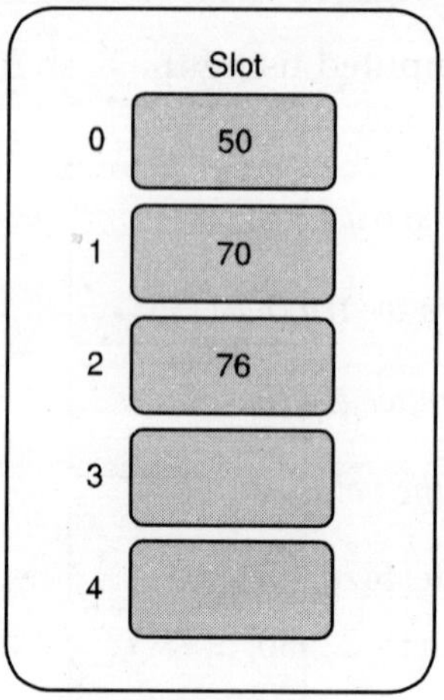

Insert 76 into hash table

- **Step 5:** The next key is 93. It will map to slot number 3 because 93%5=3, So insert it into slot number 3.

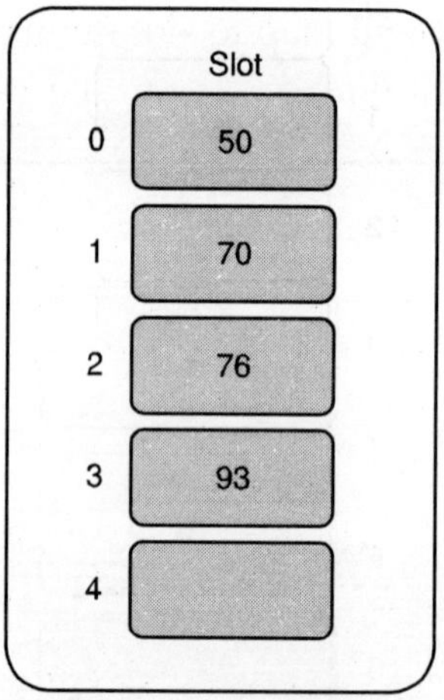

Insert 93 into hash table

2.(b) Quadratic Probing

Quadratic probing is an open addressing scheme in computer programming for resolving hash collisions in hash tables. Quadratic probing operates by taking the original hash index and adding successive values of an arbitrary quadratic polynomial until an open slot is found.

An example sequence using quadratic probing is:

$$H + 1_2, H + 2_2, H + 3_2, H + 4_2 \ldots\ldots\ldots\ldots\ldots\ldots\ldots H + k_2$$

This method is also known as the mid-square method because in this method we look for i_2 'th probe (slot) in i'th iteration and the value of $i = 0, 1, \dots n - 1$. We always start from the original hash location. If only the location is occupied then we check the other slots.

Let hash(x) be the slot index computed using the hash function and n be the size of the hash table.

If the slot hash(x) % n is full, then we try (hash(x) + 1_2*) % n.*

If (hash(x) + 1_2*) % n is also full, then we try (hash(x) +* 2_2*) % n.*

If (hash(x) + 2_2*) % n is also full, then we try (hash(x) +* 3_2*) % n.*

This process will be repeated for all the values of i until an empty slot is found

EXAMPLE: Let us consider table Size = 7, hash function as Hash(x) = x % 7 and collision resolution strategy to be $f(i) = i_2$. Insert = 22, 30, and 50

- **Step 1:** Create a table of size 7.

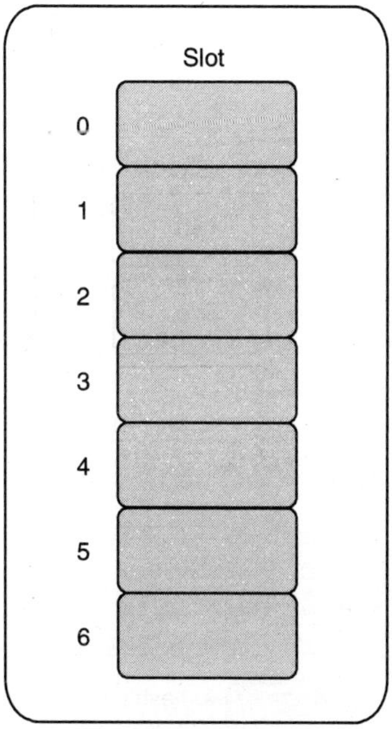

Hash table

- **Step 2** – Insert 22 and 30
  - Hash(22) = 22 % 7 = 1, Since the cell at index 1 is empty, we can easily insert 22 at slot 1.
  - Hash(30) = 30 % 7 = 2, Since the cell at index 2 is empty, we can easily insert 30 at slot 2.

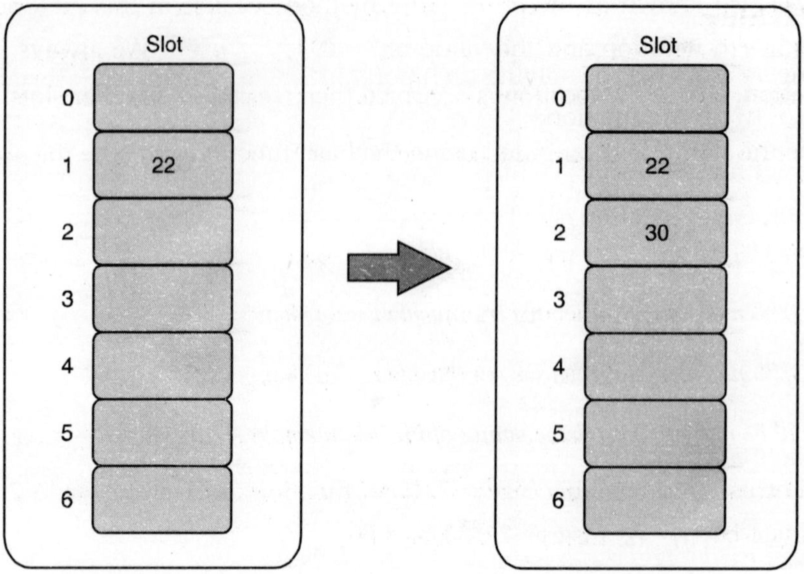

Insert key 22 and 30 in the hash table

- **Step 3:** Inserting 50
  - Hash(50) = 50 % 7 = 1
  - In our hash table slot 1 is already occupied. So, we will search for slot $1+1_2$, i.e. 1+1 = 2,
  - Again slot 2 is found occupied, so we will search for cell $1 + 2_2$, i.e. 1 + 4 = 5,
  - Now, cell 5 is not occupied so we will place 50 in slot 5.

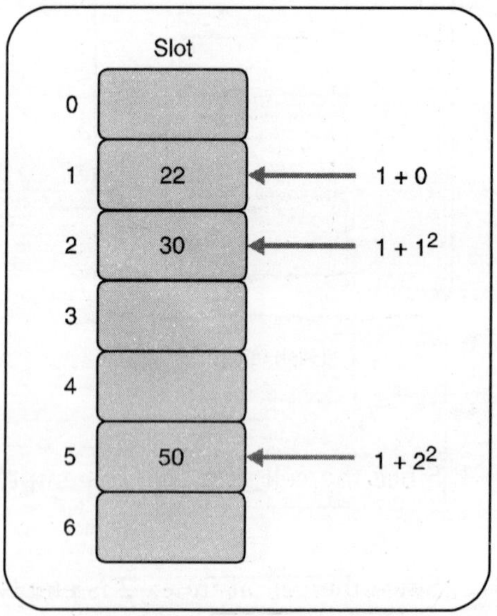

Insert key 50 in the hash table

2. (c) Double Hashing

Double hashing is a collision resolving technique in Open Addressed Hash tables. Double hashing make use of two hash function,

- The first hash function is $h_1(k)$ which takes the key and gives out a location on the hash table. But if the new location is not occupied or empty then we can easily place our key.
- But in case the location is occupied (collision) we will use secondary hash-function $h_2(k)$ in combination with the first hash-function $h_1(k)$ to find the new location on the hash table.

This combination of hash functions is of the form

$h(k, i) = (h_1(k) + i * h_2(k)) \% n$

where

- i is a non-negative integer that indicates a collision number,
- k = element/key which is being hashed
- n = hash table size.

Complexity of the Double hashing algorithm:

Time complexity: $O(n)$

Example: Insert the keys 27, 43, 692, 72 into the Hash Table of size 7. where first hash-function is $h_1(k) = k \bmod 7$ and second hash-function is $h_2(k) = 1 + (k \bmod 5)$

- **Step 1:** Insert 27
  - 27 % 7 = 6, location 6 is empty so insert 27 into 6 slot.

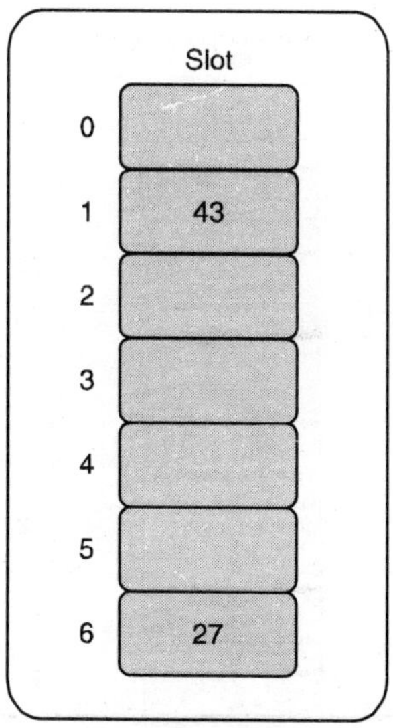

Insert key 27 in the hash table

- **Step 2:** Insert 43
  - 43 % 7 = 1, location 1 is empty so insert 43 into 1 slot.

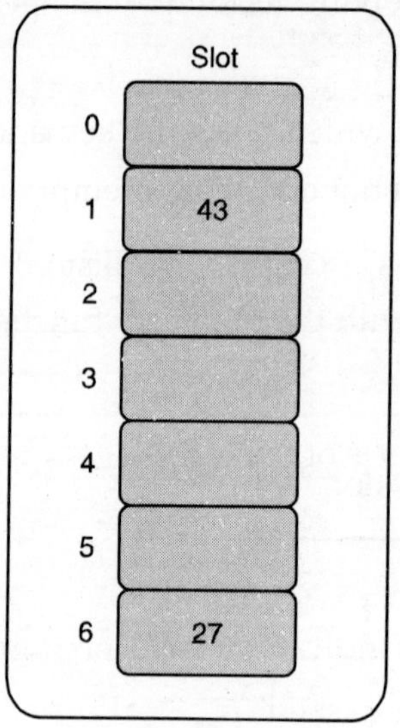

Insert key 43 in the hash table

- **Step 3:** Insert 692
  - 692 % 7 = 6, but location 6 is already being occupied and this is a collision
  - So we need to resolve this collision using double hashing.

$h_{new} = [h_1(692) + i \times (h_2(692))] \% 7$

$= [6 + 1 \times (1 + 692 \% 5)] \% 7$

$= 9 \% 7$

$= 2$

Now, as 2 is an empty slot, so we can insert 692 into 2nd slot.

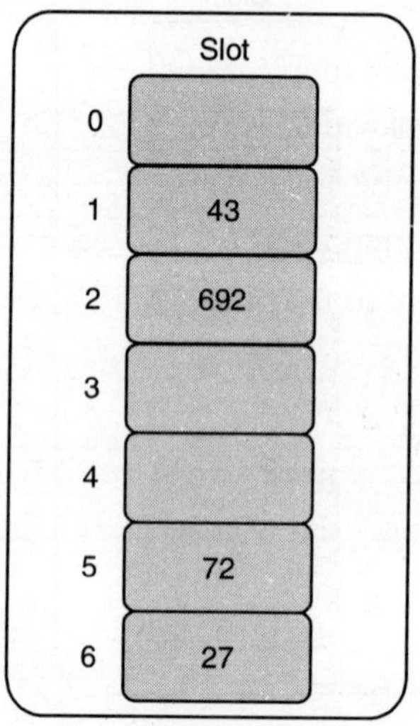

Insert key 692 in the hash table

- **Step 4:** Insert 72
  - 72 % 7 = 2, but location 2 is already being occupied and this is a collision.
  - So we need to resolve this collision using double hashing.

$h_{new} = [h_1(72) + i\,t\,(h_2(72)]\ \%\ 7$

$= [2 + 1 \times (1 + 72\ \%\ 5)]\ \%\ 7$

$= 5\ \%\ 7$

$= 5,$

Now, as 5 is an empty slot,

so we can insert 72 into 5th slot.

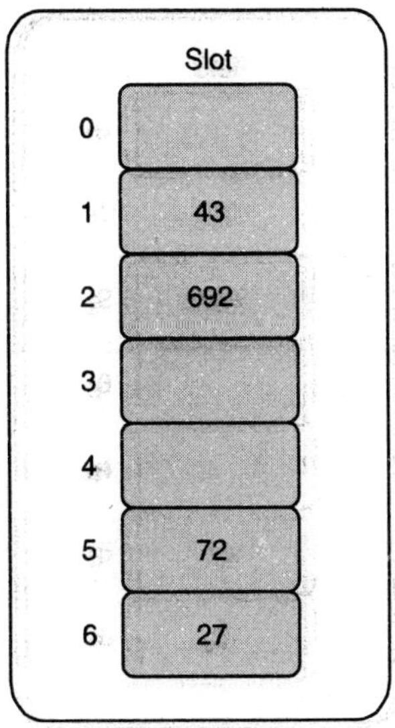

Rehashing:

Rehashing means hashing again. Basically, when the load factor increases to more than its predefined value (the default value of the load factor is 0.75), the complexity increases. So, to overcome this, the size of the array is increased (doubled) and all the values are hashed again and stored in the new double-sized array to maintain a low load factor and low complexity.

❍❍❍

UNIT 7

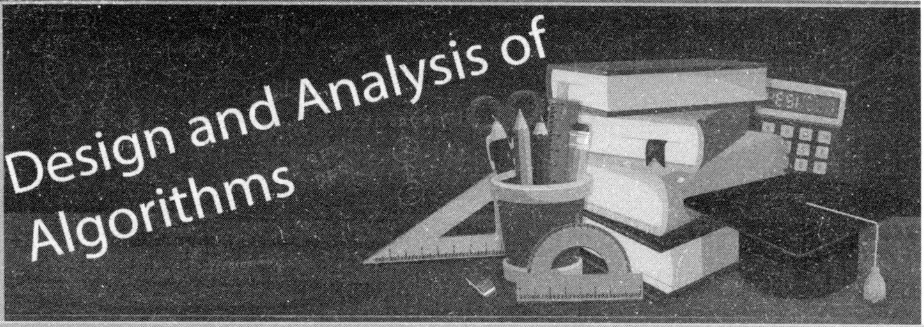

DYNAMIC PROGRAMMING

This chapter discusses dynamic programming, a method to solve optimization problems that involve a dynamical process. In a dynamical process, we make decisions in stages, where current decisions impact future decisions. In other words, decisions cannot be made in isolation. We must balance immediate cost with future costs. The main concept of dynamic programming is straight-forward. We divide a problem into smaller nested subproblems, and then combine the solutions to reach an overall solution. This concept is known as the principle of optimality, and a more formal exposition is provided in this chapter. The term "dynamic programming" was first used in the 1940's by Richard Bellman to describe problems where one needs to find the best decisions one after another. In the 1950's, he refined it to describe nesting small decision problems into larger ones. The mathematical statement of principle of optimality is remembered in his name as the Bellman Equation. In this chapter, we first describe the considered class of optimization problems for dynamical systems. Then we state the Principle of Optimality equation (or Bellman's equation). This equation is non-intuitive, since it's defined in a recursive manner and solved backwards. To alleviate this, the remainder of this chapter describes examples of dynamic programming problems and their solutions.

Dynamic programming is a technique that breaks the problems into sub-problems, and saves the result for future purposes so that we do not need to compute the result again. The subproblems are optimized to optimize the overall solution is known as optimal substructure property. The main use of dynamic programming is to solve optimization problems. Here, optimization problems mean that when we are trying to find out the minimum or the maximum solution of a problem. The dynamic programming guarantees to find the optimal solution of a problem if the solution exists.

The definition of dynamic programming says that it is a technique for solving a complex problem by first breaking into a collection of simpler subproblems, solving each subproblem just once, and then storing their solutions to avoid repetitive computations.

Let's understand this approach through an example.

Consider an example of the Fibonacci series. The following series is the Fibonacci series:

0, 1, 1, 2, 3, 5, 8, 13, 21, 34, 55, 89, 144, ...

The numbers in the above series are not randomly calculated. Mathematically, we could write each of the terms using the below formula:

$$\mathbf{F(n) = F(n-1) + F(n-2),}$$

With the base values F(0) = 0, and F(1) = 1. To calculate the other numbers, we follow the above relationship. For example, F(2) is the sum **f(0)** and **f(1),** which is equal to 1.

How can we calculate F(20)?

The F(20) term will be calculated using the *n*th formula of the Fibonacci series. The below figure shows that how F(20) is calculated.

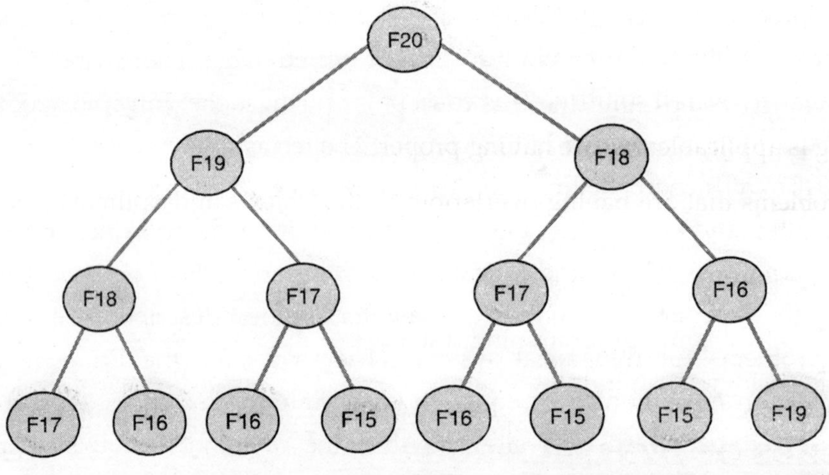

As we can observe in the above figure that F(20) is calculated as the sum of F(19) and F(18). In the dynamic programming approach, we try to divide the problem into the similar subproblems. We are following this approach in the above case where F(20) into the similar subproblems, i.e., F(19) and F(18). If we recap the definition of dynamic programming that it says the similar subproblem should not be computed more than once. Still, in the above case, the subproblem is calculated twice. In the above example, F(18) is calculated two times; similarly, F(17) is also calculated twice. However, this technique is quite useful as it solves the similar subproblems, but we need to be cautious while storing the results because we are not particular about storing the result that we have computed once, then it can lead to a wastage of resources.

In the above example, if we calculate the F(18) in the right subtree, then it leads to the tremendous usage of resources and decreases the overall performance.

The solution to the above problem is to save the computed results in an array. First, we calculate F(16) and F(17) and save their values in an array. The F(18) is calculated by summing the values of F(17) and F(16), which are already saved in an array. The computed value of F(18) is saved in an array. The value of F(19) is calculated using the sum of F(18), and F(17), and their values are already saved in an array. The computed value of F(19) is stored in an array. The value of F(20) can be calculated by adding the values of F(19) and F(18), and the values of both F(19) and F(18) are stored in an array. The final computed value of F(20) is stored in an array.

How does the dynamic programming approach work?

The following are the steps that the dynamic programming follows:

- It breaks down the complex problem into simpler subproblems.
- It finds the optimal solution to these sub-problems.
- It stores the results of subproblems (memorization). The process of storing the results of subproblems is known as memorization.
- It reuses them so that same sub-problem is calculated more than once.
- Finally, calculate the result of the complex problem.

The above five steps are the basic steps for dynamic programming. The dynamic programming is applicable that are having properties such as:

Those problems that are having overlapping subproblems and optimal substructures. Here, optimal substructure means that the solution of optimization problems can be obtained by simply combining the optimal solution of all the subproblems.

In the case of dynamic programming, the space complexity would be increased as we are storing the intermediate results, but the time complexity would be decreased.

APPROACHES OF DYNAMIC PROGRAMMING

There are two approaches to dynamic programming:

- Top-down approach
- Bottom-up approach

TOP-DOWN APPROACH

The top-down approach follows the memorization technique, while bottom-up approach follows the tabulation method. Here memorization is equal to the sum of recursion and caching. Recursion means calling the function itself, while caching means storing the intermediate results.

Advantages

- It is very easy to understand and implement.
- It solves the subproblems only when it is required.
- It is easy to debug.

Disadvantages

It uses the recursion technique that occupies more memory in the call stack. Sometimes when the recursion is too deep, the stack overflow condition will occur.

It occupies more memory that degrades the overall performance.

Let's understand dynamic programming through an example.

```
int fib(int n)
{
  if(n<0)
  error;
 if(n==0)
 return 0;
 if(n==1)
return 1;
sum = fib(n-1) + fib(n-2);
}
```

In the above code, we have used the recursive approach to find out the Fibonacci series. When the value of '*n*' increases, the function calls will also increase, and computations will also increase. In this case, the time complexity increases exponentially, and it becomes 2^n.

One solution to this problem is to use the dynamic programming approach. Rather than generating the recursive tree again and again, we can reuse the previously calculated value. If we use the dynamic programming approach, then the time complexity would be $O(n)$.

When we apply the dynamic programming approach in the implementation of the Fibonacci series, then the code would look like:

```
static int count = 0;
int fib(int n)
{
if(memo[n]!= NULL)
return memo[n];
```

```
count++;
  if(n<0)
  error;
if(n==0)
return 0;
if(n==1)
return 1;
sum = fib(n-1) + fib(n-2);
memo[n] = sum;
}
```

In the above code, we have used the memorization technique in which we store the results in an array to reuse the values. This is also known as a top-down approach in which we move from the top and break the problem into sub-problems.

BOTTOM-UP APPROACH

The bottom-up approach is also one of the techniques which can be used to implement the dynamic programming. It uses the tabulation technique to implement the dynamic programming approach. It solves the same kind of problems but it removes the recursion. If we remove the recursion, there is no stack overflow issue and no overhead of the recursive functions. In this tabulation technique, we solve the problems and store the results in a matrix.

There are two ways of applying dynamic programming:

- Top-Down
- Bottom-Up

The bottom-up is the approach used to avoid the recursion, thus saving the memory space. The bottom-up is an algorithm that starts from the beginning, whereas the recursive algorithm starts from the end and works backward. In the bottom-up approach, we start from the base case to find the answer for the end. As we know, the base cases in the Fibonacci series are 0 and 1. Since the bottom approach starts from the base cases, so we will start from 0 and 1.

Key points

- We solve all the smaller sub-problems that will be needed to solve the larger sub-problems then move to the larger problems using smaller sub-problems.

- We use for loop to iterate over the sub-problems.
- The bottom-up approach is also known as the tabulation or table filling method.

Let's understand through an example.

Suppose we have an array that has 0 and 1 values at a[0] and a[1] positions, respectively shown as below:

0	1	
a[0]	*a*[1]	

Since the bottom-up approach starts from the lower values, so the values at a[0] and a[1] are added to find the value of a[2] shown as below:

0	1	1	
a[0]	*a*[1]	*a*[2]	

The value of a[3] will be calculated by adding a[1] and a[2], and it becomes 2 shown as below:

0	1	1	2	
a[0]	*a*[1]	*a*[2]	*a*[3]	

The value of a[4] will be calculated by adding a[2] and a[3], and it becomes 3 shown as below:

0	1	1	2	3	
a[0]	*a*[1]	*a*[2]	*a*[3]	*a*[4]	

The value of a[5] will be calculated by adding the values of a[4] and a[3], and it becomes 5 shown as below:

0	1	1	2	3	5	
a[0]	*a*[1]	*a*[2]	*a*[3]	*a*[4]	*a*[5]	

The code for implementing the Fibonacci series using the bottom-up approach is given below:

```
int fib(int n)
{
    int A[];
    A[0] = 0, A[1] = 1;
```

```
    for(i=2; i<=n; i++)
    {
        A[i] = A[i-1] + A[i-2]
    }
    return A[n];
}
```

In the above code, base cases are 0 and 1 and then we have used for loop to find other values of Fibonacci series.

Let's understand through the diagrammatic representation.

Initially, the first two values, i.e., 0 and 1 can be represented as:

When $i = 2$ then the values 0 and 1 are added shown as below:

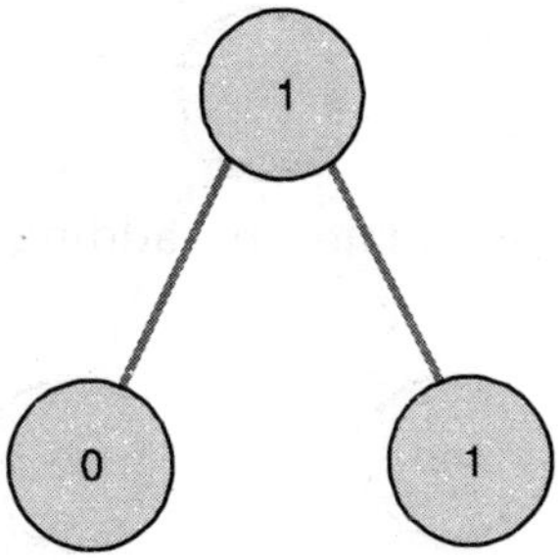

When $i = 3$ then the values 1 and 1 are added shown as below:

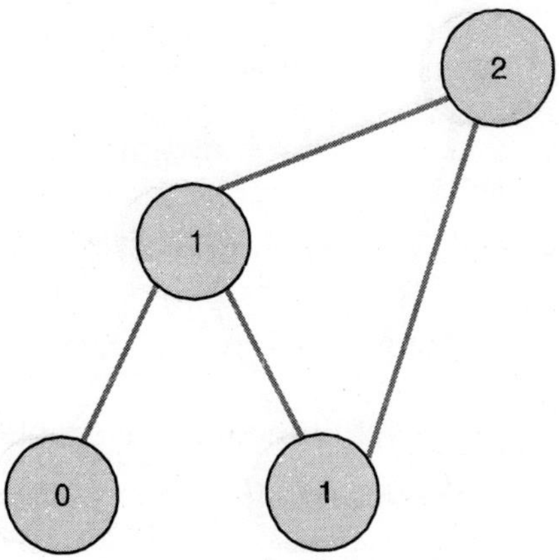

When $i = 4$ then the values 2 and 1 are added shown as below:

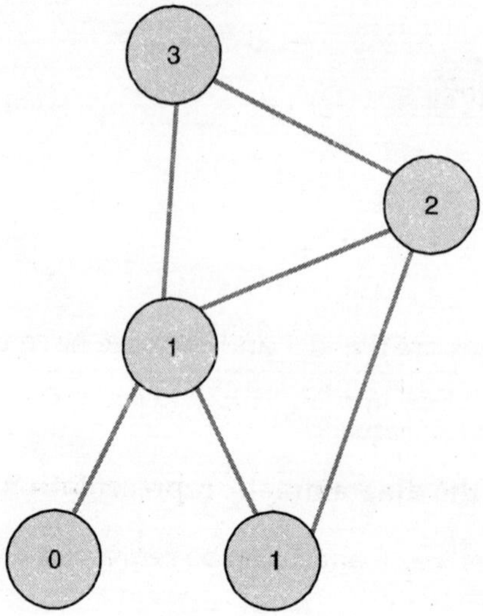

When $i = 5$, then the values 3 and 2 are added shown as below:

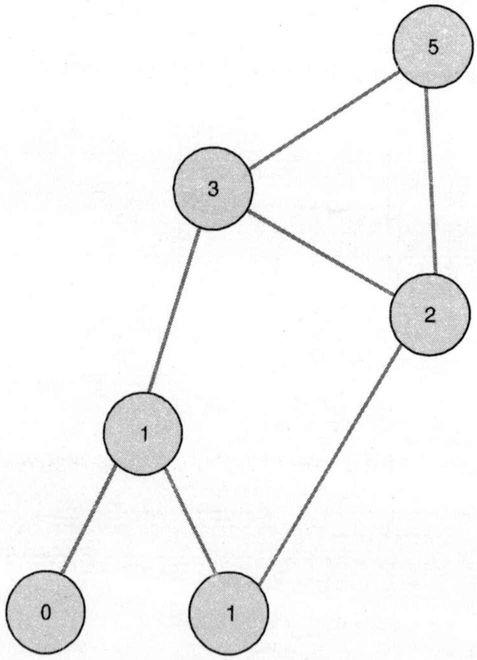

In the above case, we are starting from the bottom and reaching to the top.

THE BINOMIAL COEFFICIENT

Computing binomial coefficient is very fundamental problem of mathematics and computer science. Binomial coefficient C(n, k) defines coefficient of the term x^n in the expansion of $(1 + x)^n$.

C(*n*, *k*) also defines the number of ways to select any *k* items out of *n* items. Mathematically it is defined as,

$$C(n, k) = \frac{n!}{(n-k)!k!}(0 \le k \le n)$$

C(*n*, *k*) can be found in different ways.

Dynamic Programming Approach.

- Many sub problems are called again and again, since they have an overlapping sub problems property. Re-computations of the same sub problems is avoided by storing their results in the temporary array C[*i*, *j*] in a bottom up manner.
- The optimal substructure for using dynamic programming is stated as,

$$C[i, j] = \begin{cases} 1 & , \text{ if } i=j \text{ or } j=0 \\ C[i-1, j-1], + C[i-1, j] & \text{otherwise} \end{cases}$$

In Table, index *i* indicates row and index *j* indicates column

n/k	0	1	2	3	4	.	.	.	(*k* – 1)	*k*
0	1									
1	1	1								
2	1	2	1							
3	1	3	3	1						
4	1	4	6	4	1					
.	.									
.	.									
K	1									
.	.									
.	.									
n – 1	1								C(*n* – 1, *k* – 1)	C(*n* – 1, *k*)
N	1									C(*n*, *k*)

- This tabular representation of binomial coefficients is also known as Pascal's triangle.
- Algorithm to solve this problem using dynamic programming is shown below

```
Algorithm BINOMIAL_DC (n, k)
// n is total number of items
// k is the number of items to be selected from n
```

```
if k == 0 or k == n then
    return 1
else
    return DC_BINOMIAL(n – 1, k – 1) + DC_BINOMIAL(n – 1, k)
end
```

Input: The algorithm takes two parameters: n (the total number of items) and k (the number of items to be selected from n).

Base Case: If k equals 0 (indicating that we're choosing 0 items from n) or if k equals n (meaning we're choosing all n items), the algorithm returns 1. These are the base cases for the recursive function because there's only one way to choose either 0 or all n items.

Recursive Step: If the base cases aren't met, the algorithm recursively calls itself to calculate the binomial coefficient. It uses the formula $\binom{n}{k}=\binom{n-1}{k-1}+\binom{n-1}{k}$ which reflects the fundamental property of binomial coefficients.

Optimal Binary Search Tree

Optimal Binary Search Tree extends the concept of Binary searc tree. Binary Search Tree (BST) is a *nonlinear* data structure which is used in many scientific applications for reducing the search time. In BST, left child is smaller than root and right child is greater than root. This arrangement simplifies the search procedure.

Optimal Binary Search Tree (OBST) is very useful in dictionary search. The probability of searching is different for different words. OBST has great application in translation. If we translate the book from English to German, equivalent words are searched from English to German dictionary and replaced in translation. Words are searched same as in binary search tree order.

Binary search tree simply arranges the words in lexicographical order. Words like *'the'*, *'is'*, *'there'* are very frequent words, whereas words like *'xylophone'*, *'anthropology'* etc. appears rarely.

It is not a wise idea to keep less frequent words near root in binary search tree. Instead of storing words in binary search tree in lexicographical order, we shall arrange them according to their probabilities. This arrangement facilitates few searches for frequent words as they would be near the root. Such tree is called **Optimal Binary Search Tree**.

Consider the sequence of $n$keys K = < k_1, k_2, k_3, …, k_n> of distinct probability in sorted order such that $k_1 < k_2 < \ldots < k_n$. Words between each pair of key lead to unsuccessful search, so for n keys, binary search tree contains $n + 1$ dummy keys d_i, representing unsuccessful searches.

Two different representation of BST with same five keys $\{k_1, k_2, k_3, k_4, k_5\}$ probability is shown in following figure

With n nodes, there exist $(2n)!/((n + 1)! * n!)$ different binary search trees. An exhaustive search for optimal binary search tree leads to huge amount of time.

The goal is to construct a tree which minimizes the total search cost. Such tree is called optimal binary search tree. OBST does not claim minimum height. It is also not necessary that parent of sub tree has higher priority than its child.

Dynamic programming can help us to find such optima tree.

Binary search trees with 5 keys

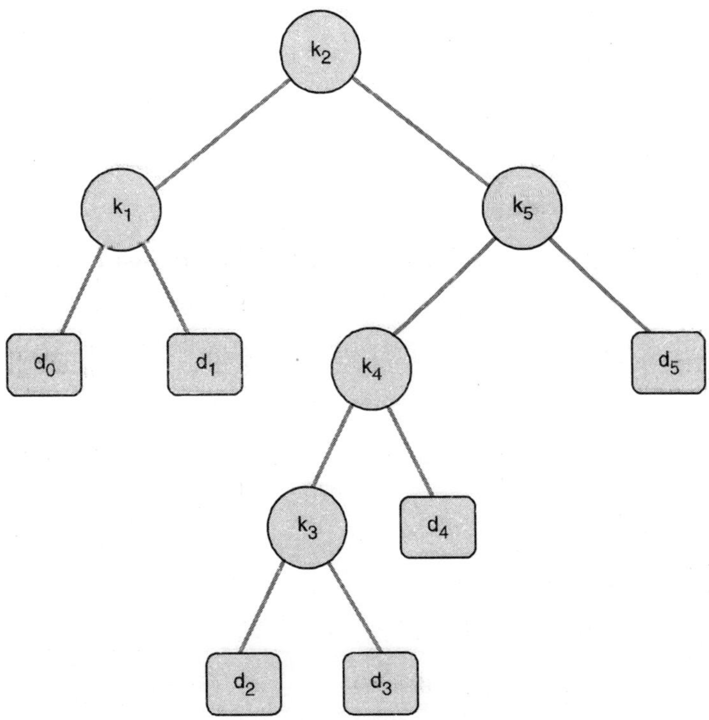

Binary search trees with 5 keys

Mathematical formulation

We formulate the OBST with following observations

Any sub tree in OBST contains keys in sorted order $k_i \ldots k_j$, where $1 \leq i \leq j \leq n$.

Sub tree containing keys $k_i \ldots k_j$ has leaves with dummy keys $d_{i-1} \ldots d_j$.

Suppose k_r is the root of sub tree containing keys k_i.....k_j. So, left sub tree of root k_r contains keys k_i....k_{r-1} and right sub tree contain keys k_{r+1} to k_j. Recursively, optimal sub trees are constructed from the left and right sub trees of k_r.

- Let e[i, j] represents the expected cost of searching OBST. With n keys, our aim is to find and minimize e[1, n].
- Base case occurs when $j = i - 1$, because we just have the dummy key d_{i-1} for this case. Expected search cost for this case would be $e[i, j] = e[i, i-1] = q_{i-1}$.
- For the case $j \geq i$, we have to select any key k_r from $k_i \ldots k_j$ as a root of the tree.
- With k_r as a root key and sub tree $k_i \ldots k_j$, sum of probability is defined as

$$w(i, j) = \sum_{m=i}^{j} p_m + \sum_{m=i-1}^{j} q_m$$

Actual key starts at index 1 and dummy key starts at index 0)

Thus, a recursive formula for forming the OBST is stated below :

$$e[i, j] = \begin{cases} q_{i-1} & \text{if } j = i-1 \\ \min\{e[i, r-1] + e[r+1, j] + w(i, j) i \leq r \leq j\} & \text{if } i \leq j \end{cases}$$

e[i, j] gives the expected cost in the optimal binary search tree.

The algorithm for optimal binary search tree is specified below :

```
Algorithm OBST(p, q, n)
// e[1...n+1, 0...n ] : Optimal sub tree
// w[1...n+1, 0...n] : Sum of probability
// root[1...n, 1...n] : Used to construct OBST


for i ← 1 to n + 1 do
e[i, i – 1] ← qi – 1
w[i, i – 1] ← qi – 1
end


for m ← 1 to n do
   for i ← 1 to n – m + 1 do
      j ← i + m – 1
```

```
e[i, j] ← ∞
w[i, j] ← w[i, j – 1] + pj + qj
    for r ← i to j do
        t ← e[i, r – 1] + e[r + 1, j] + w[i, j]
        if t <e[i, j] then
e[i, j] ← t
root[i, j] ← r
        end
    end
  end
end
return (e, root)
```

Principle of Optimality

Consider a multi-stage decision process, i.e. an equality constrained NLP with dynamics

$$\min_{x_k, u_k} \quad J = \sum_{k=0}^{N-1} g_k(x_k, u_k) + g_N(x_N)$$

s.t.

$$x_{k+1} = f(x_k, u_k), \quad k = 0, 1, \ldots, N-1$$

$$x_0 = x_{init}$$

where k is the discrete time index, xk is the state at time k, uk is the control decision applied at time *k*, N is the time horizon, $g_k(\cdot, \cdot)$ is the instantaneous cost, and $g_N(\cdot)$ is the final or terminal cost.

In words, the principle of optimality is the following. Assume at time step *k*, you know all the future optimal decisions, i.e. $u \times (k + 1)$, $u \times (k + 2)$, $\cdots$, $u \times (N - 1)$. Then you may compute the best solution for the current time step, and pair with the future decisions. This can be done recursively by starting from the end N – 1, and working your way backwards.

Mathematically, the principle of optimality can be expressed precisely as follows. Define $V_k(x_k)$ as the optimal "cost-to-go" (a.k.a. "value function") from time step *k* to the end of the time horizon N, given the current state is x_k. Then the principle of optimality can be written in recursive form as :

$$V_k(x_k) = \min_{u_k} \{g(x_k, u_k) + V_{k+1}(x_{k+1})\}, \quad k = 0, 1, \ldots, N-1$$

with the boundary condition

$$V_N(x_N) = g_N(x_N)$$

Let us illustrate this with two examples

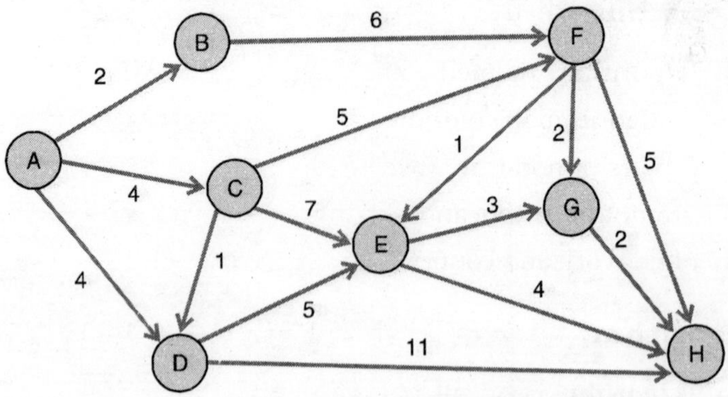

Example 1.1 (Shortest Path Problem). Consider the network shown in Fig. 2. The goal is to find the shortest path from node A to node H, where path length is indicated by the edge numbers. Let us define the cost-to-go as V (i). That is, V (i) is the shortest path length from node i to node H. For example V (H) = 0. Let $c(i, j)$ denote the cost of traveling from node i to node j. For example, c(C, E) = 7. Then $c(i, j)$ + V (j) represents the cost of traveling from node i to node j, and then from node j to H along the shortest path. This enables us to write the principle of optimality equation and boundary conditions:

$$V(i) = \min_{j \in N_i^d} \{c(i,j) + V(j)\}$$

$$V(H) = 0$$

where the set Nd i represents the nodes that descend from node i. For example Nd C = {D, E, F}. We can solve these equations recursively, starting from node H and working our way backward to node A as follows:

$$V(G) = c(G, H) + V(H) = 2 + 0 = 2$$

$$V(E) - \min \{c(E, G) + V(G), c(E, H) + V(H)\} = \min \{3 + 2, 4 + 0\} = 4$$

$$V(F) = \min \{c(F, G) + V(G), c(F, H) + V(H), c(F, E) + V(E)\}$$

$$= \min \{2 + 2, 5 + 0, 1 + 4\} = 4$$

$$V(D) = \min \{c(D, E) + V(E), c(D, H) + V(H)\} = \min \{5 + 4, 11 + 0\} = 9$$

$$V(C) = \min \{c(C, F) + V(F), c(C, E) + V(E), c(C, D) + V(D)\}$$

$$= \min \{5 + 4, 7 + 4, 1 + 9\} = 9$$

$$V(B) = c(B, F) + V(F) = 6 + 4 = 10$$

$$V(A) = \min \{c(A, B) + V(B), c(A, C) + V(C), c(A, D) + V(D)\}$$
$$= \min \{2 + 10, 4 + 9, 4 + 9\} = 12$$

Consequently, we arrive at the optimal path $A \to B \to F \to G \to H$.

Floyd Warshall Algorithm

The **Floyd-Warshall algorithm,** named after its creators **Robert Floyd** and **Stephen Warshall,** is a fundamental algorithm in computer science and graph theory. It is used to find the shortest paths between all pairs of nodes in a weighted graph. This algorithm is highly efficient and can handle graphs with both **positive** and **negative edge weights,** making it a versatile tool for solving a wide range of network and connectivity problems.

Floyd Warshall Algorithm:

The **Floyd Warshall Algorithm** is an all pair shortest path algorithm unlike Dijkstra and Bellman Ford which are single source shortest path algorithms. This algorithm works for both the **directed and undirected weighted** graphs. But, it does not work for the graphs with negative cycles (where the sum of the edges in a cycle is negative). It follows Dynamic Programming approach to check every possible path going via every possible node in order to calculate shortest distance between every pair of nodes.

Idea Behind Floyd Warshall Algortihm:

Suppose we have a graph *G[][]* with *V* vertices from *1* to *N*. Now we have to evaluate a ***shortestPathMatrix[][]*** where ***shortestPathMatrix[i][j]*** represents the shortest path between vertices *i* and *j*.

Obviously the shortest path between *i* to *j* will have some *k* number of intermediate nodes. The idea behind floydwarshall algorithm is to treat each and every vertex from *1* to *N* as an intermediate node one by one.

The following figure shows the above optimal substructure property in floydwarshall algorithm:

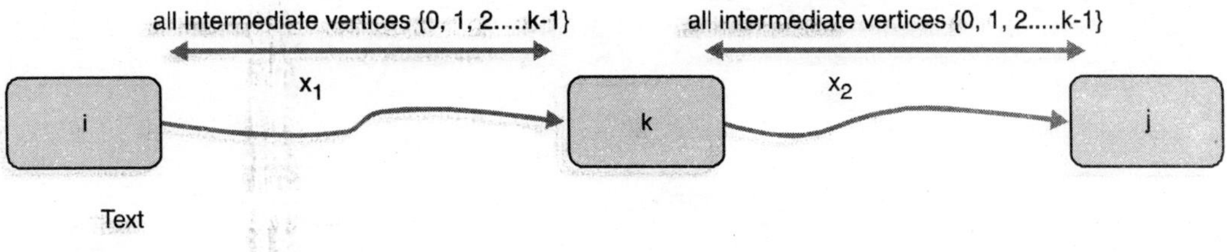

Algorithm:

- Initialize the solution matrix same as the input graph matrix as a first step.

- Then update the solution matrix by considering all vertices as an intermediate vertex.
- The idea is to pick all vertices one by one and updates all shortest paths which include the picked vertex as an intermediate vertex in the shortest path.
- When we pick vertex number *k* as an intermediate vertex, we already have considered vertices **{0, 1, 2, .. *k*–1}** as intermediate vertices.
- For every pair **(*i*, *j*)** of the source and destination vertices respectively, there are two possible cases.
- *k* is not an intermediate vertex in shortest path from *i* to *j*. We keep the value of **dist[*i*][*j*]** as it is.
- *k* is an intermediate vertex in shortest path from *i* to **j**. We update the value of **dist[*i*][*j*]** as **dist[*i*][*k*] + dist[*k*][*j*]**, if **dist[*i*][*j*] >dist[*i*][*k*] + dist[*k*][*j*]**

Pseudo-Code:

For $k = 0$ to $n - 1$

For $i = 0$ to $n - 1$

For $j = 0$ to $n - 1$

Distance[*i*, *j*] = min(Distance[*i*, *j*], Distance[*i*, *k*] + Distance[*k*, *j*])

where *i* = source Node, *j* = Destination Node, *k* = Intermediate Node

Illustration:

Suppose we have a graph as shown in the image:

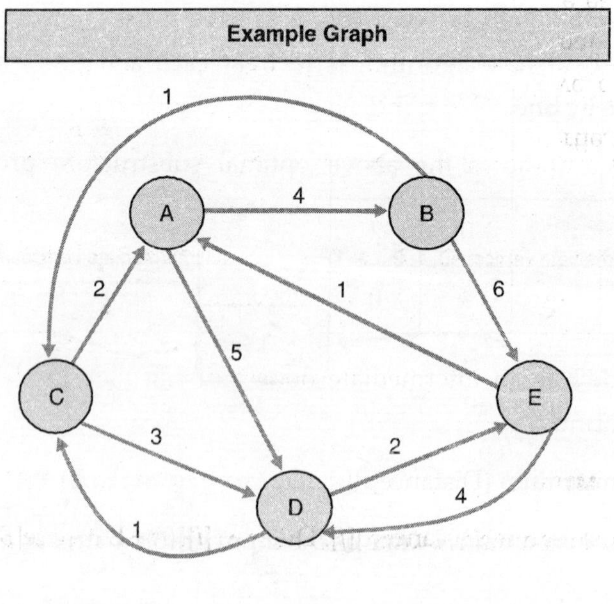

Step 1: Initialize the Distance[][] matrix using the input graph such that Distance[*i*][*j*]= weight of edge from *i* to *j*, also Distance[*i*][*j*] = Infinity if there is no edge from *i* to *j*.

Step 1: Initializing Distance [ ][ ] using the Input Graph

	A	B	C	D	E
A	0	4	∞	5	∞
B	∞	0	1	∞	6
C	2	∞	0	3	∞
D	∞	∞	1	0	2
E	1	∞	∞	4	0

Step 2: Treat node *A* as an intermediate node and calculate the Distance[][] for every {i,j} node pair using the formula:

= Distance[*i*][*j*] = minimum (Distance[*i*][*j*], (Distance from *i* to *A*) + (Distance from *A* to *j*))

= Distance[*i*][*j*] = minimum (Distance[*i*][*j*], Distance[*i*][*A*] + Distance[*A*][*j*])

Step 2: Using Node A as the Intermediate node

Distance[I][j] = min (Distance[I][j], Distance [I][A] + Distance[A][j])

	A	B	C	D	E
A	0	4	∞	5	∞
B	∞	0	1	∞	6
C	2	∞	0	3	∞
D	∞	∞	1	0	2
E	1	∞	∞	4	0

→

	A	B	C	D	E
A	0	4	∞	5	∞
B	∞	0	1	∞	6
C	2	6	0	3	12
D	∞	∞	1	0	2
E	1	5	∞	4	0

Step 3: Treat node *B* as an intermediate node and calculate the Distance[][] for every {*i,j*} node pair using the formula:

= Distance[*i*][*j*] = minimum (Distance[*i*][*j*], (Distance from *i* to *B*) + (Distance from *B* to *j*))

= Distance[*i*][*j*] = minimum (Distance[*i*][*j*], Distance[*i*][*B*] + Distance[*B*][*j*])

Step 3: Using Node B as the Intermediate node

Distance[i][j] = min (Distance [i][j], Distance [i][B] + Distance [B][j]

	A	B	C	D	E
A	?	4	?	?	?
B	∞	0	1	∞	6
C	?	6	?	?	?
D	?	∞	?	?	?
E	?	5	?	?	?

	A	B	C	D	E
A	0	4	5	5	10
B	∞	0	1	∞	6
C	2	6	0	3	12
D	∞	∞	1	0	2
E	1	5	6	4	0

Step 4: Treat node *C* as an intermediate node and calculate the Distance[][] for every {*i,j*} node pair using the formula:

= Distance[*i*][*j*] = minimum (Distance[*i*][*j*], (Distance from i to C) + (Distance from C to *j*))

= Distance[*i*][*j*] = minimum (Distance[*i*][*j*], Distance[*i*][C] + Distance[C][*j*])

Step 4: Using Node C as the Intermediate node

Distance [i][j] = min (Distance [i][j], Distance [i][C] + Distance [C][j]

	A	B	C	D	E
A	?	?	5	?	?
B	?	?	1	?	?
C	2	6	0	3	12
D	?	?	1	?	?
E	?	?	6	?	?

	A	B	C	D	E
A	0	4	5	5	10
B	3	0	1	4	6
C	2	6	0	3	12
D	3	7	1	0	2
E	1	5	6	4	0

Step 5: Treat node *D* as an intermediate node and calculate the Distance[][] for every {*i,j*} node pair using the formula:

= Distance[*i*][*j*] = minimum (Distance[*i*][*j*], (Distance from *i* to *D*) + (Distance from *D* to *j*))

= Distance[*i*][*j*] = minimum (Distance[*i*][*j*], Distance[*i*][*D*] + Distance[*D*][*j*])

Step 5: Using Node D as the Intermediate node

Distance[i][j] = min (Distance[i][j], Distance[i][D] + Distance[D][j])

	A	B	C	D	E
A	?	?	?	5	?
B	?	?	?	4	?
C	?	?	?	3	?
D	3	7	1	0	2
E	?	?	?	4	?

	A	B	C	D	E
A	0	4	5	5	7
B	3	0	1	4	6
C	2	6	0	3	5
D	3	7	1	0	2
E	1	5	5	4	0

Step 6: Treat node *E* as an intermediate node and calculate the Distance[][] for every $\{i,j\}$ node pair using the formula:

= Distance[i][j] = minimum (Distance[i][j], (Distance from i to E) + (Distance from E to j))

= Distance[i][j] = minimum (Distance[i][j], Distance[i][E] + Distance[E][j])

Step 6: Using Node E as the Intermediate node

Distance[i][j] = min (Distance[i][j], Distance[i][E] + Distance[E][j])

	A	B	C	D	E
A	?	?	?	?	7
B	?	?	?	?	6
C	?	?	?	?	5
D	?	?	?	?	2
E	1	5	5	4	0

	A	B	C	D	E
A	0	4	5	5	7
B	3	0	1	4	6
C	2	6	0	3	5
D	3	7	1	0	2
E	1	5	5	4	0

Step 7: Since all the nodes have been treated as an intermediate node, we can now return the updated Distance[][] matrix as our answer matrix.

Step 7: Return Distance[ ][ ] matrix as the result

	A	B	C	D	E
A	0	4	5	5	7
B	3	0	1	4	6
C	2	6	0	3	5
D	3	7	1	0	2
E	1	5	5	4	0

Complexity Analysis:

- **Time Complexity:** O(V3), where V is the number of vertices in the graph and we run three nested loops each of size V
- **Auxiliary Space:** O(V2), to create a 2-D matrix in order to store the shortest distance for each pair of nodes.

Why is Floyd-Warshall algorithm better for Dense Graphs and not for Sparse Graphs ?

***Dense Graph*:** A graph in which the number of edges are significantly much higher than the number of vertices.

***Sparse Graph*:** A graph in which the number of edges are very much low.

Applications of Floyd-Warshall Algorithm:

- In computer networking, the algorithm can be used to find the shortest path between all pairs of nodes in a network. This is termed as **network routing**.
- Flight Connectivity In the aviation industry to find the shortest path between the airports.
- **GIS(Geographic Information Systems)** applications often involve analyzing spatial data, such as road networks, to find the shortest paths between locations.
- Kleene's algorithm which is a generalization of floydwarshall, can be used to find regular expression for a regular language.

❍❍❍

UNIT

8

GREEDY METHOD

INTRODUCTION

The Greedy approach constructs the solution through a sequence of steps. Each step is chosen such that it is the best alternative among all feasible choices that are available. The choice of a step once made cannot be changed in subsequent steps.

Let us consider the problem of coin change. Suppose a greedy person has some 25p, 20p, 10p, 5paise coins. When someone asks him for some change then he wants to give the change with minimum number of coins. Now, let someone requests for a change of top then he first selects 25p. Then the remaining amount is 45p. Next, he selects the largest coin that is less than or equal to 45p i.e. 25p. The remaining 20p is paid by selecting a 20p coin. So the demand for top is paid by giving total 3 numbers of coins. This solution is an optimal solution. Now, let someone requests for a change of 40p then the Greedy approach first selects 25p coin, then a 10p coin and finally a 5p coin. However, the some could be paid with two 20p coins. So it is clear from this example that Greedy approach tries to find the optimal solution by selecting the elements one by one that are locally optimal. But Greedy method never gives the guarantee to find the optimal solution.

The choice of each step in a greedy approach is done based in the following:

- It must be feasible
- It must be locally optimal
- It must be unalterable

A greedy algorithm works if a problem has the following two properties:

Greedy choice property: Greedy Choice property tells us that we can obtain a globally optimal solution by obtaining a solution that is either a locally optimal solution or a Greedy solution. The choice made by a Greedy algorithm may depend on the earlier choices but will never depend on the future. A Greedy choice is made one after another and this helps to reduce the given problem to a smaller one.

Optimal substructure: A problem is said to exhibit an optimal substructure if and only if an optimal solution to the problem also contains the optimal solutions to the subproblems. That means we can solve subproblems and build up the solutions which could help us to solve larger problems.

Examples:

Following are a few examples of Greedy algorithms

- Machine scheduling
- Fractional Knapsack Problem
- Minimum Spanning Tree
- Huffman Code
- Job Sequencing
- Activity Selection Problem

General Method

```
Greedy(int a[], int n)
{
Y = 0 ; // the Y is initialized to be empty
for i = 1 to n do
{
 X = Select(a);
If feasible(Y, X) then
Y = Union(Y,X);
}
return(Y);
```

Explanation:

1. The arraya[1...*n*] contains '*n*' inputs.
2. The Y is initialized to be empty.

3. The function Select selects an input from an array a[] and removes it. The selected inputs value is assigned to X.
4. Feasible is a Boolean valued function that determines whether X can be included into the selection vector.
5. The function union combines X with Y and updates the objective function.

Prim's Algorithm

1. Prim's algorithm is a type of greedy algorithm for finding the minimum spanning tree (MST) of an undirected and weighted graph.
2. A minimum spanning tree (MST) is the subset of the edges of a graph that connects all the vertices (the point where the sides meet) together so that the total weight of the edges is minimized without forming a cycle.
3. For example, if A links to B and B links to C, C cannot link to A again because that would make a cycle.
4. One of the goals of Prim's algorithm is to get the minimum cost tree that covers the vertices in the graph without leaving any of them behind.
5. All the vertices must be involved in getting the minimum spanning tree (MST).
6. Prim's algorithm is also called **Jarník's algorithm** because it was initially developed by Czech Mathematician Vojtěch Jarník in 1930. It was later rediscovered and published by Robert C. Prim in 1957 – hence the name Prim's algorithm.

Algorithm:

```
Algorithm Prim (E, cost, n, t)
// E is the set of edges in G, cost [1 : n, 1 : n] is the cost
// adjacency matrix of an n vertex graph such that cost [i, j] is
// either a positive real number or ∞ if no edge (i, j) exists.
// A minimum spanning tree is computed and stored as a set of
// edges in the array t[1 : n – 1, 1 : 2]. (t [i, 1], t[i, 2]) is an edge in
// the minimum-cost spanning tree. The final cost is returned.
{
    Let (k, l) be an edge of minimum cost in E;
    mincost := cost [k, l];
    t[1, 1] := k; t[1, 2] := l;
    for i := 1 to n do // Initialize near.
```

```
            if (cost [i, l] < cost [i, k]) then near [i] := l;
            else near [i] := k;
        near [k] := near [l] := 0;
        for i := 2 to n – 1 do
        { // Find n – 2 additional edges for t.
            Let j be an index such that near [j] ≠ 0 and
            cost [j, near [j]] is minimum ;
            t[i, 1] := j; t[i, 2] : = near [j];
            mincost := mincost + cost [j, near [j]];
            near [j] : = 0 ;
        for k := 1 to n do // update near [ ].
            If ((near [k] ≠ 0) and (cost [k, near [k]] > cost [k, j]))
                Then near [k] := j;
        }
        return mincost;
}
```

Consider the graph below :

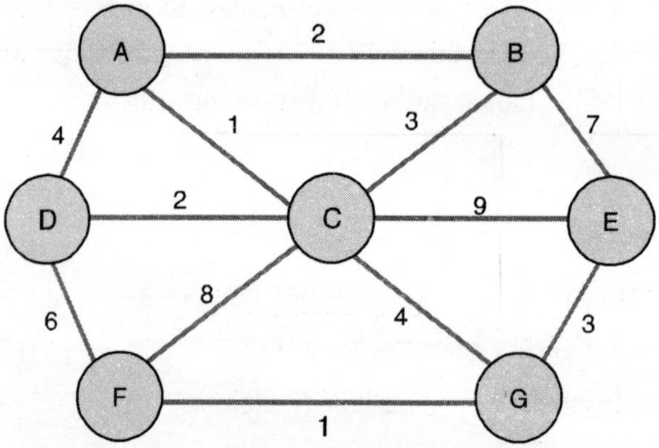

You have to start by choosing an arbitrary vertex as the starting point and adding it to the tree.

For the next step, you have to select the edge with the minimum weight that connects a vertex in the tree to a vertex not yet in the tree, and then add the new vertex to the tree.

Choosing D as the starting vertex resulted in this:

- D was the starting point.
- the next minimum weight connected to D is 2 – the line between D and C. So, I chose it.

- looking at vertex C, the next minimum weight to it is 1 – the line between C and A. So, I chose it as the next one
- looking at A, lines 2 and 4 are connected to it. We cannot choose 4 because it's bigger than 2 and it'll lead us back to the starting point D. So, we have to choose 2 – the line connecting vertices A and B.
- looking at B, line 3 connects it to C and line 7 connects it to E. We cannot choose line 3 because that will form a cycle between C, A, and B. We also should think twice before choosing line 7 because it's a big number. There's a line 4 connecting C to G, so, I chose it
- On the vertex G, there's a connection to F with line 1 and line 3 to E, so I'll choose the minimum weight which is 1
- At this point, E is the only vertex not connected yet. It's possible to connect it because it won't form a cycle at any point. So, I connected it.
- The Step by step process:

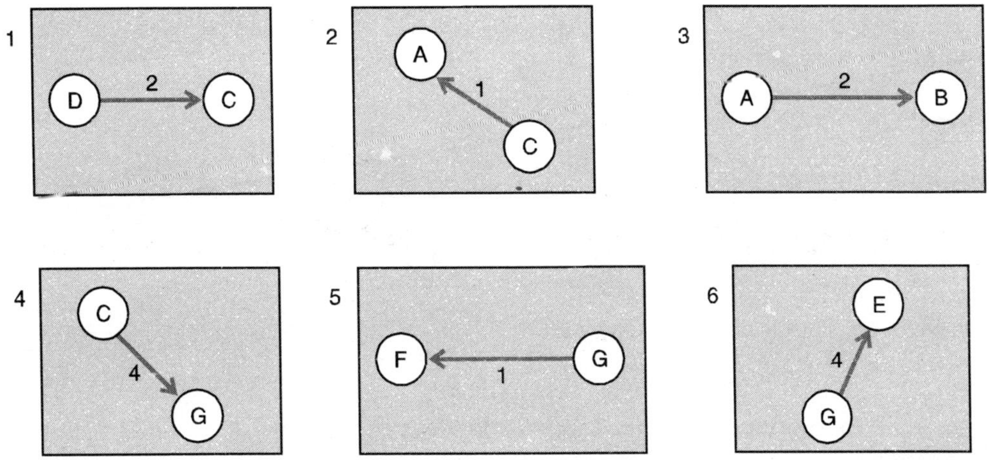

- Choosing D as the starting vertex resulted in this:

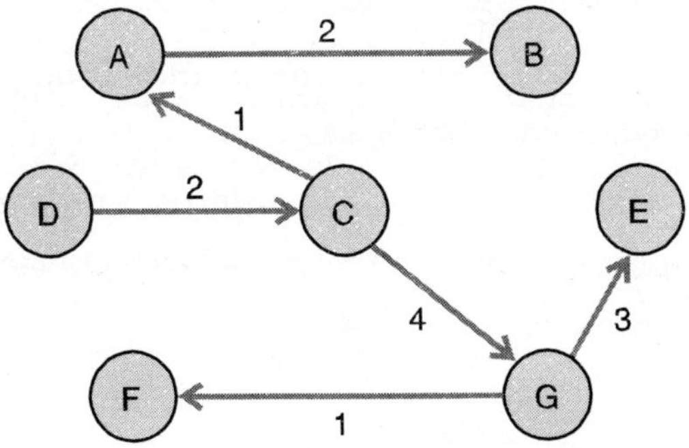

Cost = 2 + 1 + 2 + 4 + 3 + 1 = 13

Kruskal's algorithm is a greedy algorithm used to find out the shortest path in a minimum spanning tree. The algorithm aims to traverse the graph and detect the subset of edges with minimal value and cover all the vertices of the graph. At every step of the algorithm and analysis, it follows a greedy approach for an overall optimized result.

Kruskal's algorithm can be summed up as it is a minimum spanning tree algorithm that takes a graph as input and forms a subset of the edges of the graph,

- which has a minimum sum of edge weight among all the trees that can be formed from that graph.
- that form a tree including each vertex of the graph, without forming any cycle between the vertex.

Necessary conditions for Kruskal's algorithm

It works on the graph. So,

- The graph must be undirected.
- The graph must be weighted.
- The graph must be connected.

Algorithm:

```
Algorithm Krushal (E, cost, n, t)
// E is the set of edges in G. G has n vertices, cost [u, v] is the
// cost of edge (u, v). t is the set of edges in the minimum-cost
// spanning tree. The final cost is returned.
{
    Construct a heap out of the edge costs using Heapify;
    for i := 1 to n do parent [i] := –1;
    // Each vertex is in a different set.
    i := 0; mincost := 0.0;
    while ((i < n – 1) and (heap not empty)) do
    {
        Delete a mninimum cost edge (u, v) from the heap and reheapify using Adjust ;
        j := Find(u); k := Find(v);
        if (j ≠ k) the
        {
```

```
            i := i + 1;
            t[i, 1] := u; t[i, 2] := v;
            mincost := mincost + cost [u, v];
            Union (j, k);
        }
    }
    if (i ≠ n – 1) then write ("No spanning tree");
    else return mincost;
}
```

Working

Kruskal's algorithm follows a greedy approach that always tries to find a local optimum result and hopes to obtain a global optimum result.

Being a greedy algorithm, Kruskal's algorithm begins with selecting the edge with minimum weight and keeps adding edges until all the vertices aren't covered.

Step-wise working of Kruskal's algorithm is as follows:

- Keep all the edges sorted and in ascending order or sort all the edges in increasing weight order.
- Select the edge with the smallest or minimum edge weight.
- Add the selected edge to the spanning tree.
- Check whether the added edge is creating a cycle or loop. If yes, then reject that edge.
- Repeat until all the vertices are added to the graph.

Example

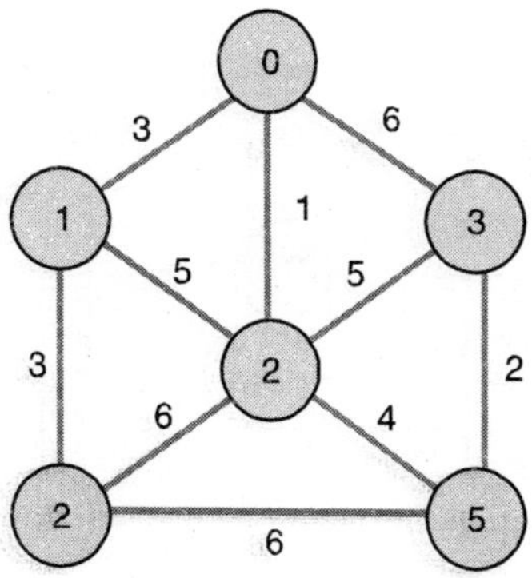

Procedure for finding Minimum Spanning Tree

Step 1. Edges are sorted in ascending order by weight.

Edge No.	Vertex Pair	Edge Weight
E1	(0,2)	1
E2	(3,5)	2
E3	(0,1)	3
E4	(1,4)	3
E5	(2,5)	4
E6	(1,2)	5
E7	(2,3)	5
E8	(0,3)	6
E9	(2,4)	6
E10	(4,5)	6

Step 2. Edges are added in sequence.

Graph

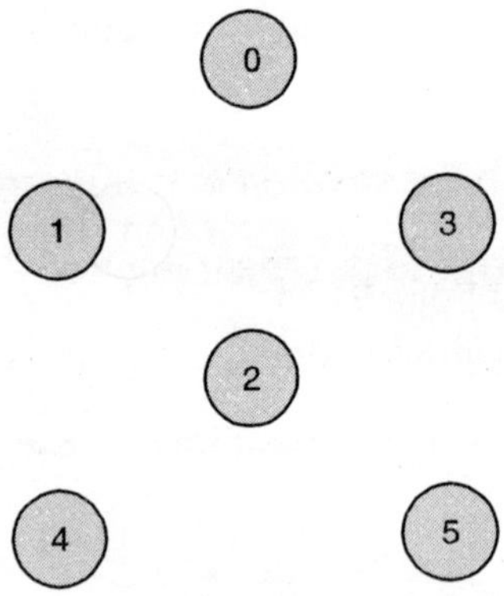

Add Edge E1

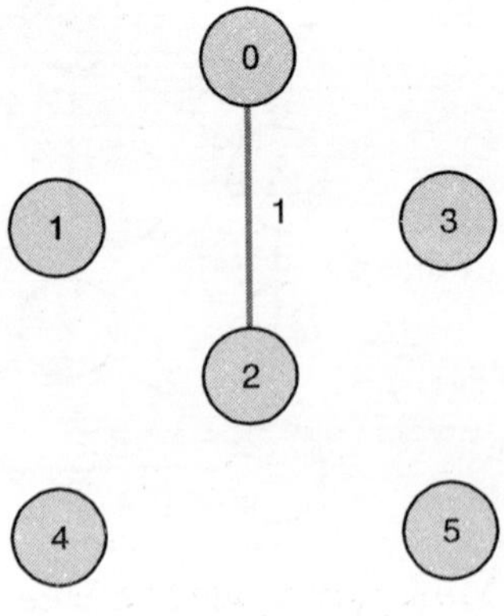

Add Edge E2

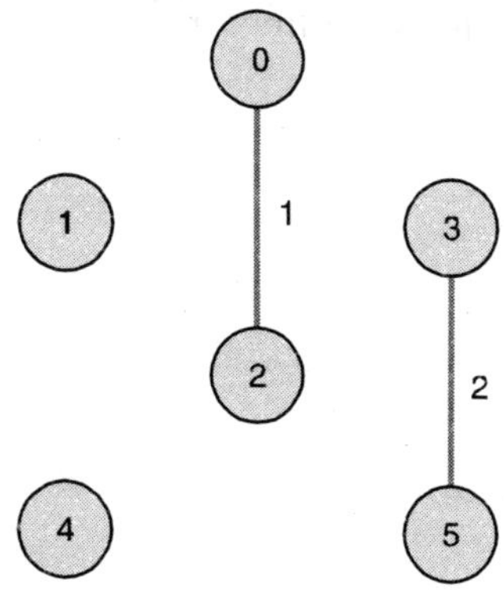

Add Edge E3

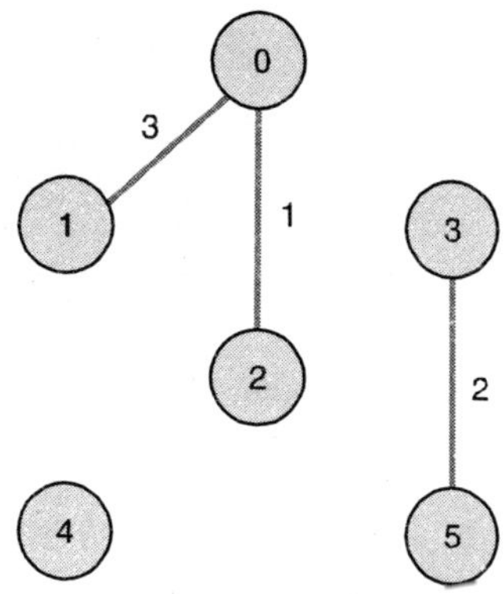

Add Edge E4

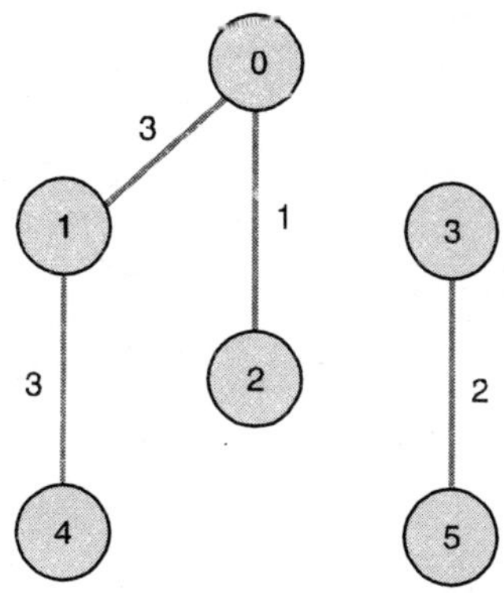

Add Edge E5

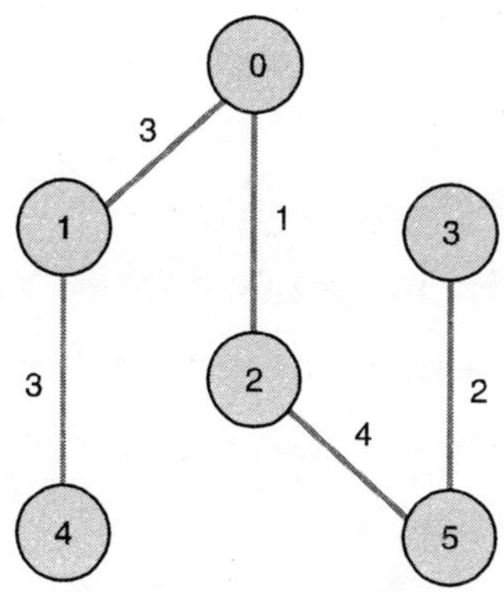

Total Cost = 1 + 2 + 3 + 3 + 4 = 13

Differences between Prim's Algorithm and Kruskal's Algorithm

Prim's Algorithm	Kruskal's Algorithm
Prim's algorithm is fast and easy to implement.	Kruskal's algorithm is more efficient but takes longer to calculate.
Requires less storage and less computational power than Kruskal's algorithm.	More storage space and more computational power than Prim's algorithm
Has no limit on the number of vertices in a graph.	May have limits on the number of vertices depending on the algorithm used.
Prim's algorithm is used to find the minimum cost path in a graph	Kruskal's algorithm is used to find the shortest path in a graph.
The route is chosen based on vertices	The route is chosen based on edges
Initiates with a node	Initiates with an edge

Dijkstra's Algorithm – Single Source Shortest Path

Dijkstra's algorithm, given by a brilliant Dutch computer scientist and software engineer Dr. Edsger Dijkstra in 1959. Dijkstra's algorithm is a greedy algorithm that solves the single-source shortest path problem for a directed and undirected graph that has non-negative edge weight.

This algorithm is used to find the shortest path in Google Maps, in network routing protocols, in social networking applications, and also in many places. For a given graph G Dijkstra's algorithm is helpful to find the shortest path between a source node to a destination node.

For example, if we draw a graph in which nodes represent the cities and weighted edges represent the driving distances between pairs of cities connected by a direct road, then Dijkstra's algorithm when applied gives the shortest route between one city and all other cities.

This algorithm is also used in GPS devices to find the shortest path between the current location and the destination. It has broad applications in industry, specially in domains that require modeling networks.

```
Algorithm ShortestPaths (v, cost, dist, n)
// dist [j], 1 ≤ j ≤ n, is set to the length of the shortest
// path from vertex v to vertex j in a digraph G with n
// vertices. Dist[v] is set to zero. G is represented by its
// cost adjacency matrix cost [1 : n, 1 : n].
{
```

```
        for i := 1 to n do
        { // Initialize S.
            S[i] := false; dist[i] := cost [v, i];
        }
        S [v] := true; dist[v] := 0.0; // Put v in S.
        For num := 2 to n – 1 do
        {
            // Determine n – 1 paths from v.
            Choose u from among those vertices not in S such that dist[u] is minimum;
            S[u] := true; // Put u in S.
            for (each w adjacent to u with S[w] = false) do
                // Update distances.
                if (dist[w] > dist[u] + cost[u, w[)) then
                    dist[w] := dist[u] + cost[u, w];
        }
}
```

1. The very first step is to mark all nodes as unvisited.
2. Mark the picked starting node with a current distance of 0 and the rest nodes with infinity.
3. Now, fix the starting node as the current node.
4. For the current node, analyseall of its unvisited neighbours and measure their distances by adding the current distance of the current node to the weight of the edge that connects the neighbour node and current node.
5. Compare the recently measured distance with the current distance assigned to the neighbouring node and make it as the new current distance of the neighbouring node.
6. After that, consider all of the unvisited neighbours of the current node, mark the current node as visited.
7. If the destination node has been marked visited then stop, an algorithm has ended. and
8. Else, choose the unvisited node that is marked with the least distance, fix it as the new current node, and repeat the process again from step 4.

Example:

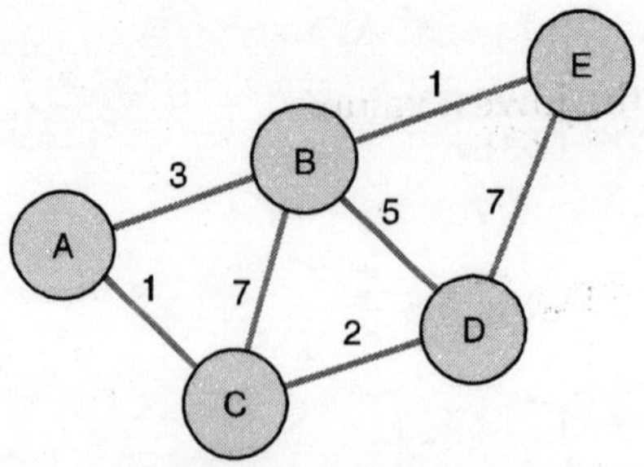

Example of Dijkstra's Algorithm

1. During the execution of the algorithm, each node will be marked with its minimum distance to node C as we have selected node C.

   In this case, the minimum distance is 0 for node C. Also, for the rest of the nodes, as we don't know this distance, they will be marked as infinity (∞), except node C (currently marked as red dot).

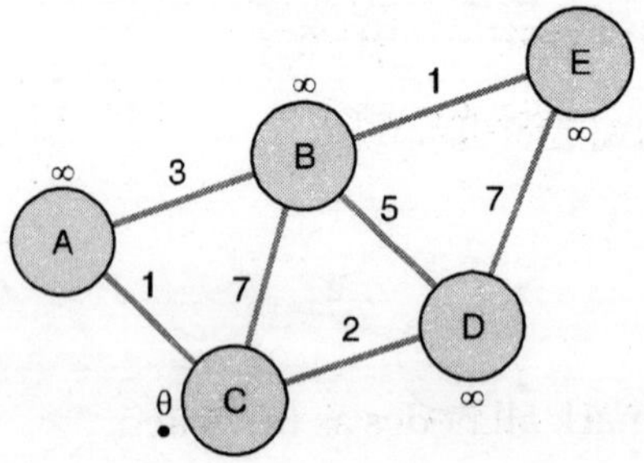

Graphical Representation of Node C as Current Node

2. Now the neighbours of node C will be checked, i.e, node A, B, and D. We start with B, here we will add the minimum distance of current node (0) with the weight of the edge (7) that linked the node C to node B and get 0+ 7= 7.

   Now, this value will be compared with the minimum distance of B (infinity), the least value is the one that remains the minimum distance of B, like in this case, 7 is less than infinity, and marks the least value to node B.

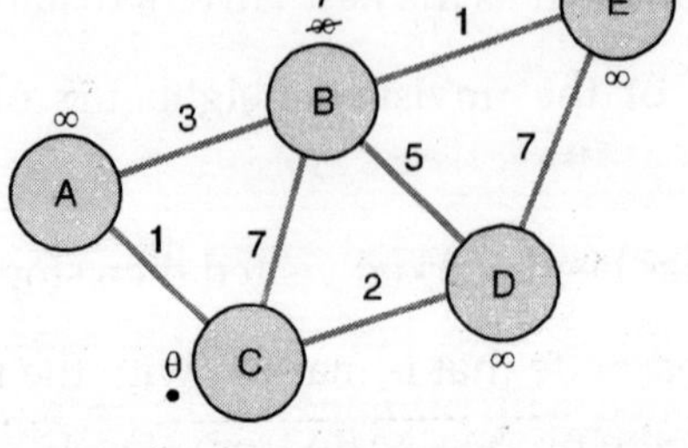

Assign Node B a minimum distance value

3. Now, the same process is checked with neighbour A. We add 0 with 1 (weight of edge that connects node C to A), and get 1. Again, 1 is compared with the minimum distance of A (infinity), and marks the lowest value.

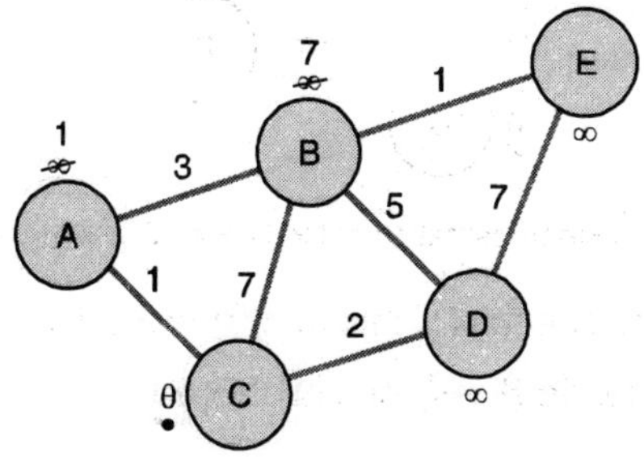

Assign Node A a minimum distance value

The same is repeated with node D, and marked 2 as lowest value at D.

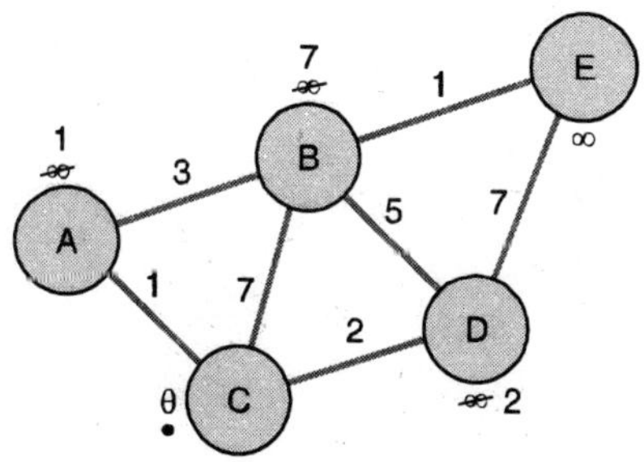

Assign Node D a minimum distance value

Since, all the neighbours of node C have checked, so node C is marked as visited with a green check mark.

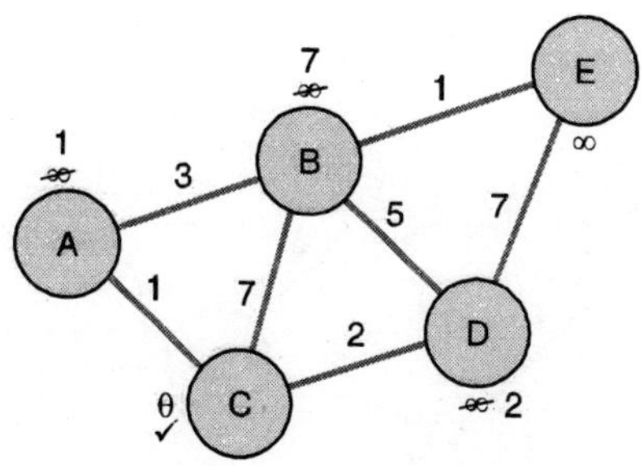

Marked Node C as visited

4. Now, we will select the new current node such that the node must be unvisited with the lowest minimum distance, or the node with the least number and no check mark. Here, node A is the unvisited with minimum distance 1, marked as current node with red dot.

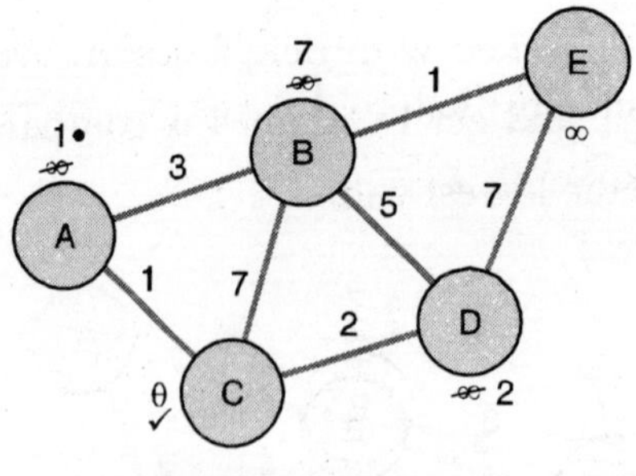

Graphical Representation of Node A as Current Node

We repeat the algorithm, checking the neighbour of the current node while ignoring the visited node, so only node B will be checked.

For node B, we add 1 with 3 (weight of the edge connecting node A to B) and obtain 4. This value, 4, will be compared with the minimum distance of B, 7, and mark the lowest value at B as 4.

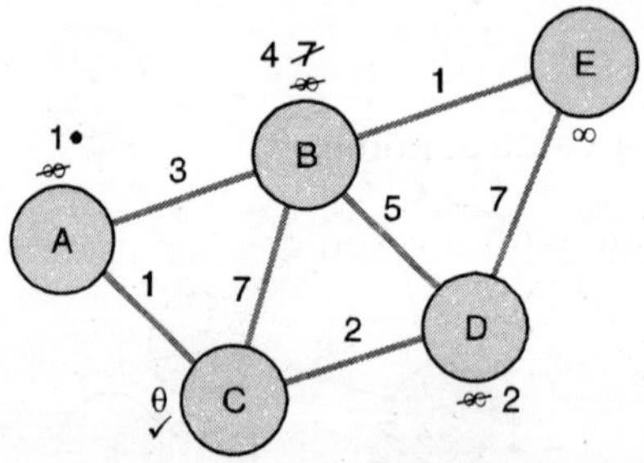

Assign Node B a minimum distance value

5. After this, node A marked as visited with a green check mark. The current node is selected as node D, it is unvisited and has a smallest recent distance. We repeat the algorithm and check for node B and E.

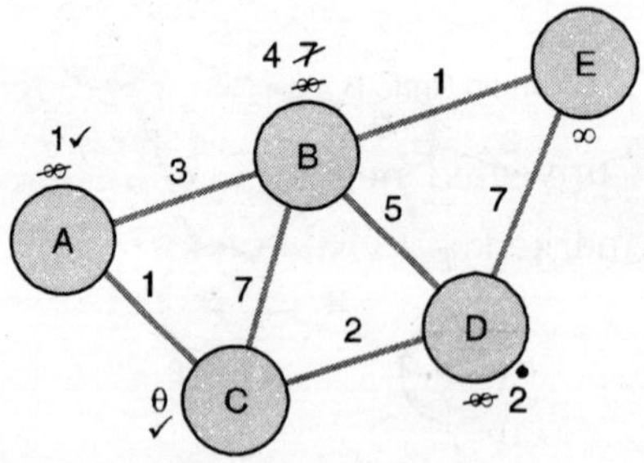

Graphical Representation of Node D as Current Node

For node B, we add 2 to 5, get 7 and compare it with the minimum distance value of B, since 7>4, so leave the smallest distance value at node B as 4.

For node E, we obtain 2+ 7= 9, and compare it with the minimum distance of E which is infinity, and mark the smallest value as node E as 9. The node D is marked as visited with a green check mark.

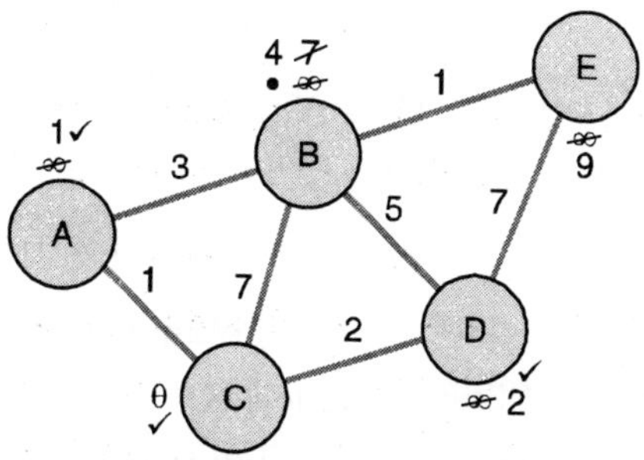

Marked Node D as visited

6. The current node is set as node B, here we need to check only node E as it is unvisited and the node D is visited. We obtain 4+ 1=5, compare it with the minimum distance of the node.

   As 9 > 5, leave the smallest value at node node E as 5.

   We mark D as visited node with a green check mark, and node E is set as the current node.

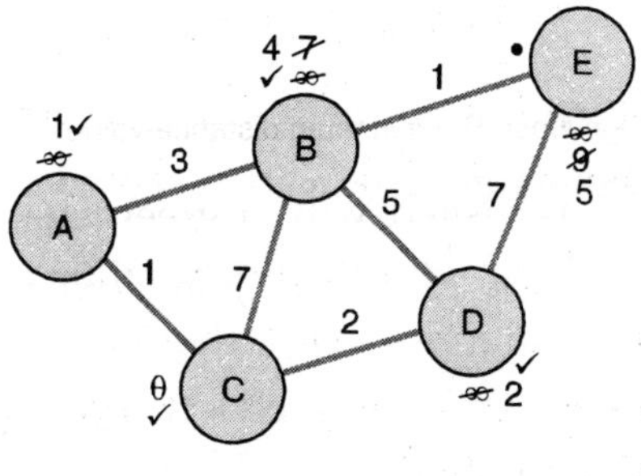

Marked Node B as visited

7. Since it doesn't have any unvisited neighbours, so there is not any requirement to check anything. Node E is marked as a visited node with a green mark.

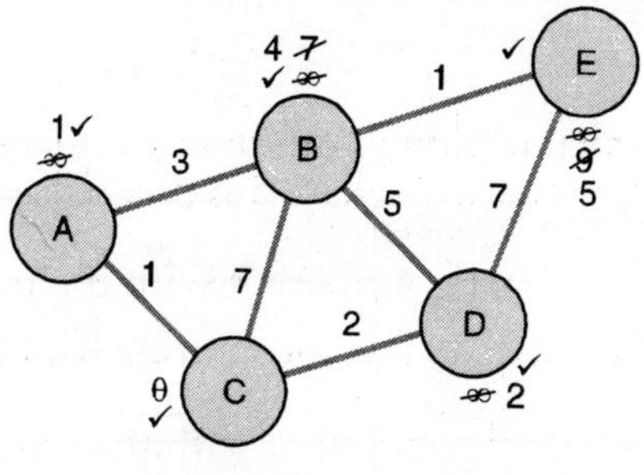

Marked Node E as visited

So, we are done as no unvisited node is left. The minimum distance of each node is now representing the minimum distance of that node from node C.

HUFFMAN TREE

Huffman trees, named after David A. Huffman, are a type of efficient binary tree used for data compression. They are primarily utilized in Huffman coding, a widely used method for lossless data compression.

The Huffman coding algorithm assigns variable-length codes to input characters, where the character codes are based on their frequencies in the input data. Characters that occur more frequently are assigned shorter codes, while those that occur less frequently are assigned longer codes, resulting in an optimal prefix-free encoding scheme.

The process of building a Huffman tree involves:

1. **Frequency Calculation:** Determine the frequency of each character in the input data.
2. **Constructing the Huffman Tree:** Create a binary tree where each leaf node represents a character along with its frequency, and internal nodes represent merged frequencies.

- Start by creating leaf nodes for each character and their frequencies.
- Merge the two nodes with the lowest frequencies into a new internal node, summing their frequencies. Repeat this process until all nodes are part of the tree.

Assigning Codes: Traverse the Huffman tree to assign binary codes to each character. Left edges are typically assigned a '0', while right edges are assigned a '1'.

Huffman coding and the resulting Huffman tree allow for efficient compression by representing frequently occurring characters with shorter bit sequences and less frequent characters with longer bit sequences. This compression technique is commonly used in file compression formats like ZIP, JPEG, and MP3.

The decompression process involves using the Huffman tree structure to decode the compressed data back into its original form by following the encoded bit sequences.

An example demonstrating how a Huffman tree is constructed for a given set of characters and their frequencies:

Let's consider the following characters along with their frequencies:

Character	Frequency
A	5
B	9
C	12

D	13
E	16
F	45

Steps to construct the Huffman tree:

Create leaf nodes for each character and its frequency:

A: 5

B: 9

C: 12

D: 13

E: 16

F: 45

Create a min-heap (priority queue) based on the frequencies.

Combine the two nodes with the lowest frequencies into a new internal node, summing their frequencies. Repeat until all nodes are part of the tree.

Constructing the Huffman tree:

Combine A(5) and B(9) to create AB(14)

Combine AB(14) and C(12) to create ABC(26)

Combine D(13) and E(16) to create DE(29)

Combine ABC(26) and F(45) to create ABCF(71)

Combine ABCF(71) and DE(29) to create the root of the tree with a frequency of 100

The resulting Huffman tree would look like this:

```
   (Root)
   /   \
 100     DE(29)
       /   \
ABCF(71)  E(16)
    /   \
ABC(26)  F(45)
  /  \
A(5)  B(9)
  \
C(12)
```

After constructing the Huffman tree, you can assign binary codes by traversing the tree. For example:

- A: 0
- B: 10
- C: 110
- D: 1110
- E: 1111
- F: 111

Note: These codes represent the unique binary representations of the characters based on their frequencies in the input. This method allows for efficient compression, where characters with higher frequencies have shorter codes, reducing the overall size of the encoded data.

❍❍❍

UNIT

9

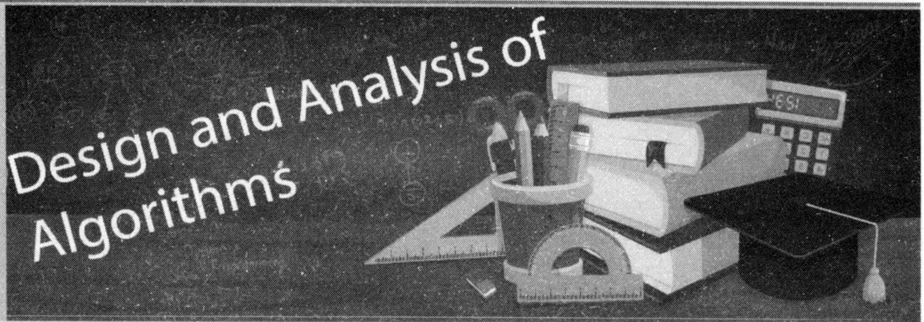

LIMITATIONS OF ALGORITHM POWER

P-CLASS

- The class P consists of those problems that are solvable in polynomial time, i.e. these problems can be solved in time O(n k) in the worst-case, where k is constant.
- These types of problems are called tractable and others are called intractable or super polynomial.
- Generally, an algorithm is a polynomial time algorithm, if there exists a polynomial $p(n)$ such that the algorithm can solve any instance of size n in a time O($p(n)$).
- Problems requiring Ω(50) time to solve are essentially intractable for large n. Most known polynomial time algorithms run in time O(n^k) for a fairly low value of k.
- The advantage in the class of polynomial-time algorithms is that all reasonable deterministic single processor models of computation can be simulated on each other with at most a polynomial slow-d.

NP-CLASS

- The class NP consists of problems that are verifiable in polynomial time. NP is a class of decision problems for which it is easy to check the correctness of a given answer, with the aid of a little extra information. Hence, we are not asking for a way to find a solution, but only to verify that a solution really is correct.

- Every problem in the given class can be solved in exponential time using exhaustive search.

Example

Consider an example to check if a problem is in P class or NP class

Step 1 – If a problem is in class P, it is nothing but we can find a solution to that type of problem in polynomial time.

Step 2 – If a problem is in class NP, it is nothing but that we can verify a possible solution in polynomial time.

Step 3 – Consider another way, NP means that a problem is Nondeterministically Polynomial. Specifically, that means that if you could build a machine that had the ability to try all the possible solutions of your problem at once, it could finish in polynomial time.

We know this to be true because we know that we can verify a possible solution in polynomial time, and what that machine is basically doing is trying to verify (test) all of the potential answers to the problem at the same time.

Step 4 – So, if you can solve a problem in polynomial time, you can certainly verify that your answer is correct in polynomial time, can't you? Sure, if you can prove that your algorithm is correct and that it can find an answer in polynomial time, which it must to be in P.

Difference between P and NP Problems

Sr. No	P class Problem	NP class Problem
1.	P problems are a set of problems that can be solved in polynomial time by deterministic algorithms.	NP problems are problems that can be solved in nondeterministic polynomial time.
2.	P problems can be solved and verified in polynomial time.	The solution to NP problems cannot be obtained in polynomial time, but if the solution is given, it can be verified in polynomial time.
3.	P problems are a subset of NP problems.	NP problems are a superset of P problems.
4.	All P problems are deterministic in nature.	All the NP problems are non-deterministic in nature.
5.	It takes polynomial time to solve a problem like n, n^2, n*logn, etc.	It takes non-deterministic polynomial time to quickly check a problem.

6.	The solution to P class problems is easy to find.	The solution to NP class problems is hard to find.
7.	**Examples of P problems are:** Selection sort, Linear Search	**Examples of NP problems are** the Travelling salesman problem and the knapsack problem.

Definition of NP-Completeness

A language M is NP-complete, if it satisfies the two conditions which are given below –

- M is in NP.
- Every A in NP is polynomial time reducible to M.

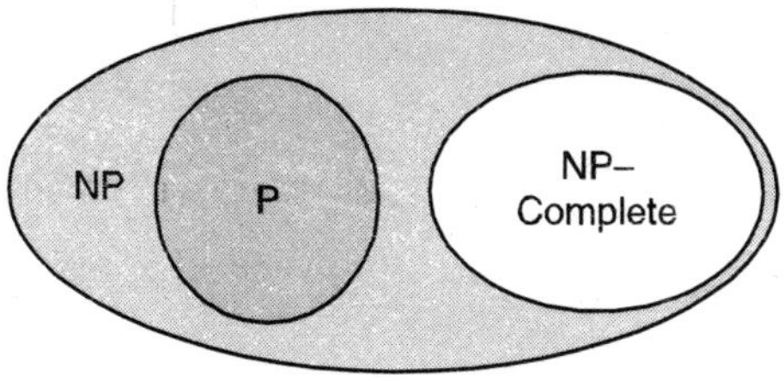

NP-Complete Problems

NP-Complete (NPC) problems are problems that are present in both the NP and NP-Hard classes. That is NP-Complete problems can be verified in polynomial time and any NP problem can be reduced to this problem in polynomial time.

A problem is in class NPC if it is in NP and is as hard as any problem in NP. A problem is said to be NP-hard if all problems in NP are polynomial time reducible to it, even though it may not be in NP itself.

If a polynomial time algorithm exists for any of these types of problems, all problems in NP can be polynomial time solvable. These problems are called NP-complete. NPcompleteness is important for both theoretical and practical reasons.

Lower Bound Theory

Lower Bound Theory Concept is based upon the calculation of minimum time that is required to execute an algorithm is known as a lower bound theory or Base Bound Theory.

Lower Bound Theory uses a number of methods/techniques to find out the lower bound.

Concept/Aim: The main aim is to calculate a minimum number of comparisons required to execute an algorithm.

Techniques:

The techniques which are used by lower Bound Theory are:

1. Comparisons Trees.
2. Oracle and adversary argument
3. State Space Method

1. Comparison trees:

In a comparison sort, we use only comparisons between elements to gain order information about an input sequence $(a_1; a_2......a_n)$.

Given a_i, a_j from $(a_1, a_2.....a_n)$We Perform One of the Comparisons

- $a_i < a_j$ less than
- $a_i \leq a_j$ less than or equal to
- $a_i > a_j$ greater than
- $a_i \geq a_j$ greater than or equal to
- $a_i = a_j$ equal to

To determine their relative order, if we assume all elements are distinct, then we just need to consider $a_i \leq a_j$ '=' is excluded &, ≥,≤,>,< are equivalent.

Consider sorting three numbers a_1, a_2, and a_3. There are 3! = 6 possible combinations:

1. (a_1, a_2, a_3), (a_1, a_3, a_2),
2. (a_2, a_1, a_3), (a_2, a_3, a_1)
3. (a_3, a_1, a_2), (a_3, a_2, a_1)

The Comparison based algorithm defines a decision tree.

Decision Tree: A decision tree is a full binary tree that shows the comparisons between elements that are executed by an appropriate sorting algorithm operating on an input of a given size. Control, data movement, and all other conditions of the algorithm are ignored.

In a decision tree, there will be an array of length n.

So, total leaves will be $n!$ (i.e. total number of comparisons)

If tree height is h, then surely

$n! \leq 2^n$ (tree will be binary)

Taking an Example of comparing a_1, a_2, and a_3.

Left subtree will be true condition i.e. $a_i \leq a_j$

Right subtree will be false condition i.e. $a_i > a_j$

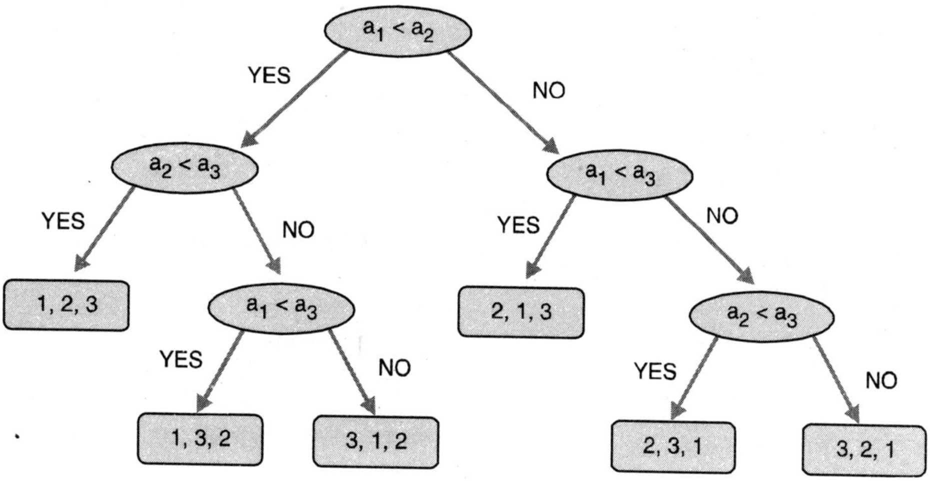

Decision Tree

So from above, we got

$$N! \leq 2^n$$

Taking Log both sides

$$\log n! \leq h \log 2$$

$$h \log 2 \geq \log n!$$

$$h \geq \log 2\ n!$$

$$h \geq \log 2\ [1, 2, 3\ldots\ldots.n]$$

$$h \geq \log_2 1 + \log_2 2 + \log_2 3 + \ldots.\ \log_2 n$$

$$h \geq \sum_{i=1}^{n} \log_2 i$$

$$h \geq \int_i^n \log_2 i - 1 d^i$$

$$h \geq \log_2 i.x^0 \int_1^n - \int_1^n \frac{1}{i} xi\, di$$

$$h \geq n\log_2 n - \int_1^n 1 di$$

$$h \geq n\log_2 n - i \int_1^n$$

$$h \geq n\log_2 n - n + 1$$

Ignoring the Constant terms

$$h \geq n \log_2 n$$

$$h = \pi\, n\, (\log n)$$

Comparison tree for Binary Search:

Example: Suppose we have a list of items according to the following Position:

1, 2, 3, 4, 5, 6, 7, 8, 9, 10, 11, 12, 13, 14

Mid = $\left[\left(\frac{1+14}{2}\right)\right] = \frac{15}{2} = 7.5 = 7$	**Note:** Choose the greatest integer.
1, 2, 3, 4, 5, 6, Mid = $\left(\frac{1+6}{2}\right)$ = **3**	8, 9, 10, 11, 12, 13, 14 Mid = $\left(\frac{8+14}{2}\right)$ = **11**

1, 2 Mid = $\left(\frac{1+2}{2}\right)$ = **1**	4, 5, 6 Mid = $\left(\frac{4+6}{2}\right)$ = **5**	8, 9, 10 Mid = $\left(\frac{8+10}{2}\right)$ = **9**	12, 13, 14 Mid = $\left(\frac{12+14}{2}\right)$ = **13**

And the last midpoint is:

2, 4, 6, 8, 10, 12, 14

Thus, we will consider all the midpoints and we will make a tree of it by having stepwise midpoints.

The Bold letters are Mid-Points Here

According to Mid-Point, the tree will be:

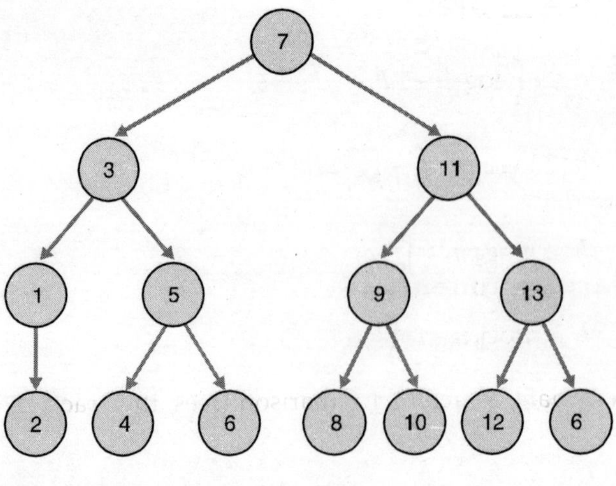

Step 1: Maximum number of nodes up to k level of the internal node is 2^k-1

For Example

$$2^k - 1$$

$$2^3 - 1 = 8 - 1 = 7$$

Where k = level = 3

Step 2: Maximum number of internal nodes in the comparisons tree is n!

Note: Here Internal Nodes are Leaves.

Step 3: From Condition1 & Condition 2 we get

$$N! \le 2^k - 1$$

$$14 < 15$$

Where N = Nodes

Step 4: Now, $n+1 \le 2^k$

Here, Internal Nodes will always be less than 2^k in the Binary Search.

Step 5:

$$n+1 <= 2^k$$

$$\text{Log}\,(n+1) = k \log 2$$

$$k >= \frac{\log(n+1)}{\log 2}$$

$$k >= \log_2(n + 1)$$

Step 6:

$$T\,(n) = k$$

Step 7:

$$T\,(n) >= \log_2(n + 1)$$

Here, the minimum number of Comparisons to perform a task of the search of n terms using Binary Search

2. Oracle and adversary argument:

Another technique for obtaining lower bounds consists of making use of an "oracle."

Given some model of estimation such as comparison trees, the oracle tells us the outcome of each comparison.

In order to derive a good lower bound, the oracle efforts it's finest to cause the algorithm to work as hard as it might.

It does this by deciding as the outcome of the next analysis, the result which matters the most work to be needed to determine the final answer.

And by keeping step of the work that is finished, a worst-case lower bound for the problem can be derived.

Example: (Merging Problem) given the sets A (1: *m*) and B (1: *n*), where the information in A and in B are sorted. Consider lower bounds for algorithms combining these two sets to give an individual sorted set.

Consider that all of the m+n elements are specific and A (1) < A (2) <....< A (*m*) and B (1) < B (2) < ....< B (*n*).

Elementary combinatory tells us that there are C ((*m* + *n*), *n*)) ways that the A's and B's may merge together while still preserving the ordering within A and B.

Thus, if we need comparison trees as our model for combining algorithms, then there will be C ((*m* + *n*), *n*)) external nodes and therefore at least log C ((*m* + *n*), *m*) comparisons are needed by any comparison-based merging algorithm.

If we let MERGE (*m, n*) be the minimum number of comparisons used to merge *m* items with n items then we have the inequality

Log C ((*m*+*n*), *m*) MERGE (*m, n*) *m*+*n*-1.

The upper bound and lower bound can get promptly far apart as *m* gets much smaller than *n*.

3. State Space Method:

1. State Space Method is a set of rules that show the possible states (*n*-tuples) that an algorithm can assume from a given state of a single comparison.
2. Once the state transitions are given, it is possible to derive lower bounds by arguing that the finished state cannot be reached using any fewer transitions.
3. Given *n* distinct items, find winner and loser.
4. Aim: When state changed count it that is the aim of State Space Method.
5. In this approach, we will count the number of comparison by counting the number of changes in state.
6. Analysis of the problem to find out the smallest and biggest items by using the state space method.

7. State: It is a collection of attributes.
8. Through this we sort out two types of Problems:
    1. Find the largest & smallest element from an array of elements.
    2. To find out largest & second largest elements from an array of an element.
9. For the largest item, we need 7 comparisons and what will be the second largest item?

   Now we count those teams who lose the match with team A

   Teams are: B, D, and E

   So the total no of comparisons are: 7

   Let n is the total number of items, then

   Comparisons = n-1 (to find the biggest item)

   No. of Comparisons to find out the 2nd biggest item = $\log_2 n$-1
10. In this no of comparisons are equal to the number of changes of states during the execution of the algorithm.

Example: State (A, B, C, D)

A. No of items that can never be compared.

B. No of items that win but never lost (ultimate winner).

C. No of items that lost but never win (ultimate loser)

D. No of items who sometimes lost & sometimes win.

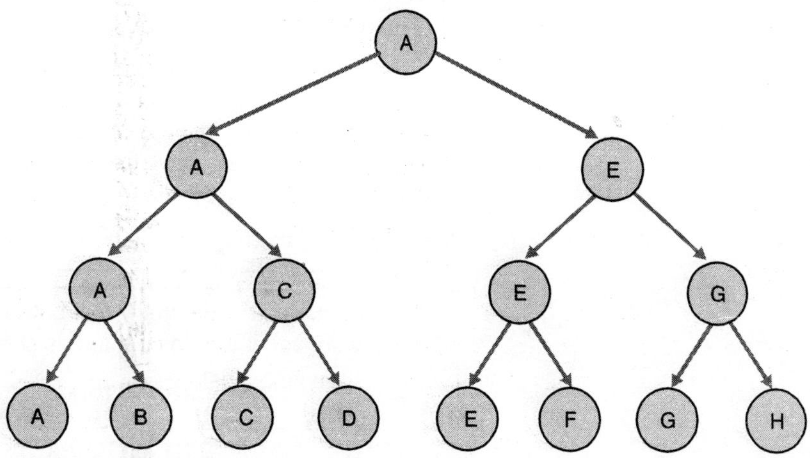

Firstly, A, B compare out or match between them. A wins and in C, D.C wins and so on. We can assume that B wins and so on. We can assume that B wins in place of A it can be anything depending on our self.

Phase-1:

A	B	C	D
8	0	0	0
6	1	1	0
4	2	2	0
2	3	3	0
0	4	4	0

8 0 0 0 — No match occurs; there are total 8 external nodes or 8 teams

6 1 1 0 — Match between A & B,6 left in A state as only one match is done between A & B.1 add to B and 1 add to C .

4 2 2 0 — C & D match out 4 left out 1 for C wins and 1 for D's lost and 0 for there is no team that sometimes wins or lost.

2 3 3 0 — Match between E & F

0 4 4 0 — Match between E & F and Match between G & H are compare out.

In Phase-1 there are 4 states,

If the team is 8 then 4 states

As if n team the $n/2$ states.

Phase-2

A	B	C	D
0	4	4	0
0	3	4	1
0	2	4	2
0	1	4	3

0 4 4 0 — Started at point where Phase 1 ends. Initial States for Phase-2

0 3 4 1 — A & C both wins from lower level. But now A wins and C lost. But, C wins from lower level so C will be counted as sometimes wins & sometimes lost.

0 2 4 2 — E & G are match E wins but G lost but G wins from lower level. It will be counted as sometimes wins & sometimes lost.

0 1 4 3 — A & C both wins at Phase-1 but now A wins and C lost. So, C wins before and last now A will come in state- D

4 is Constant in C-State as B, D, F, H are lost teams that never win.

Thus there are 3 states in Phase-2, If n is 8 then states are 3

If n teams that are $\left(\frac{n}{2}-1\right)$ states.

Phase-3: This is a Phase in which teams which come under C-State are considered and there will be matches between them to find out the team which is never winning at all.

In this Structure, we are going to move upward for denoting who is not winning after the match.

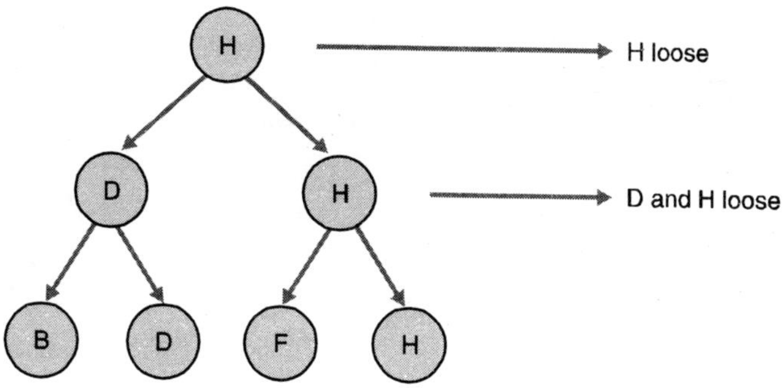

Here H is the team which is never winning at all. By this, we fulfill our second aim to.

A	B	C	D
0	1	4	3
0	1	3	4
0	1	2	5
0	1	1	6

Here by match out of B & D .We find that B wins and D looses But B at lower level looses∴ It will be counted as sometimes wins and lost and it will be removed from lost team.∴ 4 will turn to 3 from lost team.

After match out F & H, F wins and H looses but F looses at lower level ∴F will be counted as sometimes wins & lost also removed from lost team thus 2 turn to 1 from lost team.

Match between F & H

After match out of D & H.H wins and D lost but H looses from lower level ∴it will be counted as sometimes wins & lost also removed from lost team thus 2 turn to 1 from lost team.

Thus there are 3 states in Phase –3

If n teams that are $\left(\frac{n}{2}-1\right)$ states

Note: The total of all states value is always equal to '*n*'.

Thus, by adding all phase's states we will get:-

Phase1 + Phase 2 + Phase 3

$$\frac{n}{2}+\left(\frac{n}{2}-1\right)+\left(\frac{n}{2}\right)-1$$

$$\frac{n}{2}+\frac{n}{2}-1+\frac{n}{2}-1$$

$$\frac{n+n-2+n-2}{2}=\frac{3n-4}{2}$$

$$\frac{3n-2}{2}$$

Suppose we have 8 teams then $\left[3\left(\frac{8}{2}\right)-2\right]=10$ states are there (as minimum) to find out which one is never wins team.

Thus, Equation is:

$$\text{T}(n) = \frac{3n-2}{2}$$

Lower bound (L(n)) is a property of the particular issue i.e. the sorting problem, matrix multiplication not of any particular algorithm solving that problem.

Lower bound theory says that no calculation can carry out the activity in less than that of (L(n)) times the units for arbitrary inputs i.e. that for every comparison based sorting algorithm must take at least L(n) time in he worst case.

L(n) is the base overall conceivable calculation which is greatest finished.

Trivial lower bounds are utilized to yield the bound best alternative is to count the number of elements in the problems input that must be prepared and the number of output items that need to be produced.

The lower bound theory is the method that has been utilized to establish the given algorithm in the most efficient way which is possible. This is done by discovering a function g(n) that is a lower bound on the time that any algorithm must take to solve the given problem. Now if we have an algorithm whose computing time is the same order as $g(n)$, then we know that asymptotically we cannot do better.

If $f(n)$ is the time for some algorithm, then we write $f(n) = \Omega(g(n))$ to mean that $g(n)$ is the lower bound of $f(n)$. This equation can be formally written, if there exists positive constants c and n_0 such that $|f(n)| \geq c|g(n)|$ for all $n > n_0$. In addition for developing lower bounds within the constant factor, we are more conscious of the fact to determine more exact bounds whenever this is possible.

Deriving good lower bounds is more challenging than arrange efficient algorithms. This happens because a lower bound states a fact about all possible algorithms for solving a problem. Generally, we cannot enumerate and analyze all these algorithms, so lower bound proofs are often hard to obtain.

Challenges in Numerical Algorithms:

Memory access is a major bottleneck in computations. Therefore, algorithms need to maximise the number of useful calculations per memory access. Scheduling methods, memory affinity schemes, load balancing methods, are challenged.

A lot of overheads is generated by load-balancing, synchronisation, communication or fault tolerance mechanisms, that hinders the path toward exascale.

Additionally, some technologies solve issues but create new problems, eg stability of the overall system, overhead of asynchronous methods. For example, data structures using octree features face irregular computation patterns with load-balancing issues.

New applications, such as Big Data, or low rank approximations and compression methods require to adapt methods to matrix structures.

Challenges in Numerical Algorithms:

Memory access is a major bottleneck in computations. Therefore algorithms need to maximise the number of useful calculations per memory access. Scheduling methods, memory affinity schemes, load balancing methods, are challenged.

A lot of overheads is generated by load-balancing, synchronisation, communication or fault tolerance mechanisms, that hinders the path toward exascale.

Additionally, some technologies solve issues but create new problems, eg stability of the overall system, overhead of asynchronous methods. For example, data structures using octree features face irregular computation patterns with load-balancing issues.

New applications, such as Big Data, or low rank approximations and compression methods require to adapt methods to matrix structures.

```
// Kruskal's algorithm in C
#include <stdio.h>
#define MAX 30
```

```
typedef struct edge {
 int u, v, w;
} edge;

typedef struct edge_list {
  edge data[MAX];
  int n;
}  edge_list;

edge_listelist;

int Graph[MAX][MAX], n;
edge_listspanlist;

void kruskalAlgo();
int find(int belongs[], int vertexno);
void applyUnion(int belongs[], int c1, int c2);
void sort();
void print();

// Applying Krushkal Algo
void kruskalAlgo() {
 int belongs[MAX], i, j, cno1, cno2;
elist.n = 0;

 for (i = 1; i< n; i++)
   for (j = 0; j < i; j++) {
     if (Graph[i][j] != 0) {
elist.data[elist.n].u = i;
elist.data[elist.n].v = j;
elist.data[elist.n].w = Graph[i][j];
elist.n++;
```

```
    }
   }

 sort();

  for (i = 0; i< n; i++)
    belongs[i] = i;

 spanlist.n = 0;

  for (i = 0; i<elist.n; i++) {
    cno1 = find(belongs, elist.data[i].u);
    cno2 = find(belongs, elist.data[i].v);

    if (cno1 != cno2) {
spanlist.data[spanlist.n] = elist.data[i];
spanlist.n = spanlist.n + 1;
applyUnion(belongs, cno1, cno2);
   }
  }
}

int find(int belongs[], int vertexno) {
 return (belongs[vertexno]);
}

void applyUnion(int belongs[], int c1, int c2) {
 int i;

 for (i = 0; i < n; i++)
  if (belongs[i] == c2)
   belongs[i] = c1;
```

```
}

// Sorting algo
void sort() {
 int i, j;
 edge temp;

 for (i = 1; i<elist.n; i++)
  for (j = 0; j <elist.n - 1; j++)
   if (elist.data[j].w>elist.data[j + 1].w) {
    temp = elist.data[j];
elist.data[j] = elist.data[j + 1];
elist.data[j + 1] = temp;
   }
}

// Printing the result
void print() {
 int i, cost = 0;

 for (i = 0; i<spanlist.n; i++) {
printf("\n%d - %d : %d", spanlist.data[i].u, spanlist.data[i].v, spanlist.data[i].w);
  cost = cost + spanlist.data[i].w;
 }

printf("\nSpanning tree cost: %d", cost);
}

int main() {
 int i, j, total_cost;

 n = 6;
```

```
Graph[0][0] = 0;
Graph[0][1] = 4;
Graph[0][2] = 4;
Graph[0][3] = 0;
Graph[0][4] = 0;
Graph[0][5] = 0;
Graph[0][6] = 0;

Graph[1][0] = 4;
Graph[1][1] = 0;
Graph[1][2] = 2;
Graph[1][3] = 0;
Graph[1][4] = 0;
Graph[1][5] = 0;
Graph[1][6] = 0;

Graph[2][0] = 4;
Graph[2][1] = 2;
Graph[2][2] = 0;
Graph[2][3] = 3;
Graph[2][4] = 4;
Graph[2][5] = 0;
Graph[2][6] = 0;

Graph[3][0] = 0;
Graph[3][1] = 0;
Graph[3][2] = 3;
Graph[3][3] = 0;
Graph[3][4] = 3;
Graph[3][5] = 0;
Graph[3][6] = 0;
```

```
Graph[4][0] = 0;
Graph[4][1] = 0;
Graph[4][2] = 4;
Graph[4][3] = 3;
Graph[4][4] = 0;
Graph[4][5] = 0;
Graph[4][6] = 0;

Graph[5][0] = 0;
Graph[5][1] = 0;
Graph[5][2] = 2;
Graph[5][3] = 0;
Graph[5][4] = 3;
Graph[5][5] = 0;
Graph[5][6] = 0;

kruskalAlgo();
print();
}
```

Output:

```
2 - 1 : 2
5 - 2 : 2
3 - 2 : 3
4 - 3 : 3
1 - 0 : 4
Spanning tree cost: 14
```

```
// Prim's Algorithm in C
#include<stdio.h>
#include<stdbool.h>
```

```
#define INF 9999999

// number of vertices in graph
#define V 5

// create a 2d array of size 5x5
//for adjacency matrix to represent graph
int G[V][V] = {
 {0, 9, 75, 0, 0},
 {9, 0, 95, 19, 42},
 {75, 95, 0, 51, 66},
 {0, 19, 51, 0, 31},
 {0, 42, 66, 31, 0}};

int main() {
 int no_edge;  // number of edge

 // create a array to track selected vertex
 // selected will become true otherwise false
 int selected[V];

 // set selected false initially
memset(selected, false, sizeof(selected));

 // set number of edge to 0
no_edge = 0;

 // the number of egde in minimum spanning tree will be
 // always less than (V -1), where V is number of vertices in
 //graph

 // choose 0th vertex and make it true
```

```
selected[0] = true;

 int x; //  row number
 int y; //  col number

 // print for edge and weight
printf("Edge : Weight\n");

 while (no_edge< V - 1) {
  //For every vertex in the set S, find the all adjacent vertices
  // , calculate the distance from the vertex selected at step 1.
  // if the vertex is already in the set S, discard it otherwise
  //choose another vertex nearest to selected vertex  at step 1.

  int min = INF;
  x = 0;
  y = 0;

  for (int i = 0; i < V; i++) {
   if (selected[i]) {
    for (int j = 0; j < V; j++) {
     if (!selected[j] && G[i][j]) {  // not in selected and there is an edge
      if (min > G[i][j]) {
       min = G[i][j];
       x = i;
       y = j;
      }
     }
    }
   }
  }
```

```
printf("%d - %d : %d\n", x, y, G[x][y]);
  selected[y] = true;
no_edge++;
 }

 return 0;
}
```

Output:

Edge : Weight

0 - 1 : 9

1 - 3 : 19

3 - 4 : 31

3 - 2 : 51

QUESTIONS

Short Answers:

1. Define NP hard problems.
2. Describe the relationship between P and NP.
3. What is meant by deterministic algorithm and non deterministic algorithm.
4. Define decision problem.
5. Define graphic coloring and chromatic number.
6. Define polynomial bounded.
7. Define Class P and Class NP.
8. Define prim's algorithm.
9. Define kruskal'salgorithm.
10. What is Dijkstra's algorithm?
11. What is lower bound arguments?
12. What is decision trees?
13. Define P problems.

14. List the challenges of numerical algorithms.
15. List the Advantages of Dijkstra's algorithm.

Long Answers:

1. Write an algorithm and explain the prim's algorithm with example.
2. Write and explain the Kruskal's algorithm with an example.
3. Explain the NP problem & P problem with an example.
4. Write short note on challenges of numerical algorithms.
5. Differences between prim's & Kruskal's algorithms.
6. Explain decision tree with and example.
7. Explain the complete concept of Dijkstra's algorithm with an example.
8. What is lower bound argument. Give an example.

❍❍❍

UNIT

10

COPING WITH THE LIMITATIONS OF ALGORITHM POWER

Introduce two algorithm design techniques—backtracking and branch-and-bound—that often make it possible to solve at least some large instances of difficult combinatorial problems, Both strategies can be considered an improvement over exhaustive search, Unlike exhaustive search, they construct candidate solutions one component at a time and evaluate the partially constructed solutions: if no potential values of the remaining components can lead to a solution, the remaining components are not generated at all. This approach makes it possible to solve some large instances of difficult combinatorial problems, though, in the worst case.

Both backtracking and branch-and-bound are based on the construction of a state-space tree whose nodes reflect specific choices made for a solution's components. Both techniques terminate a node as soon as it can be guaranteed that no solution to the problem can be obtained by considering choices that correspond to the node's descendants. The techniques differ in problems they can be applied to. Branch-and-bound is applicable only to optimization problems because it is based on computing a bound on possible values of the problem's objective function. Backtracking is not constrained by this demand, but often, it applies to non-optimization problems. The other distinction between backtracking and branch-and-bound lies in the order in which nodes of thestate-space tree are generated. For backtracking, this tree is usually developed depth-first (i.e., like DFS).

BACK TRACKING

Backtracking is a more intelligent variation of this approach. The principal idea is to construct solutions one component at a time and evaluate such partially constructed candidates as follows. If a partially constructed solution can be developed further without violating the problem's constraints, it is done by taking the first remaining legitimate option for the next component. If there is no legitimate option for the next component, no alternatives for any remaining component need to be considered. In this case, the algorithm backtracks to replace the last component of the partially constructed solution with its next option. It is convenient to implement this kind of processing by constructing a tree of choices being made, called the state-space tree. Its root represents an initial state before the search for a solution begins. The nodes of the first level in the tree represent the choices made for the first component of a solution, the nodes of the second level represent the choices for the second component, and so on. A node in a state-space tree is said to be promising if it corresponds to a partially constructed solution that may still lead to a complete solution; otherwise, it is called nonpromising. Leaves represent either nonpromising dead ends or complete solutions found by the algorithm. In the majority of cases, a statespace tree for a backtracking algorithm is constructed in the manner of depthfirst search. If the current node is promising, its child is generated by adding the first remaining legitimate option for the next component of a solution, and the processing moves to this child. If the current node turns out to be nonpromising, the algorithm backtracks to the node's parent to consider the next possible option for its last component; if there is no such option, it backtracks one more level up the tree, and so on. Finally, if the algorithm reaches a complete solution to the problem, it either stops (if just one solution is required) or continues searching for other possible solutions.

Backtracking is a problem-solving algorithmic technique that involves finding a solution incrementally by trying different options and undoing them if they lead to a dead end. It is commonly used in situations where you need to explore multiple possibilities to solve a problem, like searching for a path in a maze or solving puzzles like Sudoku. When a dead end is reached, the algorithm backtracks to the previous decision point and explores a different path until a solution is found or all possibilities have been exhausted.

Backtracking can be defined as a general algorithmic technique that considers searching every possible combination in order to solve a computational problem.

Basic Terminologies

- **Candidate:** A candidate is a potential choice or element that can be added to the current solution.
- **Solution:** The solution is a valid and complete configuration that satisfies all problem constraints.

- **Partial Solution:** A partial solution is an intermediate or incomplete configuration being constructed during the backtracking process.
- **Decision Space:** The decision space is the set of all possible candidates or choices at each decision point.
- **Decision Point:** A decision point is a specific step in the algorithm where a candidate is chosen and added to the partial solution.
- **Feasible Solution:** A feasible solution is a partial or complete solution that adheres to all constraints.
- **Dead End:** A dead end occurs when a partial solution cannot be extended without violating constraints.
- **Backtrack:** Backtracking involves undoing previous decisions and returning to a prior decision point.
- **Search Space:** The search space includes all possible combinations of candidates and choices.
- **Optimal Solution:** In optimization problems, the optimal solution is the best possible solution.

n-Queens Problem

The problem is to place n queens on an $n \times n$ chessboard so that no two queens attack each other by being in the same row or in the same column or on the same diagonal. For $n = 1$, the problem has a trivial solution, and it is easy to see that there is no solution for $n = 2$ and $n = 3$. So let us consider the four-queens problem and solve it by the backtracking technique. Since each of the four queens has to be placed in its own row, all we need to do is to assign a column for each queen on the board presented in Figure below.

We start with the empty board and then place queen 1 in the first possible position of its row, which is in column 1 of row 1. Then we place queen 2, after trying unsuccessfully columns 1 and 2, in the first acceptable position for it, which is square (2, 3), the square in row 2 and column 3. This proves to be a dead end because there is no acceptable position for queen 3. So, the algorithm backtracks and puts queen 2 in the next possible position at (2, 4). Then queen 3 is placed at (3, 2), which proves to be another dead end. The algorithm then backtracks all the way to queen 1 and moves it to (1, 2). Queen 2 then goes to (2, 4), queen 3 to (3, 1), and queen 4 to (4, 3), which is a solution to the problem. The state-space tree of this search is shown in Figure. If other solutions need to be found (how many of them are there for the fourqueens problem?), the algorithm can simply resume its operations at the leaf at which it stopped. Alternatively, we can use the board's symmetry for this purpose.

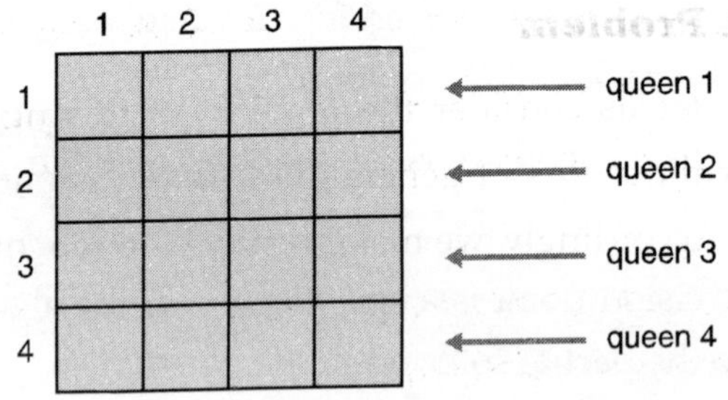

Board for the four-queens problem.

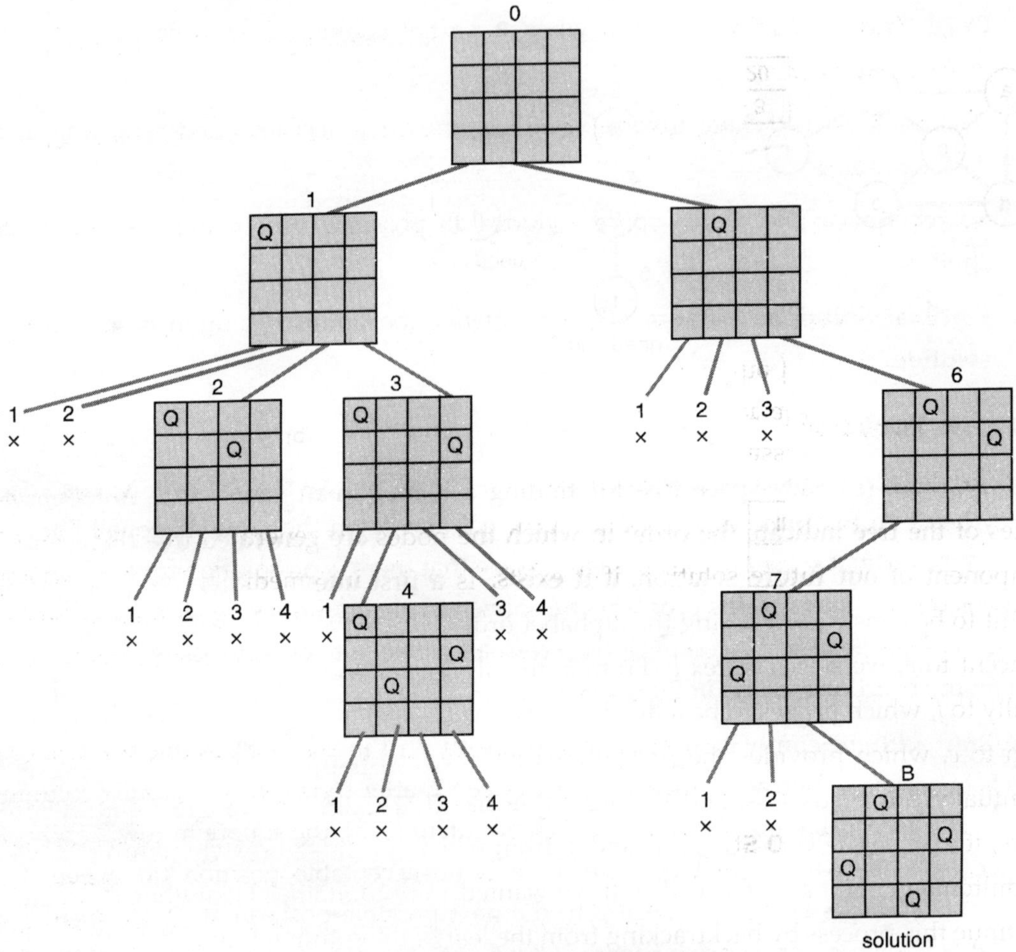

State-space tree of solving the four-queens problem by backtracking. × denotes an unsuccessful attempt to place a queen in the indicated column. The numbers above the nodes indicate the order in which the nodes are generated.

Finally, it should be pointed out that a single solution to the n-queens problem for any $n \geq 4$ can be found in linear time.

Hamiltonian Circuit Problem

As our next example, let us consider the problem of finding a Hamiltonian circuit in the graph in Figure below. Without loss of generality, we can assume that if a Hamiltonian circuit exists, it starts at vertex a. Accordingly, we make vertex a the root of the state-space.

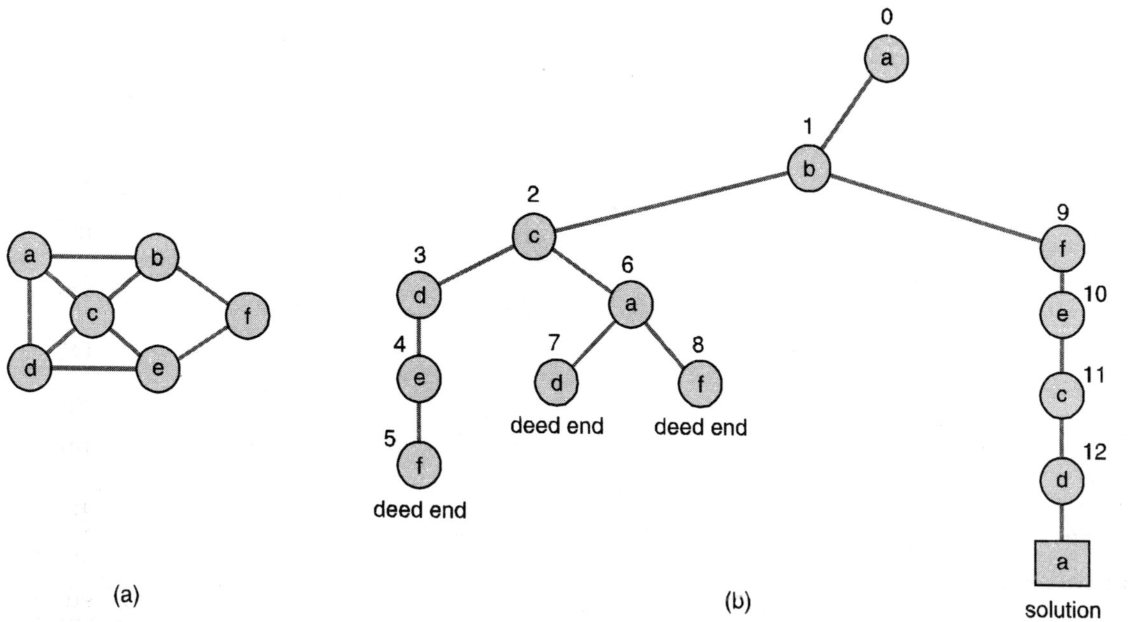

(a) Graph. (b) State-space tree for finding a Hamiltonian circuit. The numbers above the nodes of the tree indicate the order in which the nodes are generated tree (Figure b). The first component of our future solution, if it exists, is a first intermediate vertex of a Hamiltonian circuit to be constructed. Using the alphabet order to break the three-way tie among the vertices adjacent to *a*, we select vertex *b*. From *b*, the algorithm proceeds to *c*, then to *d*, then to *e*, and finally to *f*, which proves to be a dead end. So the algorithm backtracks from *f* to *e*, then to *d*, and then to *c*, which provides the first alternative for the algorithm to pursue. Going from *c* to *e* eventually proves useless, and the algorithm has to backtrack from *e* to *c* and then to *b*. From there, it goes to the vertices *f* , *e*, *c*, and *d*, from which it can legitimately return to *a*, yielding the Hamiltonian circuit *a*, *b*, *f*, *e*, *c*, *d*, *a*. If we wanted to find another Hamiltonian circuit, we could continue this process by backtracking from the leaf of the solution found.

Subset-Sum Problem

As our last example, we consider the subset-sum problem: find a subset of a given set A = $\{a_1,..., a_n\}$ of n positive integers whose sum is equal to a given positive integer d. For example, for A = {1, 2, 5, 6, 8} and $d = 9$, there are two solutions: {1, 2, 6} and {1, 8}. Of course, some instances of this problem may have no solutions. It is convenient to sort the set's elements in increasing order. So, we will assume that

$$a_1 < a_2 < \ldots < a_n.$$

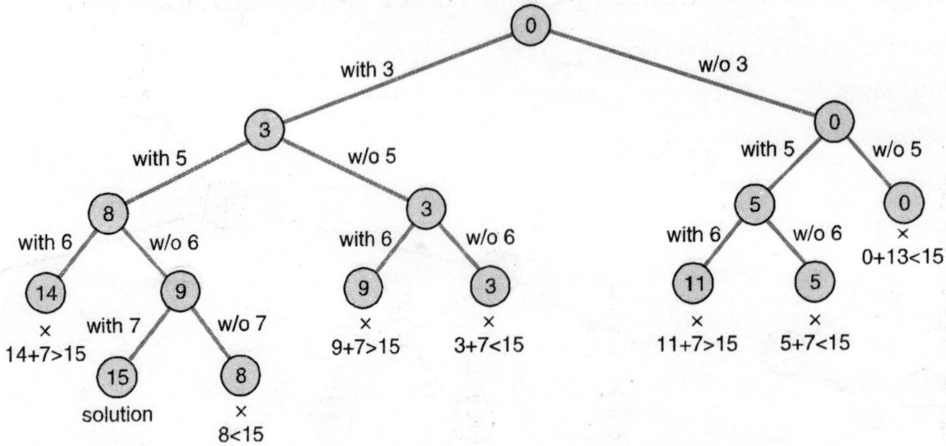

Complete state-space tree of the backtracking algorithm applied to the instance A = {3, 5, 6, 7} and d = 15 of the subset-sum problem. The number inside a node is the sum of the elements already included in the subsets represented by the node. The inequality below a leaf indicates the reason for its termination.

The state-space tree can be constructed as a binary tree like that in Figure 12.4 for the instance A = {3, 5, 6, 7} and d = 15. The root of the tree represents the starting point, with no decisions about the given elements made as yet. Its left and right children represent, respectively, inclusion and exclusion of $a1$ in a set being sought. Similarly, going to the left from a node of the first level corresponds to inclusion of a_2 while going to the right corresponds to its exclusion, and so on. Thus, a path from the root to a node on the ith level of the tree indicates which of the first i numbers have been included in the subsets represented by that node. We record the value of s, the sum of these numbers, in the node. If s is equal to d, we have a solution to the problem. We can either report this result and stop or, if all the solutions need to be found, continue by backtracking to the node's parent. If s is not equal to d, we can terminate the node as nonpromising if either of the following two inequalities holds:

$$s + a_{i+1} > d \text{ (the sum } s \text{ is too large)},$$

$$s + \sum_{j=i+1}^{n} a_j < d \text{ (the sum } s \text{ is too small)}.$$

A more general perspective, most backtracking algorithms fit the following description. An output of a backtracking algorithm can be thought of as an n-tuple $(x_1, x_2, \ldots, x_n)$ where each coordinate x_i is an element of some finite lin-early ordered set S*i*. For example, for the *n*-queens problem, each S*i* is the setof integers (column numbers) 1 through *n*. The tuple may need to satisfy some additional constraints (e.g., the nonattacking requirements in the *n*-queens problem). Depending on the problem, all solution tuples can be of the same length(the *n*-queens and the Hamiltonian circuit problem) and of different lengths (thesubset-sum problem). A backtracking algorithm generates, explicitly or implicitly, a state-space tree; its nodes represent partially constructed tuples with thefirst *i* coordinates defined by the earlier actions of the algorithm. If such a tuple($x_1, x_2,...,x_i$) is not a solution, the algorithm finds the next element in S*i*+1 thatis consistent with the values of ($x_1, x_2,..., x_i$) and the problem's constraints, andadds it to the tuple as its (i + 1)st coordinate. If such an element does not exist,the algorithm backtracks to consider the next value of x_i, and so on.

To start a backtracking algorithm, the following pseudocode can be called for $i = 0$; X[1..0] represents the empty tuple.

```
ALGORITHM Backtrack(X[1..i])
//Gives a template of a generic backtracking algorithm
//Input: X[1..i] specifies first i promising components of a solution
//Output: All the tuples representing the problem's solutions
if X[1..i] is a solution write X[1..i]
else //see Problem 9 in this section's exercises
for each element x → Si+1 consistent with X[1..i] and the constraints do
X[i + 1] → x
Backtrack(X[1..i + 1])
```

Branch-and-Bound

Recall that the central idea of backtracking, discussed in the previous section, is tocut off a branch of the problem's state-space tree as soon as we can deduce that itcannot lead to a solution. This idea can be strengthened further if we deal with anoptimization problem. An optimization problem seeks to minimize or maximizesome objective function (a tour length, the value of items selected, the cost ofan assignment, and the like), usually subject to some constraints. Note that inthe standard terminology of optimization problems, a feasible solution is a pointin the problem's search space that satisfies all the problem's constraints (e.g., aHamiltonian circuit in the traveling salesman problem or a subset of items whosetotal weight does not exceed the knapsack's capacity in the knapsack problem),whereas an optimal solution is a feasible solution with the best value of theobjective function (e.g., the shortest Hamiltonian circuit or the most valuablesubset of items that fit the knapsack).

Compared to backtracking, branch-and-bound requires two additional items:

- a way to provide, for every node of a state-space tree, a bound on the bestvalue of the objective function1 on any solution that can be obtained by addingfurther components to the partiallyconstructed solution represented by thenode
- the value of the best solution seen so far
- If this information is available, we can compare a node's bound value withthe value of the best solution seen so far. If the bound value is not better than thevalue of the best solution seen so far—i.e., not smaller for a minimization problem

and not larger for a maximization problem—the node is nonpromising and can be terminated (some people say the branch is "pruned"). Indeed, no solution obtained from it can yield a better solution than the one already available. This is the principal idea of the branch-and-bound technique. In general, we terminate a search path at the current node in a state-space tree of a branch-and-bound algorithm for any one of the following three reasons:

- The value of the node's bound is not better than the value of the best solution seen so far.
- The node represents no feasible solutions because the constraints of the problem are already violated.
- The subset of feasible solutions represented by the node consists of a single point (and hence no further choices can be made)—in this case, we compare the value of the objective function for this feasible solution with that of the best solution seen so far and update the latter with the former if the new solution is better.

Let us illustrate the branch-and-bound approach by applying it to the problem of assigning n people to n jobs so that the total cost of the assignment is as small as possible. where we solved it by exhaustive search. Recall that an instance of the assignment problem is specified by an $n \times n$ cost matrix C so that we can state the problem as follows: select one element in each row of the matrix so that no two selected elements are in the same column and their sum is the smallest possible. We will demonstrate how this problem can be solved using the branch-and-bound technique by considering the same small instance of the problem that we investigated.

$$\begin{array}{cccccl} & \text{job 1} & \text{job 2} & \text{job 3} & \text{job 4} & \\ C = & \left[\begin{array}{c} 9 \\ 6 \\ 5 \\ 7 \end{array}\right. & \begin{array}{c} 2 \\ 4 \\ 8 \\ 6 \end{array} & \begin{array}{c} 7 \\ 3 \\ 1 \\ 9 \end{array} & \left.\begin{array}{c} 8 \\ 7 \\ 8 \\ 4 \end{array}\right] & \begin{array}{l} \text{Person } a \\ \text{Person } b \\ \text{Person } c \\ \text{Person } d \end{array} \end{array}$$

How can we find a lower bound on the cost of an optimal selection without actually solving the problem? We can do this by several methods. For example, it is clear that the cost of any solution, including an optimal one, cannot be smaller than the sum of the smallest elements in each of the matrix's rows. For the instance here, this sum is 2 + 3 + 1 + 4 = 10. It is important to stress that this is not the cost of any legitimate selection (3 and 1 came from the same column of the matrix); it is just a lower bound on the cost of any legitimate selection. We can and will apply the same thinking to partially constructed solutions. For example, for any legitimate selection that selects 9 from the first row, the lower bound will be 9 + 3 + 1 + 4 = 17.

One more comment is in order before we embark on constructing the problem's state-space tree. It deals with the order in which the tree nodes will begenerated. Rather than generating a single child of the last promising node as we did in backtracking, we will generate all the children of the most promising node among nonterminated leaves in the current tree. (Nonterminated, i.e., still promising, leaves are also called live.) How can we tell which of the nodes is most promising? We can do this by comparing the lower bounds of the live nodes. It is sensible to consider a node with the best bound as most promising, although this does not, of course, preclude the possibility that an optimal solution will ultimately belong to a different branch of the state-space tree. This variation of the strategy is called the best-first branch-and-bound.

So, returning to the instance of the assignment problem given earlier, we start with the root that corresponds to no elements selected from the cost matrix. As we already discussed, the lower-bound value for the root, denoted lb, is 10. The nodes on the first level of the tree correspond to selections of an element in the first row of the matrix, i.e., a job for person a (Figure below).

So we have four live leaves—nodes 1 through 4—that may contain an optimal solution. The most promising of them is node 2 because it has the smallest lowerbound value. Following our best-first search strategy, we branch out from that node first by considering the three different ways of selecting an element from the second row and not in the second column—the three different jobs that can be assigned to person b (Figure below).

Of the six live leaves—nodes 1, 3, 4, 5, 6, and 7—that may contain an optimal solution, we again choose the one with the smallest lower bound, node 5. First, we consider selecting the third column's element from c's row (i.e., assigning person c to job 3); this leaves us with no choice but to select the element from the fourth column of d's row (assigning person d to job 4). This yields leaf 8 (Figure 12.7), which corresponds to the feasible solution $\{a \rightarrow 2, b \rightarrow 1, c \rightarrow 3, d \rightarrow 4\}$ with the total cost of 13. Its sibling, node 9, corresponds to the feasible solution $\{a \rightarrow 2, b \rightarrow 1, c \rightarrow 4, d \rightarrow 3\}$ with the total cost of 25. Since its cost is larger than the cost of the solution represented by leaf 8, node 9 is simply terminated. (Of course, ifits cost were smaller than 13, we would have to replace the information about the best solution seen so far with the data provided by this node.)

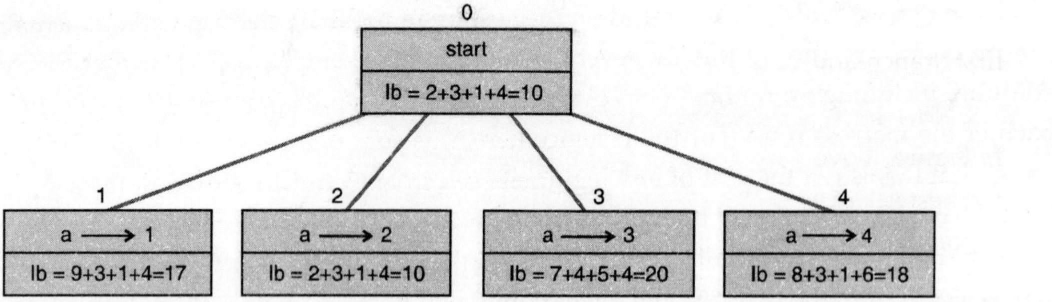

5 Levels 0 and 1 of the state-space tree for the instance of the assignment problem being solved with the best-first branch-and-bound algorithm. The number above a node shows the order in which the node was generated. A node's fields indicate the job number assigned to person a and the lower bound value, lb, for this node.

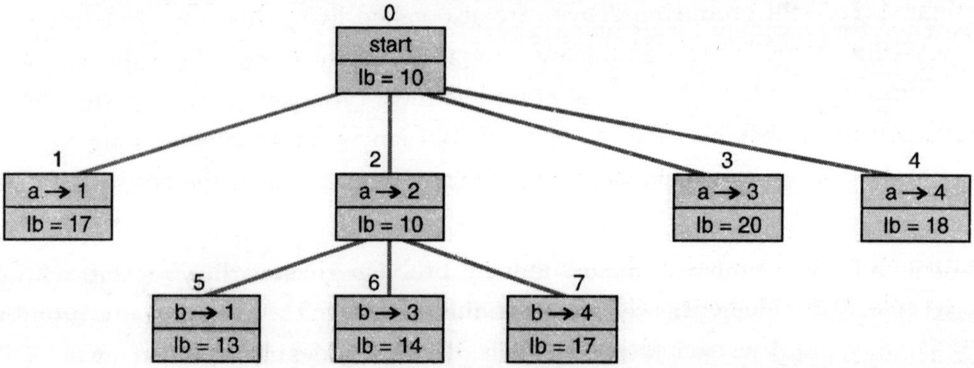

Levels 0, 1, and 2 of the state-space tree for the instance of the assignment problem being solved with the best-first branch-and-bound algorithm.

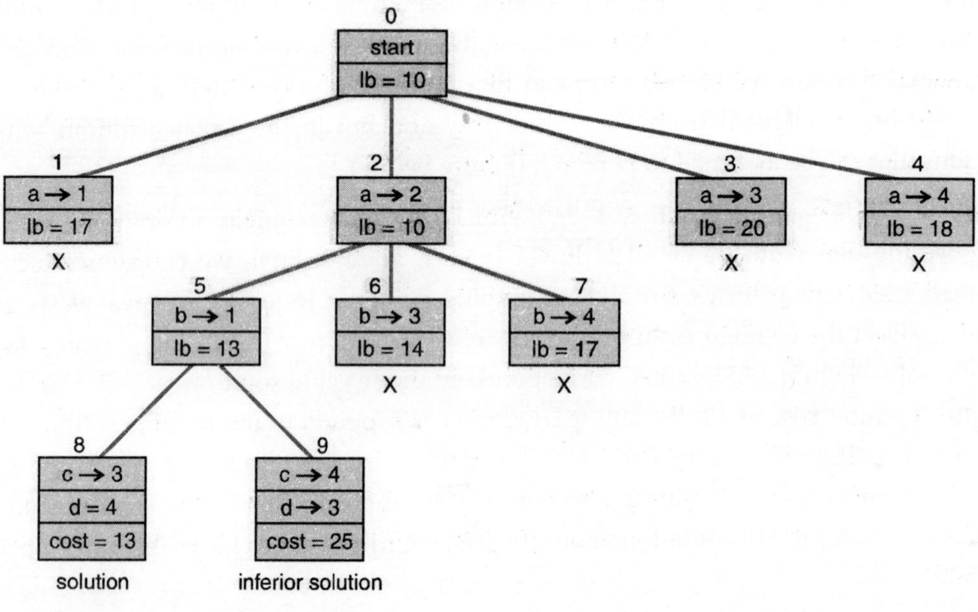

7 Complete state-space tree for the instance of the assignment problem solved with the best-first branch-and-bound algorithm.

Now, as we inspect each of the live leaves of the last state-space tree—nodes 1, 3, 4, 6, and 7 in Figure above—we discover that their lower-bound values are not smaller than 13, the value of the best selection seen so far (leaf 8). Hence, we terminate all of them and recognize the solution represented by leaf 8 as the optimal solution to the problem.

Knapsack Problem

Let us now discuss how we can apply the branch-and-bound technique to solving the knapsack problem. Given n items of known weights wi and values vi, $i = 1, 2, \dots, n$, and a knapsack of capacity W, find the most valuable subset of the items that fit in the knapsack. It is convenient to order the items of a given instance in descending order by their value-to-weight ratios. Then the first item gives the best payoff per weight unit and the last one gives the worst payoff per weight unit, with ties resolved arbitrarily:

$$v_1/w_1 \geq v_2/w_2 \geq \dots \geq v_n/w_n.$$

It is natural to structure the state-space tree for this problem as a binary tree constructed as follows (see Figure below for an example). Each node on the ith level of this tree, $0 \leq i \leq n$, represents all the subsets of n items that include a particular selection made from the first i ordered items. This particular selection is uniquely determined by the path from the root to the node: a branch going to the left indicates the inclusion of the next item, and a branch going to the right indicates its exclusion. We record the total weight w and the total value v of this selection in the node, along with some upper bound ub on the value of any subset that can be obtained by adding zero or more items to this selection. A simple way to compute the upper bound ub is to add to v, the total value of the items already selected, the product of the remaining capacity of the knapsack W – w and the best per unit payoff among the remaining items, which is v_i+1/w_i+1:

$$ub = v + (W - w)(v_i + 1/w_i + 1).$$

As a specific example, let us apply the branch-and-bound algorithm to the same instance of the knapsack problem we solved by exhaustive search. (We reorder the items in descending order of their value-to-weight ratios, though.)

Item	Weight	Value	Value/Weight
1	4	\$40	10
2	7	\$42	6
3	5	\$25	5
4	3	\$12	4

The knapsack's capacity W is 10.

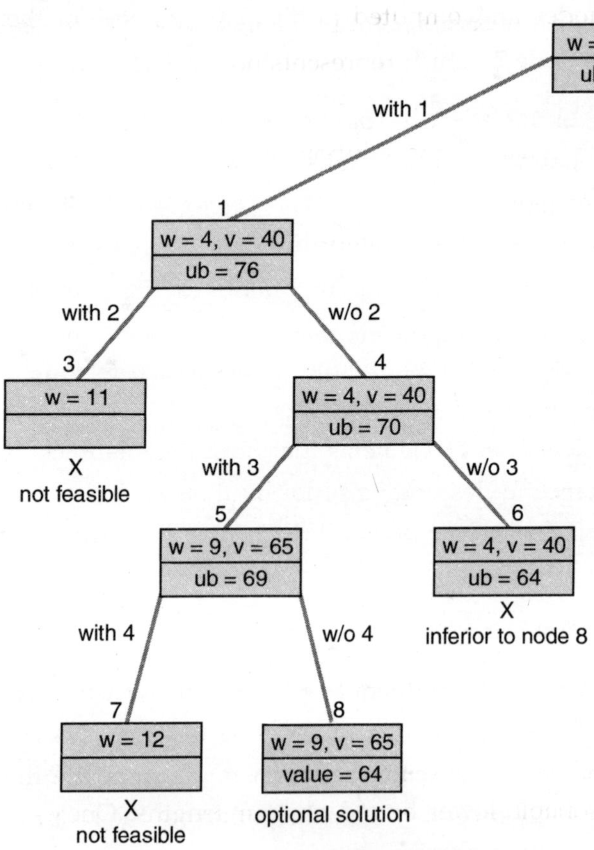

State-space tree of the best-first branch-and-bound algorithm for the instance of the knapsack problem.

At the root of the state-space tree (see Figure above), no items have been selected as yet. Hence, both the total weight of the items already selected w and their total value v are equal to 0. The value of the upper bound computed by formula (12.1) is \$100. Node 1, the left child of the root, represents the subsets that include item 1. The total weight and value of the items already included are 4 and \$40, respectively; the value of the upper bound is 40 + (10 – 4) × 6 = \$76. Node 2 represents the subsets that do not include item 1. Accordingly, w = 0, v = \$0, and ub = 0+ (10 – 0) × 6 = \$60. Since node 1 has a larger upper bound than the upper bound of node 2, it is more promising for this maximization problem, and we branch from node 1 first. Its children—nodes 3 and 4—represent subsets with item 1 and with and without item 2, respectively. Since the total weight w of every subset represented by node 3 exceeds the knapsack's capacity, node 3 can be terminated immediately. Node 4 has the same values of w and v as its parent; the upper bound ub is equal to 40 + (10 – 4) × 5 = \$70. Selecting node 4 over node 2 for the next branching (why?), we get nodes 5 and 6 by respectively including and excluding item 3. The total weights and values as well as the upper bounds forthese nodes are computed in the same way as for the preceding nodes. Branching from node 5 yields node 7, which represents no feasible solutions, and node 8, which represents just a single subset {1, 3} of value $65. The remaining live nodes 2 and 6 have smaller upper-bound values than the value of the solution represented by node 8. Hence, both can be terminated making the subset {1, 3} of node 8 the optimal solution to the problem. Solving the knapsack problem by a branch-and-bound algorithm has a rather unusual characteristic. Typically, internal nodes of a state-space tree do not define a point of the problem's search space, because some of the solution's components remain undefined. (See, for example, the branch-and-bound tree for the assignment problem discussed in the preceding subsection.) For the knapsack problem, however, every node of the tree represents a subset of the items given. We can use this fact to update the information about the best subset seen so far after generating each new node in the tree. If we had done this for the instance investigated above, we could have terminated nodes 2 and 6 before node 8 was generated because they both are inferior to the subset of value $65 of node 5.

Travelling Salesman Problem

We will be able to apply the branch-and-bound technique to instances of the traveling salesman problem if we come up with a reasonable lower bound on tour lengths. One very simple lower bound can be obtained by finding the smallest element in the intercity distance matrix D and multiplying it by the number of cities n. But there is a less obvious and more informative lower bound for instances with symmetric matrix D, which does not require a lot of work to compute. It is not difficult to show that we can compute a lower bound on the length l of any tour as follows. For each city i, $1 \leq i \leq n$, find the sum si of the distances from city i to the two nearest cities; compute the sum s of these n numbers, divide the result by 2, and, if all the distances are integers, round up the result to the nearest integer:

$$lb = [s/2]$$

For example, for the instance in Figure below,formula (12.2) yields $lb = [[(1 + 3) + (3 + 6) + (1 + 2) + (3 + 4) + (2 + 3)]/2] = 14$.

Moreover, for any subset of tours that must include particular edges of a given graph, we can modify lower bound accordingly. For example, for all the Hamiltonian circuits of the graph in Figure below that must include edge (a, d), we get the following lower bound by summing up the lengths of the two shortest edges incident with each of the vertices, with the required inclusion of edges(a, d) and (d, a):

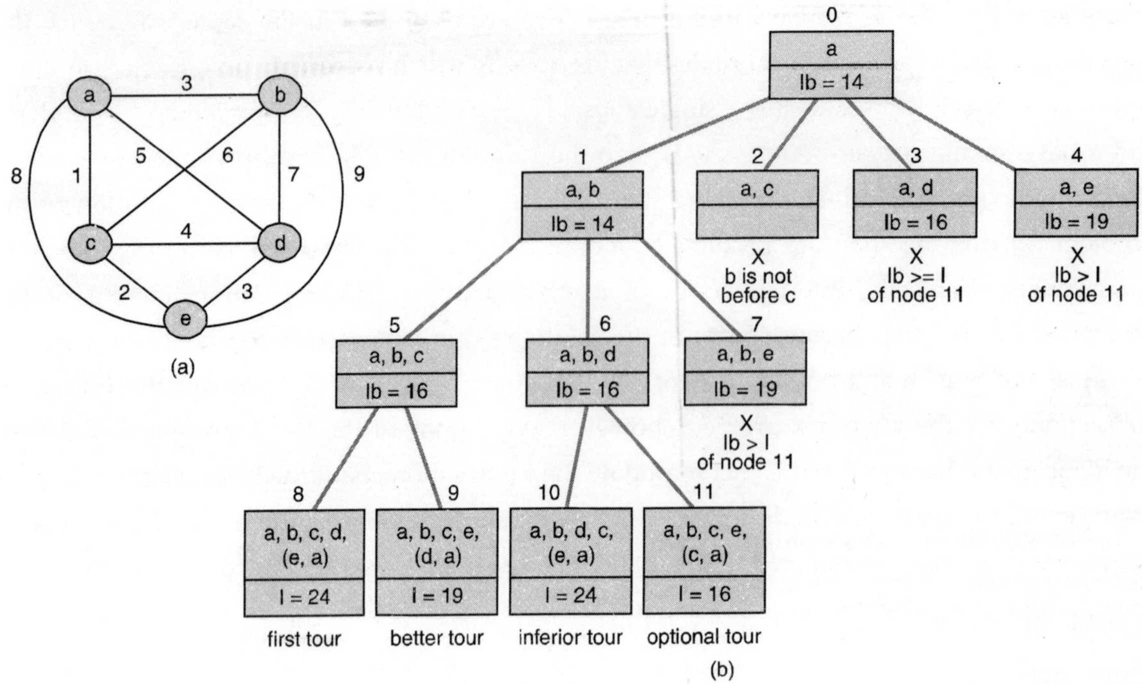

(a) Weighted graph. (b) State-space tree of the branch-and-bound algorithm to find a shortest Hamiltonian circuit in this graph. The list of vertices in a node specifies a beginning part of the Hamiltonian circuits represented by the node.

❍❍❍

ALGORITHMS LAB MANNUAL

1. Implement Recursive Binary search and Linear search and determine the time taken to search an element. Repeat the experiment for different values of *n*, the number of elements in the list to be searched and plot a graph of the time taken versus *n*.

```
/* Implementation of recursive binary search and sequential search */

#include<stdio.h>
#include<conio.h>
#include<time.h>
#include<stdlib.h>
#define max 20

int pos;
int binsearch(int,int[],int,int,int);
int linsearch(int,int[],int);

void main()
{
 int ch=1;
 double t;
 int n, i, a[max], k, op, low, high, pos;
 clock_t begin,end;
```

```
clrscr();
while(ch)
{
printf("\n.....MENU.....\n 1.Binary Search\n 2.Linear    Search\n 3.Exit\n");
printf("\nEnter your choice\n");
scanf("%d",& op);

switch(op)
{
   case 1:printf("\nEnter the number of elements \n");
           scanf("%d",& n);
      printf("\nEnter the elements of an array in order\n");
           for(i=0; i<n; i++)
                 scanf("%d",& a[i]);
      printf("\nEnter the elements to be searched\n");
           scanf("%d", & k);
           low = 0; high = n-1;
           begin = clock();
           pos = binsearch(n, a, k, low, high);
           end = clock();
           if(pos==-1)
            printf("\n\n Unsuccessful search");
           else
       printf("\n Element %d is found at position %d", k, pos+1);
                       printf("\n Time taken is % lf CPU1 cycles\n",(end-begin)/CLK_TCK);
            getch();
            break;
   case 2:printf("\nEnter the number of elements\n");
           scanf("%d",&n);
           printf("\nEnter the elements of an array\n");
           for(i=0; i<n; i++)
                 scanf("%d",& a[i]);
```

```
                    printf("\nEnter the elements to be searched\n");
            scanf("%d",& k);
            begin=clock();
            pos=linsearch(n, a, k);
            end=clock();
            if(pos==-1)
                  printf("\n\n Unsuccessful search");
            else
                        printf("\n Element %d is found at position %d", k, pos+1);
                  printf("\n Time taken is %lf CPU cycles\n",(end-begin)/CLK_TCK);
            getch();
            break;
   default:printf("\nInvalid choice entered\n");
            exit(0);
   }

  printf("\n Do you wish to run again (1/0) \n");
  scanf("%d", &ch);
  }
  getch();
}


int binsearch(int n, int a[],int k,int low, int high)
{
 int mid;
  delay(1000);
  mid=(low+high)/2;
  if(low>high)
   return -1;
  if(k==a[mid])
   return(mid);
```

```
 else
  if(k<a[mid])
   return binsearch(n, a, k, low, mid-1);
  else
   return binsearch(n, a, k, mid+1, high);
}

int linsearch(int n, int a[], int k)
{
  delay(1000);
  if(n<0)
   return -1;
  if(k==a[n-1])
   return(n-1);
  else
   return linsearch(n-1, a, k);
}
```

Output

Case 1

.....MENU.....

1. Binary Search

2. Linear Search

3. Exit

Enter your choice

1

Enter the number of elements

3

Enter the elements of an array

4

8

12

Enter the elements to be searched

12

Element 12 is found at position 2

Time taken is 1.978022 CPU1 cycles

Case 2

.....MENU.....

1.Binary Search

2.Linear Search

3.Exit

Enter your choice

2

Enter the number of elements

4

Enter the elements of an array

3

6

9

12

Enter the elements to be searched

9

Element 9 is found at position 3

Time taken is 3.021978 CPU cycles

2. Write a C program to implement tower of Hanoi problem to execute it for different number of disks.

```
#include <stdio.h>

// Tower of Hanoi program in C using Recursion
void toH(int n, char rodA, char rodC, char rodB)
{
        if (n == 1)
        {
                printf("\n Move disk 1 from rod %c to rod %c", rodA , rodC );
                return;
        }
        toH(n-1, rodA, rodB, rodC);
        printf("\n Move disk %d from rod %c to rod %c", n, rodA, rodC);
        toH(n-1, rodB, rodC, rodA);
}

int main()
{
        int no_of_disks ;
        printf("Enter number of disks: ");
        scanf("%d", &no_of_disks);
        toH(no_of_disks, 'A','C','B');
        return 0;
}
```

Output:

```
Enter the number of disks: 4
Move disk 1 from rod A to rod B
Move disk 2 from rod A to rod C
Move disk 1 from rod B to rod C
Move disk 3 from rod A to rod B
```

Move disk 1 from rod C to rod A

Move disk 2 from rod C to rod B

Move disk 1 from rod A to rod B

Move disk 4 from rod A to rod C

Move disk 1 from rod B to rod C

Move disk 2 from rod B to rod A

Move disk 1 from rod C to rod A

Move disk 3 from rod B to rod C

Move disk 1 from rod A to rod B

Move disk 2 from rod A to rod C

Move disk 1 from rod B to rod C

---

3. Sort a given set of elements using Selection sort and hence find the time required to sort elements. Repeat the experiment for different values of n, the number of elements in the list to be sorted and plot a graph of the time taken versus *n*.

```
#include<stdio.h>
#include<conio.h>
#include<time.h>
void main()
{
        int i, n, j, min, k, a[20], ch=1;
        clock_t begin,end;
        clrscr();
        while(ch)
        {
          printf("\n enter the number of elements\n");
          scanf("%d",&n);
          printf("\n enter the elements to be sorted\n");
          for(i=0; i<n; i++)
            scanf("%d",& a[i]);
          begin=clock();
          for(i=0; i<=n-2; i++)
            {
```

```
            min=i;
            delay(200);
            for(j=i+1; j<=n-1; j++)
            {
                    if(a[j]< a[min])
                    min=j;
            }
            k=a[i];
            a[i]=a[min];
            a[min]=k;
        }
      end=clock();
      printf("\n\t the sorted list of elements are:\n");
      for(i=0; i<n; i++)
        printf("\n%d", a[i]);
      printf("\n\n\t time taken:%lf",(end-begin)/CLK_TCK);
      printf("\n\n do u wish to continue (0/1)\n");
      scanf("%d",&ch);
    }
    getch();
}
```

OUTPUT

enter the number of elements

5

enter the elements to be sorted

8

3

5

1

9

the sorted list of elements are:

1 3 5 8 9

time taken:0.824176

4.a. Program to calculate X^n using divide and conquer method

```
#include <stdio.h>
/* Function to calculate x raised to the power y */
intpower(intx, unsigned inty)
{
  if(y == 0)
    return1;
  elseif(y % 2 == 0)
    returnpower(x, y / 2) * power(x, y / 2);
  else
    returnx * power(x, y / 2) * power(x, y / 2);
}

intmain()
{
  int x = 2;
  unsigned int y = 3;

  // Function call
  printf("%d", power(x, y));
  return0;
}
```

Output

8

4.b. Program to calculate X^n using Brute Force Method

```
#include <stdio.h>
intpower(intx, intn)
{
```

```
  // If x^0 return 1
  if(n == 0)
    return1;

  if(x == 0)
    return0;

  return x * power(x, n - 1);
}

intmain()
{
  intx = 2;
  intn = 3;

  // Function call
  printf("%d\n", power(x, n));
}
```

Output

8

---

5. Sort a given set of elements using Quick sort method and determine the time taken to sort the elements. Repeat the experiment for different values of n, the number of elements in the list to be sorted and plot a graph of the time taken versus *n*.

```
#include<stdio.h>
#include<conio.h>
void quicksort(int[],int,int);
int partition(int[], int, int);
void main()
{
        int i, n, a[20], ch=1;
        clrscr();
```

```
        while(ch)
        {
          printf("\n enter the number of elements\n");
          scanf("%d",&n);
          printf("\n enter the array elements\n");
          for(i=0; i<n; i++)
                scanf("%d", & a[i]);
          quicksort(a, 0, n-1);
          printf("\n\n the sorted array elements are\n\n");
          for(i=0; i<n; i++)
                printf("\n%d", a[i]);
          printf("\n\n do u wish to continue (0/1)\n");
          scanf("%d", & ch);
        }
        getch();
}
void quicksort(int a[],int low, int high)
{
        int mid;
        if(low<high)
        {
                mid=partition(a, low, high);
                quicksort(a, low, mid-1);
                quicksort(a, mid+1, high);
        }
}
int partition(int a[], int low, int high)
{
        int key, i, j,temp, k;
        key=a[low];
        i=low+1;
        j=high;
```

```
        while(i<=j)
        {
                while(i<=high && key>=a[i])
                i=i+1;
                while(key<a[j])
                j=j-1;
                if(i<j)                                 {
                        temp=a[i];
                        a[i]=a[j];
                        a[j]=temp;
                }
                else
                {
                        k=a[j];
                        a[j]=a[low];
                        a[low]=k;
                }
        }
        return j;
}
```

OUTPUT

enter the number of elements

5

enter the elements to be sorted

8

5

2

4

1

the sorted list of elements are:

1 2 4 5 8

time taken:0.824176

6. **Write a program to find the Binomial Co-efficient using Dynamic Programming.**

```
#include<stdio.h>
#include<conio.h>
void main()
{
    int i, j, k, n, c[50][50];
    clrscr();
    printf("\n enter the value of n & k\n");
    scanf("%d%d",&n,&k);
    for(i=0; i<=n; i++)
    for(j=0; j<=k; j++)
    c[i][j]=0;
    for(i=0; i<=n; i++)
    {
        c[i][0]=1;
        c[i][i]=1;
    }
    for(i=2; i<=n; i++)
    for(j=1; j<=i-1; j++)
    c[i][j]=c[i-1][j-1]+c[i-1][j];
    printf("\n the table for valuation is\n");
    for(i=0; i<=n; i++)
    {
        for(j=0; j<=k; j++)
        if(c[i][j]!=0)
        printf("\t%d", c[i][j]);
        printf("\n");
    }
    printf("\n\t the binomial coefficient of C(%d,%d) is %d\n", n, k, c[n][k]);
    getch();
}
```

OUTPUT

enter the value of *n* & *k*

6 3

the table for valuation is

```
1
1   1
1   2   1
1   3   3   1
1   4   6   4
1   5   10  10
1   6   15  20
```

the binomial coefficient of C(6, 3) is 20

---

7. Implement All Pair Shortest paths problem using Floyd's algorithm.

```
#include<stdio.h>
#include<conio.h>
#include<stdlib.h>
int cost[10][10], a[10][10];
void all_paths(int [10][10], int [10][10], int);
int min1(int, int);

void main()
{
        int i, j, n;
        clrscr();
        printf("\n enter the number of vertices\n");
        scanf("%d", &n);
        printf("\n enter the adjacency matrix\n");
        for(i=1; i<=n; i++)
        for(j=1; j<=n; j++)
```

```
        scanf("%d", & cost[i][j]);
        all_paths(cost, a, n);
        printf("\n\t the shortest path obtained is\n");
        for(i=1; i<=n; i++)
        {
                for(j=1; j<=n; j++)
                printf("\t %d", a[i][j]);
                printf("\n");
        }
        getch();
}
void all_paths(int cost[10][10], int a[10][10], int n)
{
        int i, j, k;
        for(i=1; i<=n; i++)
        for(j=1; j<=n; j++)
        a[i][j]=cost[i][j];
        for(k=1; k<=n; k++)
        for(i=1; i<=n; i++)
        for(j=1; j<=n; j++)
        a[i][j]=min1(a[i][j], a[i][k]+ a[k][j]);
}
int min1(int a,int b)
{
        return(a<b)?a:b;
}
```

OUTPUT

enter the number of vertices

4

enter the adjacency matrix

999 999 3 999

2 999 999 999

999 7 999 1

6 999 999 999

the shortest path obtained is

10 10 3 4

2 12 5 6

7 7 10 1

6 16 9 10

8.a. Write a C program to evaluate a polynomial using brute force based algorithm

```
#include <stdio.h>
#include <stdlib.h>
#define MAXSIZE 10

void main()
{
 int a[MAXSIZE];
 int i, N, power;
 float x, polySum;
 printf("Enter the order of the polynomial\n"); /* enter order of polynomial */
 scanf("%d", & N);
 printf("Enter the value of x\n"); /* value of x */
 scanf("%f", & x);

 /*Read the coefficients into an array*/

 printf("Enter %d coefficients\n", N + 1);
 for (i = 0; i <= N; i++) {
  scanf("%d", & a[i]);
 }
```

```
 polySum = a[0];
 for (i = 1; i <= N; i++) {
  polySum = polySum * x + a[i]; /* calculating the polysum  */
 }
power = N;

  printf("Given polynomial is: \n");
  for (i = 0; i <= N; i++)
  {
    if (power < 0)
    {
      break;
    }
    /* displaying polynomial  */
    if (a[i] > 0 & i!=0)
      printf(" + ");
    else if (a[i] < 0)
      printf(" - ");
    else
      printf(" ");
    printf("%dx^%d  ", abs(a[i]), power--);
 }
 printf("\nSum of the polynomial = %6.2f\n", polySum); /* displays the sum */
}
```

Output:

Enter the order of the polynomial

2

Enter the value of *x*

2

Enter 3 coefficients

3

2

6

Given polynomial is:

3x^2 + 2x^1 + 6x^0

Sum of the polynomial = 22.00

8.b. Write a C program to evaluate a polynomial using Horners Method algorithm

```
include<stdio.h>
#include<stdlib.h>
#include<math.h>

int main(void)
{
  int deg, i, Arr[10];
  float x, Sum=0;
  printf("\nEnter the degree of the polynomial and value of x\n");
  scanf("%d%f", &deg, &x); //taking input value of degree and x //
  printf("\nEnter the coefficients in descending order of degree\n");
  for(i=0; i<=deg; i++)
  {
    scanf("%d", & Arr[i]);
  }  // taking co-efficient value polynomial //

  for(i=deg; i>0; i--)
  {
    Sum=(Sum + Arr[i])*x;
  }  //evaluating polynomial using Horner's method//
  Sum = Sum + Arr[0]; //adding sum to higher degree co-efficient //
  printf("\nValue of polynomial after evaluation=%g\n", Sum);
  //printing the result//
  return 0;
}
```

Output:

Enter the degree of the polynomial and value of x

5

2

Enter the coefficients in descending order of degree

6 5 4 3 2 1

Value of polynomial after evaluation=120.000000

9. Write a C Program to solve the string-matching problem using Boyer – Moore approach

```
# include <limits.h>
# include <string.h>
# include <stdio.h>

# define NO_OF_CHARS 256

// A utility function to get maximum of two integers
int max(int a, int b) {
   return (a > b) ? a : b;
}

// The preprocessing function for Boyer Moore's bad character heuristic
void badCharHeuristic(char *str, int size, int badchar[NO_OF_CHARS]) {
   int i;

   // Initialize all occurrences as -1
   for (i = 0; i < NO_OF_CHARS; i++)
      badchar[i] = -1;

   // Fill the actual value of last occurrence of a character
   for (i = 0; i < size; i++)
      badchar[(int) str[i]] = i;
}
```

```
void search(char *txt, char *pat) {
  int m = strlen(pat);
  int n = strlen(txt);

  int badchar[NO_OF_CHARS];

  badCharHeuristic(pat, m, badchar);

  int s = 0; // s is shift of the pattern with respect to text
  while (s <= (n - m)) {
    int j = m - 1;

    while (j >= 0 && pat[j] == txt[s + j])
      j--;

    if (j < 0) {
      printf("\n pattern occurs at shift = %d", s);

      s += (s + m < n) ? m - badchar[txt[s + m]] : 1;
    }

    else
      s += max(1, j - badchar[txt[s + j]]);
  }
}

int main() {
  char txt[] = "ABAAABCD";
  char pat[] = "ABC";
  search(txt, pat);
  return 0;
}
```

10. Write a C Program to solve the string-matching problem using KMP approach

```
#include<iostream>
#include<string.h>
using namespace std;
void prefixSuffixArray(char* pat, int M, int* pps) {
  int length = 0;
  pps[0] = 0;
  int i = 1;
  while (i < M) {
    if (pat[i] == pat[length]) {
      length++;
      pps[i] = length;
      i++;
    } else {
      if (length != 0)
      length = pps[length - 1];
      else {
        pps[i] = 0;
        i++;
      }
    }
  }
}
void KMPAlgorithm(char* text, char* pattern) {
  int M = strlen(pattern);
  int N = strlen(text);
  int pps[M];
  prefixSuffixArray(pattern, M, pps);
  int i = 0;
  int j = 0;
```

```
  while (i < N) {
    if (pattern[j] == text[i]) {
      j++;
      i++;
    }
    if (j == M) {
      printf("Found pattern at index %d
", i - j);
      j = pps[j - 1];
    }
    else if (i < N && pattern[j] != text[i]) {
      if (j != 0)
      j = pps[j - 1];
      else
      i = i + 1;
    }
  }
}
int main() {
  char text[] = "xyztrwqxyzfg";
  char pattern[] = "xyz";
  printf("The pattern is found in the text at the following index :
");
  KMPAlgorithm(text, pattern);
  return 0;
}
```

Output

The pattern is found in the text at the following index –

Found pattern at index 0

Found pattern at index 7

11. Write a program to implement BFS traversal Algorithm

```
#include<stdio.h>
int a[20][20], q[20], visited[20], n, i, j, f = 0, r = -1;
void bfs(int v) {
 for(i = 1; i <= n; i++)
 if(a[v][i] && !visited[i])
 q[++r] = i;
 if(f <= r) {
 visited[q[f]] = 1;
 bfs(q[f++]);
 }
}

void main() {
int v;
 printf("\n Enter the number of vertices:");
 scanf("%d", &n);
 for(i=1; i <= n; i++) {
 q[i] = 0;
 visited[i] = 0;
 }

 printf("\n Enter graph data in matrix form:\n");
 for(i=1; i<=n; i++) {
 for(j=1; j<=n; j++) {
 scanf("%d", & a[i][j]);
 }
 }

 printf("\n Enter the starting vertex:");
 scanf("%d", &v);
```

```
bfs(v);
printf("\n The node which are reachable are:\n");


for(i=1; i <= n; i++) {
if(visited[i])
printf("%d\t", i);
else {
printf("\n Bfs is not possible. Not all nodes are reachable");
break;
}
}
}
```

Output:

Enter the number of vertices: 4

Enter the graph in matrix form:

1 1 1 1

0 1 0 0

0 0 1 0

0 0 0 1

Enter the starting vertex : 1

The node which are reachable are

1 2 3 4

12. Obtain the Topological ordering of vertices in a given digraph.

```
#include<stdio.h>
#include<conio.h>
#define max 20


int a[max][max], n;
void topological_sort();
void main()
{
```

```
	int i, j;
	clrscr();
	printf("\n enter the number of vertices\n");
	scanf("%d",&n);
	printf("\n enter the adjacency matrix\n");
	for(i=1; i<=n; i++)
	for(j=1; j<=n; j++)
	scanf("%d", & a[i][j]);
	topological_sort();
	getch();
}

void topological_sort()
{
	int v[max], ver[max], i, j, p=1, flag=0;
	for(i=1; i<=n; i++)
	v[i]=0;
	while(p<=n)
	{
		j=1;
		while(j<=n)
		{
			flag=0;
			if(v[j]==0)
			{
				for(i=1; i<=n; i++)
				if((a[i][j]!=0) && (v[i]==0))
				{
					flag=1;
					break;
				}
				if(flag==0)
```

```
                        {
                                v[j]=1;
                                ver[p++]=j;
                                break;
                        }
                }
                j++;
                if(j>n)
                {
                        printf("\n topological order is not possible\n");
                        getch();
                        exit(0);
                }
        }
    }
    printf("\n topological order obtained is...\n");
    for(i=1; i<p; i++)
    printf("\t%d", ver[i]);
    getch();
}
```

OUTPUT

enter the number of vertices

4

enter the adjacency matrix

0 1 1 1

0 0 0 1

0 0 0 0

0 0 1 0

topological order obtained is...

1 2 4 3

13. Find a subset of a given set S == {sl,s2,......sn} of n positive integers whose sum is equal to a given positive integer d. For example, if S== (1, 2, 5, 6, 8} and d = 9 there are two solutions {1,2,6} and {1,8}. A suitable message is to be displayed if the given problem instance doesn't have a solution.

```
#include<stdio.h>
int s[10], d, n, set[10], count=0;
void display(int);
int flag = 0;

void main()
{
	int subset(int, int);
	int i;
	clrscr();
	printf("Enter the Number of elements in the set\n");
	scanf("%d", &n);
	printf("enter the set values\n");
	for(i=0; i<n; ++i)
	scanf("%d", & s[i]);
	printf("\nEnter the sum\n");
	scanf("%d", &d);
	printf(" The Program Output is:\n");
	subset(0,0);
	if(flag == 0)
	printf(" There is no solution \n");
	getch();
}
int subset(int sum, int i)
{
	if(sum == d)
	{
		flag = 1;
```

```
                display(count);
                return;
        }
        if(sum>d || i>=n) return;
        else
        {
                set[count]=s[i];
                count++;
                subset(sum+s[i], i+1);
                count--;
                subset(sum, i+1);
        }
}

void display(int count)
{
        int i;
        printf("{ ");
        for(i=0; i<count; i++)
        printf("%d ", set[i]);
        printf("}\n");
}
```

OUTPUT

Enter the Number of elements in the set

5

enter the set values

1

2

5

6

8

Enter the sum

9

The Program Output is:

{1 2 6}

{1 8}

14. Find Minimum Cost Spanning Tree of a given undirected graph using Prims algorithm.

```
#include<stdio.h>
#include<conio.h>
void main()
{
	int cost[20][20], t[20][20], near1[20], a[20];
	int i, j, n, min, minimum, k, l, mincost, c, b;
	clrscr();
	printf("\n enter the number of nodes\n");
	scanf("%d", &n);
	printf("\n enter the adjacency matrix\n");
	for(i=1; i<=n; i++)
	for(j=1; j<=n; j++)
	scanf("%d", &cost[i][j]);
	minimum=cost[1][1];
	for(i=1; i<=n; i++)
	for(j=1; j<=n; j++)
	{
		if(minimum>=cost[i][j])
		{
			minimum=cost[i][j];
			k=i;
			l=j;
		}
	}
```

```
mincost=minimum;
t[1][1]=k;
t[1][2]=l;
for(i=1; i<=n; i++)
{
        if(cost[i][l]<cost[i][k])
        near1[i]=l;
        else
        near1[i]=k;
}
near1[k]=near1[l]=0;
for(i=2; i<=n-1; i++)
{
        min=999;
        for(j=1; j<=n; j++)
        {
                if(near1[j]!=0)
                {

                a[j]=cost[j][near1[j]];
                        {
                                min=a[j];
                                c=near1[j];
                                b=j;
                                printf("\n");
                        }
                }
        }
        mincost=mincost+cost[b][c];
        near1[b]=0;
        for(k=1; k<=n; k++)
        if((near1[k]!=0) &&
```

```
            (cost[k][near1[k]]>cost[k][b]))
                near1[k]=b;
        }
        printf("\n\ the cost of minimum spanning tree is=%d", mincost);
        getch();
}
```

OUTPUT

```
enter the number of nodes
4


enter the adjacency matrix
999  1  5  2
 1  999 999 999
 5  999 999  3
 2  999  3  999
the cost of minimum spanning tree is = 6
```

15. Compute the transitive closure of a given directed graph using Warshall's algorithm.

```
#include<stdio.h>
#include<conio.h>


int a[10][10];
void main()
{
        int i, j, k, n;
        clrscr();
        printf("\n enter the number of vertices\n");
        scanf("%d", &n);
        printf("\n enter the adjacency matrix\n");
        for(i=1; i<=n; i++)
        for(j=1; j<=n; j++)
        scanf("%d",& a[i][j]);
```

```
for(k=1; k<=n; k++)
for(i=1; i<=n; i++)
for(j=1; j<=n; j++)
a[i][j]=a[i][j] || a[i][k] && a[k][j];
printf("\n\t the  tranitive closure is\n");
for(i=1;i<=n; i++)
{
        for(j=1; j<=n; j++)
        printf("\t %d", a[i][j]);
        printf("\n");
}
getch();
}
```

OUTPUT

```
enter the number of vertices
4

enter the adjacency matrix
0 1 0 0
0 0 0 1
1 0 1 0
0 0 0 0

    the  tranitive closure is
    0   1   0   1
    0   0   0   1
    1   1   1   1
    0   0   0   0
```

❍ ❍ ❍